"The Guns, They Hear Me"

John Brian Driscoll

OLD GLORY BOOKS
HELENA, MONTANA

2016

"The Guns, They Hear Me"
Copyright © 2016 by John B. Driscoll
All rights reserved. This book or any portion thereof may
not be reproduced or used in any manner whatsoever
without the express written permission of the publisher.

ISBN: 978-0-692-77909-5
First Edition

Cover design by Seth Roby, Colorblind Prints,
Helena, Montana

Dedicated to Peacemakers

Contents

Author's Note	vii
List of Pictures	viii
Acknowledgements	xii
Map: Montana Territory	1
1. Howitzer	2
2. Leader	9
3. Judge	16
4. Blackfeet	22
5. Treaty	28
6. Irish	34
7. Storm	39
8. Irregulars	47
9. Disorder	59
10. Electricity	69
11. Fetterman	74
12. Radicals	79
13. Adjutant	86
14. Gallatin	98
15. Helena	106
16. Quartermaster	121
17. Messenger	130
18. Professor	140
19. Chroniclers	147
20. Handoff	157
21. Telltale	169
22. Shanty	181
23. Volunteers	190
24. Settlers	203
25. Regiment	216
26. Muster	229

27. Ambushes	241
28. Insurrection	251
29. Discharge	259
30. Dreams	276
Endnotes	292
Index	337

Author's Note

The Creator's natural order is chaos, a self-organizing phenomenon that yields the fascinating ripples in wild rivers, the cold beauty of rock and snow, the solitude of ponderosa forests and wonderful creatures such as eagles, buffalo, wolves, grizzlies, trout, rattlesnakes, horses and human beings. As explainers with titles try to make sense for us out of the chaordic violence that's become a feature of global life, Montana remains a place on the planet, if one chooses to go out into it, where the natural order still has more presence than human interpretations. Do not expect a story about what happened here in the early years of Montana Territory to be tidily bundled into a predictable narrative.

List of Pictures

1. Mountain Howitzer and Pack Saddle, with Prairie Carriage in Background, Fort Sill Field Artillery Museum Collection.   2

2. Handbill Calling for Meeting of the Vigilantes, Montana Historical Society Collection, 1988.83.02.   9

3. Tribes in Montana in 1805, Lewis & Clark Trail Bicentennial Commission.   16

4. "Blackfeet Warriors: Back To The Wind," Blackfeet Artist, Driscoll Collection.   22

5. Fort Benton, Taken from Harper's Monthly Oct. 1867 "Rides Through Montana" by Thomas F. Meagher P. 570, Montana Historical Society Research Center Photograph Archives, Helena, MT.   28

6. 1st Regiment Irish Brigade, Civil War Colors, http://tmg110.tripod.com/union1.htm   34

7. "Ground Blizzard," Barbara Van Cleve, Holter Museum of Art Collection.   39

8. Dearborn Station after 1866, Overholser Historical Research Center.   47

9. Hanging of James Daniels, Helena, Montana Territory, March 1, 1866. (Hanged by Vigilantes

for the murder of A.J. Gartley), Montana Historical Society Research Center Photograph Archives, Helena, MT.   59

10. A Single Primary Battery Jar, Union Battery Instructions, Figure 64.   69

11. One Stand of Arms: .58 Caliber Springfield Rifle-Musket With Sling, Cartridge, Tin Inserts, Cartridges, Musket Tool, Waist Belt and Cap Pouch, Sharlot Hall Museum Collection.   74

12. Neil Howie, U.S. Marshal, Montana Territory, www.usmarshals.gov/district/mt/profiles/home/html.   79

13. Row of Field-Stacked Rifle-Muskets, Library of Congress Photograph Archives.   86

14. Gallatin City-Three Forks of the Missouri, Drawing by Bond-Chandler, from J.L. Campbell's "Idaho: 6 Months in the Open," Chicago, 1864, Montana Historical Society Research Center Photograph Archives, Helena, MT.   98

15. Saddling a Bronco the First Pull at Latigo, Photograph by L.A. Huffman, September 1904, (Cowboy Lee Warren with bucking horse, Bow Gun on Bow and Arrow Ranch on Sunday Creek), Montana Historical Society Research Center Photograph Archives, Helena, MT.   106

16. Running Cayuses in Montana Territory 1867, Driscoll Collection.   121

17. John X. Beidler Holding Rifle (no date), Photographed by E.D. Keller, Helena, Montana, Montana Historical Society Research Center Photographic Archives, Helena, MT.   130

18. Virginia City's 1867 First Class Post Office, Driscoll Collection.   140

19. Alexander K. McClure (no date), The Rembrandt Engraving Studio, Philadelphia, Montana Historical Society Research Center Photograph Archives, Helena, MT.   147

20. Packaged .58 Caliber Springfield Rifle-Musket Ammunition, angelfire.com.   157

21. Butte InterMountain Evening Edition, March 15, 1902, Chronicling America.   169

22. "The Shanty," Charles J.D.Curtis letter to Captain Duswold, Montana Historical Society Research Center Archives, F 1, SC 588.   181

23. "The Branding Fire, Big Dry, Northern Montana," Photograph by L.A. Huffman, 1902, Montana Historical Society Research Center Photograph Archives, Helena, MT.   190

24. Bull train between Lewistown and Fort Benton, Stereograph Collection and Photograph

by W.E. Hook, Sr. 1878-1879, Montana Historical Society Research Center Photograph Archives, Helena, MT.   203

25. Governor Green Clay Smith and Staff: #1. J.J. Hull, #2. Martin Beem, #3. George W. Hynson, #4. Green Clay Smith, #5. Neil Howie, #6. Hamilton Cummings, #7. M.S. Carpenter (sic.), (no date), Montana Historical Society Research Center Photograph Archives, Helena, MT.   216

26. Kirkendall's Montana Fast Freight, NE Corner of Main and Broadway, Helena, Montana, about 1871. Montana Historical Society Research Center Photograph Archives, Helena, MT.   229

27. M1841 Mountain Howitzers Limbered & Packed, Civil War Re-enactors Forum.   241

28. Fort C.F. Smith, Montana Territory, 1867, from a sketch by Captain I.D. Isay, after a drawing by Anton Schonborn. Original owned by Captain John A. Perry, National Archives, #94317, Montana Historical Society Research Center Photograph Archives, Helena, MT.   251

29. Arsenal, Virginia City (Arsenal built for Montana Militia), Photographed by Frank Garver, 1920, Montana Historical Society Research Center Photograph Archives, Helena, MT.   259

30. Big Brave as Mountain Chief with Owl Child in Cypress Hills, 1879, E. H. Train, Helena.   276

Acknowledgements

I appreciate my loving wife, Kathryn Driscoll, for creating a peaceful and supportive home and for reviewing this work. The staff of the Montana Historical Society Research Center Museum, Archives and Photograph Archives have helped by making an enduring contribution of pages from eighty Montana newspaper titles to Chronicling America, a national digitized newspaper repository hosted by the Library of Congress and supported by the National Endowment for the Humanities. Thank you to Colonel Ray Read for his encouragement and work with all the others at the Montana Military Museum at Fort Harrison, Montana. I was aided by the work already accomplished by Sergeant Kermit Edmonds who traced the diminishing numbers of Montana's Civil War rifle-muskets that remained in the Montana Territorial Arsenal after 1874.

Montana Territory in 1865 Annotated to 1871[1]

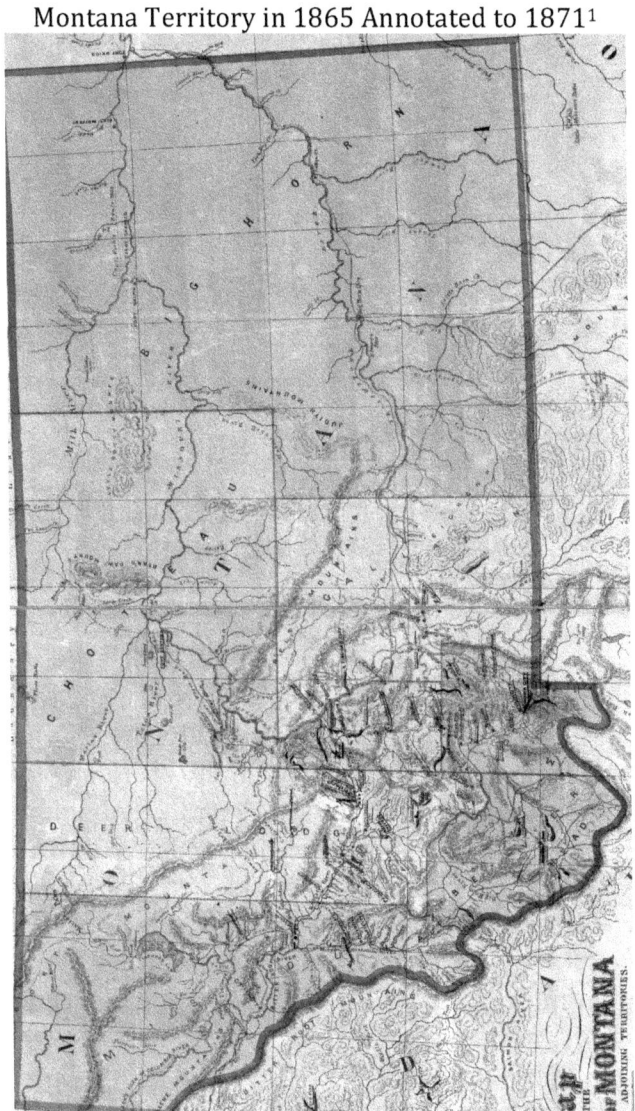

(Digitally Expandable Library of Congress JPEG2000)
Google: W.W. DeLacy 1865 Map of Montana Territory

Mountain Howitzer, Pack Saddle With Prairie Carriage in Background

1. Howitzer

The first of Montana's seven, bronze 12-pound mountain howitzers was given to Sidney Edgerton, Chief Justice for Idaho Territory, at Bannack on September 20, 1863. Capable of firing 12-pound shot, shell or canister, its tube weighed 220 pounds and could be towed behind a wagon or a single horse or broken down and carried by three pack animals along with its ammunition and tools. The howitzer had a range of 900 yards at five degrees elevation, fired by a one-half pound charge of powder. Captain James Fisk transferred the weapon to Edgerton at the end of his second immigrant wagon expedition, brought overland from Minnesota.

When President Abraham Lincoln signed legislation creating Montana Territory on May 26, 1864, the howitzer became Montana's property, Bannack became Montana's capital and Edgerton became Montana's governor.[2]

By then the piece had been fired twice. From the Mullan Military Road on top of the continental divide, Fisk set off some celebratory rounds.[3] He did this after continuing west beyond his journey's planned end at Fort Benton. The recently completed 633-mile Mullan Road followed old Indian trails to connect the Missouri River's upriver steamboat levee at Fort Benton with the Columbia River's upriver steamboat landing at Fort Walla Walla in Washington Territory. By the time he was crossing the continent's divide, with a few members of his immigration party, he had already crossed the Sun River.

The Sun flows eastward out of a steep-sided mountain canyon and joins the Missouri within the sound of its great falls. At the west end are two passes out of western Montana and at the other end lies at least one ford across the Missouri. Streams of life, including the trails of human beings, have always crisscrossed the Sun's corridor. Immigrants through Montana from Asian cultures valued the hunting and berry picking found along the Sun and used the river as a rung in a ladder of streams, allowing them to walk down two continents.[4] At the Sun they could veer southeast past a huge squared rock extruding from the prairie. Passing it and crossing the Missouri brought them to a graduated rise through the north-flowing Smith River and into the south-flowing Shields River, the northern reach of the Yellowstone River. When artist Charlie Russell painted a portrait of himself and his native friends working their way up the first low divide, he captured Square Butte and the Rocky Mountain Front as their backdrop. The Yellowstone offers its own series of north-flowing streams, serving as a ladder to and from the heart of North America. When reversed this route came to be called the Bozeman Trail. A more heavily traveled stem of the main trail from the north crosses the Sun to continue southwards.

Brings-Down-The-Sun, a member of the Blackfeet tribe of Piegan Indians, traveled south along the front of the Rockies during Montana's territorial days and described the main stem:

> There is a well-known trail we call the Old North Trail. It runs north and south along the Rocky Mountains. No one knows how long the Indians have used it. My father told me it originated in the migration of a great tribe of Indians from the distant north to the south, and all the tribes have, ever since, continued to follow in their tracks.
>
> The Old North Trail is now becoming overgrown with moss and grass, but it was worn so deeply by many generations of

travelers, that the travois tracks and horse trail are still plainly visible . . .

In many places the white man's roads and towns have obliterated the Old Trail. It forked where the city of Calgary now stands. The right fork ran north into the Barren Lands as far as people live. The main trail ran south along the eastern side of the Rockies, at a uniform distance from the mountains, keeping clear of the forest and outside of the foothills. It ran close to where the city of Helena now stands and extended south into the country inhabited by a people with dark skins and long hair falling over their faces.

My father once told me of an expedition from the Blackfeet that went south by the Old Trail to visit the people with dark skins. Elk Tongue and his wife Natoya were of this expedition, also Arrow Top and Pemmican, who was a boy of 12 at that time. He died only a few years ago at the age of 95. They were absent four years. It took them 12 moons of steady traveling to reach the country of the dark-skinned people, and 18 moons to come north again. They returned by a longer route through the 'High Trees' or Bitterroot country, where they could travel without danger of being seen. They feared going along the North Trail because it was frequented by their enemies, the Crow, Sioux, and Cheyennes (sic.). I have followed the Old North Trail so often that I know every mountain, stream, and river far to the south as well as toward the distant north.[5]

The horses that left their mark on the old trails came to the northern plains from the south in the early 1700's. They were valued for hunting and transportation and for trading even for women. Among the tribes, stealing horses became customary and a festering cause of mutual hostility. The hostility worsened between adapted and European-cultured immigrants. The latecomers considered horses to be something they called private property. They would kill a horse thief without a second thought, if they could catch them. That was difficult. In 1787, for example, a band of 250 Piegan warriors stole all the horses from a Mexican pack-train, left silver ore scattered on the ground, and trailed the stock more than a thousand miles north to the British Possessions.[6] Mexicans roamed just as far to the north.

On the morning of January 11, 1864, a man from Mexico occasioned the second use of Montana's first howitzer. In Bannack the previous day, a 29 year-old lawyer named Wilbur Fisk Sanders, Edgerton's nephew, supervised the vigilante execution of Beaverhead and Madison Counties' Sheriff Henry Plummer and two of his associates. His death-wielding power came essentially from the habitual experience of trust among Freemasons. Though not all vigilantes were Masons, freemasonry was at the core of Sanders' practical power, because all Masons, for all their wide differences, were vigilantes. Their bond was a perceived thread of common decency, even brotherly love. Non-Mason vigilantes explained their enigmatic 3-7-77 symbol as the dimensions of a grave. Nathaniel Langford, a widely respected Mason, revealed in his *Vigilante Days and Ways* the unique aspects of Montana's Freemasonry that underwrote 3-7-77.

Three Masons were in Fisk's 1862 expedition that fired the celebratory howitzer rounds on the continent's divide. Three being present allowed Langford to ceremonially open and close Montana's first lodge. Seven Masons formed the nucleus of embryonic vigilante action from Virginia City and Nevada City. Under the leadership of a non-Mason, James Williams, they pursued and captured three suspects in the murder of Nicholas Tibeault resulting in the execution of George Ives. Seventy-seven Masons, including the dead one who asked to be buried with Montana's first Masonic funeral, attended that funeral November 13, 1864. Langford said he conducted the ceremony at Bannack. Subsequent meetings to form a local lodge gave rise to Bannack's vigilantes.

After getting organized and hanging their first three men, Bannack's vigilantes decided to arrest Jose Pizanthia. They wanted to talk to him and review his record for anything he might have done wrong while in Montana. Gathering in front of the man's home, they called for the "greaser" to come out of his darkened cabin onto the sun-lit snow. He made no response to their demands. With the bodies of the Sheriff and two others swinging from a nearby wooden frame, two crowd members, Smith Ball and George Copley, ignored friendly advice and approached the cabin. The Mexican shot both, killing Copley. Enraged artillerists rushed to Edgerton's cabin and removed the howitzer's tube from under the judge's bed.[7] They positioned a box 25 feet from the windowless side of Pizanthia's log house and, without bothering to remount the tube on its axle and trail, laid and loaded the howitzer on top of the box. They pointed the tube and fired two explosive shells and one solid shot.[8]

Vigilantes' 3-7-77

2. Leader

After May 26, 1864, when Governor Edgerton became responsible for the new Territory of Montana, the first Superintendent of Public Instruction appointed by him was a private school teacher named Thomas Dimsdale. He had been writing *The Vigilantes of Montana*, capturing details of what happened with the howitzer that January morning:

> Without waiting to place it on the carriage, it was brought by willing hands to within five rods of the windowless side of the cabin and some old artillerists, placing it on a box, loaded it with shell, and laid it for the building. By one of those omissions so

common during times of excitement, the fuse was left uncut, and, being torn out in its passage through the logs, the missile never exploded, but left a clean breach through the wall, making the chips fly. A second shell was put into the gun, and this time the fuse was cut but the range was so short that the explosion took place after it had traversed the house.

Thinking that Pizanthia might have taken refuge in the chimney, the howitzer was pointed for it and sent a solid shot through it. Meanwhile the military judgment of the leader had been shown by posting of some riflemen opposite the shot-hole, with instructions to maintain so rapid a fire upon it that the beleaguered inmate should not be able to use it as a crenelle through which to fire upon the assailants. No response being given to the cannon and small arms the attacking party began to think of storming the dwelling.

The leader called for volunteers to follow him. Nevada (City) cast in her lot first, and men from the crowd joined. The half dozen stormers moved steadily, under cover of the edge of the last building, and then dashed at the house across the open space. The door had fallen from the effects of the fusillade; but, peeping in, they could not see anything until a sharp eye noticed the

Greaser's boots protruding. Two lifted the door, while Smith Ball drew his revolver and stood ready. The remainder seized the boots.

On lifting the door, Pizanthia was found lying flat and badly hurt. His revolver was beside him. He was quickly dragged out, Smith Ball paying him for the wound he had received by emptying his revolver into him.

A clothes-line was taken down and fastened round his neck; the leader climbed a pole, and the rest holding up the body, he wound the rope round the top of the stick of timber making a jamb hitch. While aloft, fastening all securely, the crowd blazed away upon the murderer swinging beneath his feet. At his request, 'Say, boys! Stop shooting a minute' the firing ceased, and he came down 'by the run.' Over one hundred shots were discharged at the swaying corpse.

A friend, one of the four Bannack originals (vigilantes) touched the leader's arms and said, 'Come and see my bonfire.' Walking down to the cabin he found that it had been razed to the ground by the maddened people, and was then in a bright glow of flame. A proposition to burn the Mexican was received with a shout of exultation.

The body was hauled down and thrown upon the pile, upon which it was burned to ashes so completely that not a trace of a bone could be seen when the fire burned out.

In the morning some women of ill fame actually panned out the ashes, to see whether the desperado had any gold in his purse. We are glad to say that they were not rewarded for their labors by striking any auriferous deposit.[9]

The leader was Edgerton's nephew, Sanders. His military judgment came from having recruited enough men for an artillery battery in Ohio. After turning down an offer to be elected by those men as their First Lieutenant, he raised a company of infantry. This led to his commission as a First Lieutenant and his appointment as Adjutant for the 64th Ohio Volunteer Infantry. Though he agreed to 36 months of service, he resigned after ten months on August 10, 1862. He still held the rank of First Lieutenant. Sanders gave illness as his reason for resigning. His family surmised the illness as "possibly caused by or aggravated by a wound." Sanders said he saw action in several engagements, including the Battle of Shiloh. The 64th reached the Shiloh battlefield on its second day, in time to help bury the many dead. Only its Company A got there in time to help chase retreating Confederates. From Shiloh until the date of his resignation, Sanders participated in the siege of Corinth, the pursuit to Booneville and helped establish defenses for the Memphis to Charleston railroad line.[10] Sanders resigned from the 64th Ohio Volunteer Infantry as a First Lieutenant. In private life Sanders had been trained as an attorney by his uncle, Judge Edgerton.

Edgerton had proven reluctant to shoulder his Idaho Territory responsibilities, protecting citizen's rights of due process under the U.S. Constitution. He alleged that no one on the Bannack side of the Bitterroot Mountains could administer to him his oath of office. In chronicling the wave of vigilante executions experienced under Edgerton's judgment, Dimsdale wrote that Sanders had "opened the ball." Twenty-one days before leading the attack on Pizanthia's home, the ball started with the lynching of George Ives.

Ives, sophisticated, popular and handsome in his misleading Union Army overcoat, had been accused of robbing and killing a man.[11] As the accused he benefited from a three-day miners' trial in Nevada City, four defense attorneys and two 12-man hung juries. Sanders, as Prosecutor, pre-planned a surprise combination of motions for Ives to be found guilty and immediately executed. At the appropriate time Sanders sent a note to his Catholic, merchant friend John Creighton. The message said, "The time is now." Creighton rushed his men to Nevada City, where they positioned themselves to pack the restless late-night crowd. At the time, Ives was standing under torchlight in front of the crowd, futilely pleading to delay immediate execution until morning so he could write about his fate to his mother and sisters in the states.[12] For some unknown reason Ives addressed Sanders as "Colonel." This dramatic public moment may explain the subsequent practice of addressing Sanders as though he was a Colonel. Judge Edgerton did not commission him a Colonel until after he became Governor Edgerton.

With Creighton's men included, more than 1000 spectators, with abundant help from forty-rod, a whiskey plied in bars and brothels of mining camps and thought capable of stupefying a man or woman at 660 feet, drowned-out the doubts of both juries by shouting their approval to hang Ives. Ives' alleged actions may have been the clearest proof of the effects of forty-rod. Forty-four years after the lynching, Ives' respected co-worker and friend, Barney Hughes, concluded, "A load of that whiskey could lead a man to rob Christ on the Cross."[13]

As vigilantes tried to impose their ideal order on the territory's new arrivals, the territory's earliest immigrants, now considered natives, found nothing good about the Mullan Road passing through their hunting areas.[14] Growing numbers of Civil War refugees, survivors and sympathizers, reinventing their lives as gold seekers, settlers and miners, were already severely agitating the Indians.

Everywhere the encroaching white men were boating, walking or riding, to and from Bannack, Virginia City, Helena, Diamond City and dozens of other mining camps.[15]

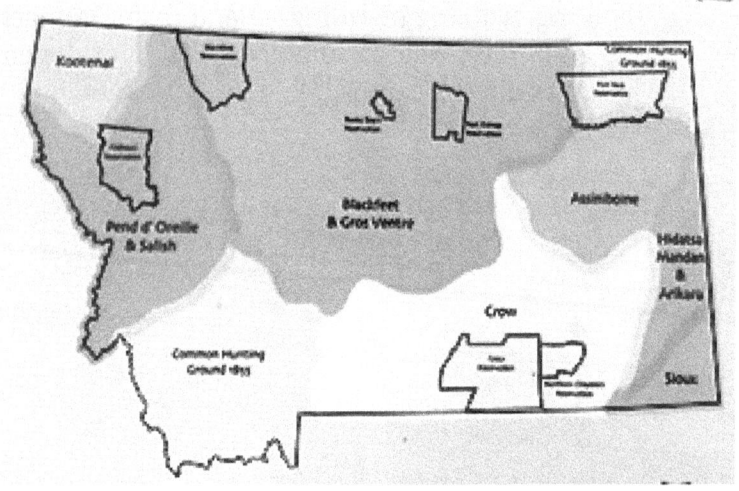

Tribes in Montana in 1805

3. Judge

Chief Justice Hezekiah Hosmer, Lincoln's new Republican appointee to Montana's Supreme Court, took his responsibilities more seriously than had Edgerton in his position as Idaho's Chief Justice. On December 5, 1864, to the Madison County Grand Jury gathered in the Planters House Hotel at Virginia City, Hosmer declared that vigilante actions would be considered criminal acts. After that he continued applying pressure on the Madison County Bar Association of which Sanders was a member. Hosmer argued that constant resort to the death penalty elevates barbarity and indifference to human life, so that:

The conscience will cease to be addressed or educated and the principle of fear, that principle which sustains despotism, instead of virtue needful to support liberty, will be the only quality of mind that will restrain men from the commission of crime. All discrimination as to the real guilt of offenders will ultimately be broken and the death penalty alone will form the only remedy...

Are we prepared for such a condition of society? Have we brought with us to these mountains the elements of refined and civilized life, surrounded ourselves with the arts and sciences in their perfection, planted here institutions of learning and religion, fashioned laws after those which we have left, to see them all gradually undermined by an instrumentality, which well enough as a desperate alternative, is ruinous and retrogressive in all its elements as a settled institution. It cannot, it must not be![16]

As Hosmer took the first steps to reign in the egregious behavior of non-Indians, the Indians under his jurisdiction were behaving badly, also aggravated by the effects of whiskey. Spiked with ginger, molasses and red pepper and colored with chewing tobacco before being watered down with river water, the good name of forty-rod changed for Indians into what they called "fire-water." Regardless of name, alcohol had its usual debilitating and malevolent influence among the tribes. Jesuit missionary Father Pierre DeSmet, during his earliest trip north of the Sun, met an Irishman vulnerable to the brew. To dry out from its effects he had followed a trader friend to escape among the Piegan. Though still speaking English with an Irish accent, he managed to make something out of his life by avoiding alcohol.[17] He became an Indian, married "as best he could," and became father to five children who he baptized by himself. His heroics in a war with another tribe elevated the man to Chief. While he succeeded, all around him firewater accelerated its devastation among the Piegan.

By January 1864 the prognosis was already near fatal. Horse thieving could buy more whiskey, resulting in no horses for someone who needed them to hunt buffalo. More horse stealing out of necessity to support families, also bought more whiskey. Indians were being killed for stealing their horses back from the newcomers, some being the whiskey traders. Jesuit Father Joseph Giorda, working among Indians at considerable distance from the active Saint Peters Mission near today's Ulm, watched whiskey traders stalk wintering bands of drink-crazed Piegan led by Little Robe and Big Lake. The traders would stay close with the camps, constantly moving their wagons through the deep snows of the upper Marias. After trying to work with Indians suffering the numbing and abnormal effects of constant drinking, Giorda wrote to Blackfeet Indian Agent Gad Upson:

> What will be the result of this whiskey trading and drinking among the Blackfeet? Of course they will grow the more poor, lazy and stupid. They will be brutalized. They will drink their robes, their homes; they will drink their daughters and their wives.[18]

Giorda's concern failed to resonate with anyone, because there was little sympathy anywhere in Montana for the Blackfeet roaming out of northern Deer Lodge County. By their sheer numbers, Indians of all the tribes, dominated all of Montana's nine counties: Missoula, Deer Lodge, Chouteau, Gallatin, Big Horn, Beaverhead, Madison and Edgerton. The Flathead or Salish, Pend d'Oreille and Kootenai lived in Missoula County's huge valleys. They and the Snake, Bannock, Coeur d'Alene, Spokane and Nez Pierce traveled eastwards to hunt across the generally neutral valleys of Beaverhead, Southern Deer Lodge, Edgerton, Madison and Gallatin counties. The Gros Ventre ranged east in Chouteau County from the Piegans' hunting areas to the Little Rocky Mountains. Assiniboine, or Mountain Sioux, roamed on the east side of the Little Rockies. Up and down the Yellowstone's ladder of streams, the Sioux, Cheyenne, Arapaho and Crow in Big Horn and Gallatin counties were focused on actively resisting the flow of more non-Indians from the east. These latest people were different in ways more important than skin color. They seemed disconnected from the land and the natural universe. For the sake of a new start they took risks insensitive or ignorant of consequences. For all their differences, the new peoples and most other Indians considered Blackfeet their worst threat. Bands of Blackfeet still roamed the lands far beyond the boundaries of the 1855 treaty signed by their famous war leader, Lame Bull.

That 1855 treaty, signed for the non-Indians by Isaac Stevens, happened at the mouth of the Judith River as an effort to end warring between all the tribes. The Crow were to stay south of the Musselshell River and the Blackfeet were to stay to its north. That arrangement ended after two years when the Crow raided across the Musselshell to ambush a Piegan movement south of the Missouri. The Crow killed 109 Piegan men, women and children while losing seven of their own. Reciprocal killings had been continuing since then.

An incident happened when the Crow and Gros Ventre, both fighting the Piegan, planned a big celebration on the Milk River. A war party of Gros Ventre, returning from raiding a Cree camp in the British Possessions, spotted a Piegan camp in the Cypress Hills. They failed to see another nearby camp of lodges enough to contain 1,000 Blood warriors. Advancing to a joint attack on the Piegan camp, the Crow and the Gros Ventre brought along their women to handle the plunder. As their approach unfolded, a Piegan hunter and his wife saw the attacking force. The man warned the Piegans while the Indian woman alerted the Bloods. There was a big slaughter.

Little Dog, Big Lake, Three Suns and other chiefs tried to have their fighters not kill the approaching defenseless women and children. By day's end, five Piegan and Bloods had been killed and a few wounded. In contrast, the bodies of 360 Crow and Gros Ventre men, women and children lay strewn for miles. The Gros Ventre settled for peace, but the Crow told the Blackfeet Confederacy, "We will see what we will see. Sleep well."[19] Territorial Supreme Court Chief Justice Hosmer's sense of order held little supremacy over Indians or non-Indians.

"Blackfeet Warriors: Back To The Wind"

4. Blackfeet

The effects of fire-water on the Blackfeet proved worse than the priest feared. In the spring of 1865, a band of Bloods appeared on the main street of Fort Benton. Their leader, challenging the courage of some new arrivals and counting coup on others, was loose-lipped enough to brag about how he and his friends stole 40 horses, a number recently missing in the area. Upon hearing his story three non-Indians drew their pistols and shot and killed the Blood warrior, then found and killed most of his companions, before throwing their bodies off the levee into the Missouri. On rumors of the murders, two weeks later a widely feared Blood chief, Calf Shirt, rode 200 miles southwards from the Belly River in the British Possessions with 200 warriors.[20] Years later he said he intended "to make some inquiries." When Calf Shirt and his party appeared along the bluffs overlooking the Marias, eleven inexperienced lumberjacks, employed to cut logs in the Marias bottoms for building the planned town of Orphir, became frightened enough to start shooting at them. Unable to make the greenhorns understand they first wanted to talk and perhaps make peace, Calf Shirt's warriors rode down, trampled and killed in brutal ways all the woodcutters and then went home.[21]

This first of at least two massacres on the Marias caused Edgerton to attempt mobilizing Montana's First Volunteer Militia of 500 men to pursue Calf Shirt. Edgerton had already appointed Scotland-born Deputy U.S. Marshall Neil Howie to be Brigadier General.[22] Howie, a self-described radical Republican with no military experience had earned a reputation in Virginia City and Bannack as an active vigilante leader respected for his personal courage and calm demeanor.[23] During this flare-up Edgerton also appointed Sanders to serve as the territory's Quartermaster Colonel. The militia mobilization under Howie and Sanders floundered. Fellow Republican Hosmer described their 1865 efforts this way:

> Our Governor and Sanders made a great fizzle over it in getting up troops to send on for the protection of the route from Benton

to Helena. We had more Generals and Colonels, etc. etc., than there were in the Army of the Potomac, trying, with beat of drum, a great display of flags, and a most melancholy waste of cheap whiskey, to raise 500 men. The result was, after a fortnight of recruiting, boys and all, the company numbered about 30, and broke up in disgust after having pressed into service, from the Ranches on the Stinking Water, about 90 of the hardest looking specimens of horse and mule flesh you ever laid eyes on. It was a tremendous exhibition of windy patriotism, out of which no buncombe could be made for any body...[24]

Much closer to the Marias killings, John J. Healy, working as Assistant Blackfeet Indian Agent managing the Sun River Government Farm, expected Captain James Stuart to lead a militia detail northwards. Healy observed in later years that Stuart wisely ended the whole matter after learning Calf Shirt had gone home.[25] The territory's howitzer could have been a small advantage, but riding into Blood country with 30 poorly mounted volunteers armed with personal weapons and small amounts of mixed ammunition would have ended badly for the volunteers. A more credible capability began evolving a few months later when a man radically different from Edgerton started calling the shots.

On September 23, 1865, President Andrew Johnson's new appointee as Territorial Secretary arrived by stagecoach. His name was Thomas Francis Meagher, famous for raising, organizing and commanding the Union Army's Irish Brigade prominent in many of the hard fought battles of the Civil War. Instead of welcoming additional help, Edgerton transferred to Meagher all of his gubernatorial duties, including the role of Indian Superintendent for the Territory and, specifically, asked him to attend Upson's pending treaty negotiations at Fort Benton. Then Edgerton and his family climbed on the same stagecoach that brought Meagher and removed their entire household to Ohio. Meagher had a month to get his feet on the ground and prepare for the treaty gathering at Fort Benton. On October 17, 1865, still enjoying his first month in Montana, Meagher signed a hand receipt for 40 Springfield .58 caliber rifle-muskets, 7320 paper-wrapped powder and mini-ball cartridges and 8795 percussion caps.[26] On behalf of the territory, he received the weapons and ammunition from Colonel James Sawyer, leader of a party just completing a preliminary survey of the Niobrara and Virginia City Wagon Road, the formal name for the Bozeman Trail. Anyone with fighting experience, including Meagher, considered these weapons obsolete. Individual Indian fighters with filled quivers were capable of launching 10 arrows in the time required for a soldier to stand, as a full view target, reloading a Civil War muzzle-loader.

During 1865 at Springfield Armory the U.S. Army had evaluated 65 versions of breech-loading rifles. They wanted to give soldiers the benefit of cover while reloading and a better rate of fire. Already, at Springfield Armory, master gunsmith Erskine Allin was supervising production of more than 5,000 Springfield .58 caliber breech-loaders, modified muzzle-loaders designed to rim-fire a copper cartridge before extracting it with a forward folding trapdoor mechanism. The change couldn't get to soldiers posted at western military assignments fast enough. General Philip Cooke, commanding the Department of the Platte, reported that one of his enlisted men posted as a cattle guard refused to fire his muzzle-loader at threatening Indians. Exhibiting the good sense of self-preservation, the enlisted man reasoned that once he fired he'd be at their mercy while reloading.[27] Already there were other weapons in Montana better suited for protecting the shooter while reloading and offered a higher rate of fire.   Civilians, once serving as soldiers, purchased these weapons as they left their Civil War units. Army Ordinance Circular No. 13, dated June 5, 1865, charged $6 for Enfield or Springfield rifle-muskets, $10 for Spencers or any other kind of carbines, and $8 for revolvers.[28] In Montana breech-loading Henry and Sharps rifles, Sharps and Spencer carbines and the versatile Navy Colt were everywhere.

Meagher wisely left behind the recently acquired Springfields when he rode north to the treaty negotiations. He opted for protection by the personal weapons of the members in his party. Also, he arranged to have a two-man escort with Montana's howitzer join them from Helena.

Meagher's Fort Benton

5. Treaty

Traveling to Fort Benton during late October and early November 1865, Meagher and his party encountered a major snowstorm. They survived by following the sound of dogs barking through the blizzard to shelter. Their refuge for several days was a sixteen-person tipi and separate walled tent that were serving as a construction crew's quarters. The crew was building the new Saint Peters Mission south of the Mullan Road near Bird Tail Rock. Jesuit Father Francis Kuppens served as their host. Meagher's escort with the howitzer waited to leave Helena on November 9, after the storm ended.[29]

That escort consisted of Howie and his assistant, John Xavier Beidler. Beidler, like Howie, figured prominently in *The Vigilantes of Montana*. Even before the serialized version of the book appeared in Dimsdale's newspaper, *The Montana Post*, Beidler had become a well-known vigilante. The first initial of his middle name meant, "Get out of town." The two men stayed overnight at Kennedy's Ranch near the east end of Little Prickly Pear Creek Canyon. The next morning they continued north, passing occasional groups of Indians traveling on the road. Along the way they offered friendly directions to a fellow who lost cattle in the storm. On November 10 they reached the Sun River Government Farm and remained overnight. They left at 2:30 the next morning and reached 28-Mile Springs before sunrise. After eating their breakfast, the two closed the distance to Fort Benton by sundown. In America's most remote riverport, the night of November 11, Howie sat down for dinner with Meagher and Connecticut Republican Lyman Munson, Helena's District Judge and member of the Territorial Supreme Court. The jurisdiction of his Helena District Court covered much of the territory subject to the upcoming treaty.

Next morning, Howie met the rest of Meagher's party and helped the general and the judge decorate the council room where the treaty would be signed. Howie noted in his diary that he and Meagher "had a good deal of fun" as wind blew hard outside. Decorating continued the next day until the wind abated, permitting Howie and Munson to row a skiff across the Missouri to a Pend d'Oreille camp on the other side. In that camp, they saw a Piegan horse thief being held prisoner.[30] For dinner that night, Howie and Meagher ate oysters together.

Next morning, 300 Gros Ventre rode into the Missouri bottoms close to town while Meagher canvassed the previous election's returns. A hard rain started at four in the afternoon and continued through midnight. With driving rain outside, Howie and Meagher enjoyed sardines and peaches for dinner together.

On November 15, the treaty-signing party watched across the river as the Pend d'Oreille moved their camp up a trail winding around the high bluff. Using that same Indian trail, William Berkin, as head of Diamond R Freight, had pioneered the Graham Wagon Road south from Fort Benton through Confederate Gulch and Diamond City providing a back way to Helena.[31] As those Indians left, thousands more from other tribes crowded into the bottoms by the next morning. Howie recorded:

> The Pagan (sic.) Chives (sic.) came in on the walk with conciderble (sic.) dignity, the Grovontes (sic.) came riding up on the gallop, s___g the Indians seemed to know their place and refused to go into the council room, where the chiefs were. We had very little trouble getting them to sign

the treaty. We expect to be two days getting them to sign, but everything was fixed up today. Weather beautiful.

Beidler was the one who memorialized that day for posterity. "X" tried to impress the 7,500 to 15,000 gathered tribesmen.[32] He intended to fire a blast from a 4-pound howitzer he saw lashed nearby onto the back of a mule in an upriver pack train. His display of might was to be against the high steep bank across the river.[33] Leaving the howitzer tube pointed over the back of the mule, he had another man steady the animal's head by holding its halter rope up close. Beidler charged the tube with gunpowder, wadding and grapeshot, then pushed and pointed the mule's back end toward the river. When a third man touched a match to the fuse in the vent, the hissing sound caused the pack animal to jump wildly in a circle around the halter rope's holder. This fascinated the thousands of gathered Indians getting to watch all the non-Indians scatter for their lives.

According to Healy's version of the story, he and his partner Alf Hamilton hit the ground, grabbed their knives and started digging for cover. Robert Vaughn, another spectator, remembered otherwise. He said Healy jumped into the river, as did many of the distinguished guests, until the grapeshot blasted into the ground behind the mule.[34] Healy's version had the grapeshot peppering a billboard painting of a buffalo hanging on the fort's outside wall.[35] Both storytellers agreed the Indians considered the incident, especially the jumping mule, wonderful entertainment.

Upson, acting as Special Commissioner, and Meagher, acting as Montana Territorial Superintendent of Indian Affairs, signed for the non-Indians.[36] The chiefs, headmen and delegates of the Gros Ventre and the Blackfeet Confederacy, mostly Piegan and some Bloods, signed for the Indians. Piegan included Chief Little Dog, the same man who in 1860 welcomed the first steamboat docking at Fort Benton. Little Dog was respected for his prowess as a warrior and leader who made hard decisions to maintain peace with the non-Indians. He was Healy's good friend and often stayed at Sun River Crossing in a cabin near Healy's home.

Whether the Indian signers realized it or not, they were releasing to the U.S. all land south of a horizontal line through the Missouri at the mouths of the Marias and the Teton Rivers. In return they expected to keep land, bounded on the south by this rough line and on the north by the smooth horizontal map boundary of the British Possessions extending east from the continental divide to a north-south line drawn at the mouth of the Milk. Non-Indians would not be able to reside on their land. They were agreeing that non-Indians could still build roads across their reserved land. The reservation they expected did not include Fort Benton, the Mullan Road or the Sun River Valley. At the discretion of its President, the U.S. was promising to spend up to $50,000 a year providing useful goods and services to the Indians. After signing, the principle chiefs expected to receive $250 per year as long as they kept peace between their tribes.

All the provisions of the treaty had been written before the start of the negotiations. They amounted to nothing more than getting the Indian leaders to place an "X" next to their written names. With the treaty's failure still in the future and the winter's wind blowing, Meagher and Howie completed the formalities by riding through the Indians' camps and visiting all the signers. Of this Howie wrote:

> ... took a ride ... to the Pagan (sic.), Blood, & Grovont (sic.) Camps. The chiefs rec'd their presents this forenoon. Went down to the Grovontres (sic.), their chives (sic.) received their presents today and were well pleased.

Of the $15,000 appropriated by Congress for negotiating expenses, a large portion bought gifts for the Indian leaders agreeing to sign.[37] All formalities were completed when the Indian signatures were in the hands of non-Indians and the gifts were in the hands of the Indians. By noon on November 19, Meagher's party left for Helena and Virginia City without Howie.

1st Regiment Irish Brigade

6. Irish

On November 19, 1865, Howie couldn't leave Fort Benton until after dark. He noted in his diary, "One of my horses is missing." When he finally did leave that night, he tied one of Hamilton's horses to his own and rode into a hard wind that was blowing from the west. He caught up with John Kennedy and the two men camped for the night seven or eight miles from Fort Benton. Kennedy was a close friend of Healy's, having long ago partnered in opening the Oro Fino gold fields of Idaho. The next day Howie caught up with Meagher and Munson who were waiting for him at 28-Mile Springs. When Howie reported the Indians being on the warpath with each other, the general and the judge decided to ride back to Fort Benton. They told Howie to come along with the howitzer. That night everything seemed quiet enough that Howie wrote, "The Indians have made another treaty." At dawn the quiet ceased. Before riding south Meagher had to work hard to convince 400 agitated warriors to disperse.

After laying over on the Sun with the Healys, Munson and Howie left Meagher there and got back to Helena on November 26. Two weeks later, Meagher reached Virginia City at the end of one day's longer ride. As happens on extended trips, Meagher, Munson and Howie had been able to realize their important differences. The biggest disagreement was that Meagher was more open to the views from both sides of the Civil War, especially from veterans and Irish. Also, Meagher felt more at home with the Healy's on the Sun. Father DeSmet concluded that Healy and Meagher grew to be good friends. The two men had a lot in common. Both were immigrants, born in Ireland and influenced by New York. They were veterans of the U.S. Army and immigrated from New York to Montana.[38]

Meagher presented Healy's schoolteacher wife, Mary Francis Sarsfield Healy, "with an American flag and a pearl-handled revolver, telling her they were her protectors."[39] The act carried great meaning between the friends. Both Meagher and Healy were dreamers. Meagher envisioned a Montana where Irish could live equally and freely. Healy imagined a Canada free from the British. In addition to being dreamers, they were practical men and the gift reflected the state of Indian affairs on the Sun.

There existed heightened concern amongst the newest immigrants about the attitudes and actions of the oldest immigrants.

The two weeks Meagher spent on the Sun coincided with the organizing phase of the Sun River Rangers. The Rangers chose Healy as their Captain. The Jesuits have always considered the Rangers part of the territorial militia organized by Meagher. Whether or not he was involved with organizing them or with executing their early actions, he certainly had the opportunity. While on the Sun he did learn from Healy's growing knowledge of Indian language and customs. The general's improved understanding surfaced in the report he sent to the Bureau of Indian Affairs about the Upson Treaty signing. He questioned the wisdom of giving pistols to Indians in return for signatures and noted the treaty had been signed by only one Chief of the Blackfeet proper and none of the hostile Bloods. He saw friendly Bloods spread through an encampment of over 1,000 lodges on the Teton and Missouri. This eyewitness report by Meagher substantiates that there were more than 8,000 Bloods in attendance at the Upson treaty signing:

> These Indians appeared to me the most peaceably disposed, and their chiefs, with an intelligent readiness, assented to the stipulations of the treaty and subscribed their names to the instrument.

Meagher's report also demonstrated a hardness of heart, possibly acquired while leading thousands of his native countrymen to their deaths. He sounded much like Healy and wrote:

> Nevertheless, I am satisfied they will continue more or less vexatiously to annoy the whites by stealing horses belonging to the latter, etc. Horse stealing is accounted rather an heroic exploit by the best of these Indians, and the habit has become so inveterate with them that until some of the thieves are severely punished I much fear it will not be relinquished.[40]

Meagher's two weeks on the Sun gave him time enough to hear Healy's strategy for entering and conquering the British Possessions. Healy planned to build trade based on personal relationships with key leaders of the tribes. In that traders' world, where a musket barrel filled with gunpowder was more valuable than if it were filled with gold dust, the Bloods were already his favorites. Healy began executing his plan by asking Meagher, as Superintendent of Indian Affairs for Montana, to give him permission to trade in Montana with the Blackfeet, Gros Ventre and Crow. Meagher, like one wave in front of another, was perfectly capable of helping Healy.

Their friendship, in the presence of so many Ireland-born Montanans, naturally caused others to dream or fret over the possibility of Meagher leading a force of Fenians north into Canada. Organizing and leading such a body of men to assault such a huge space made no sense at all. Healy's more practical non-violent concept was to make a living by trade while accelerating the acquisition of hides and meat. He would sap the economic foundation from the Hudson's Bay Company. Meagher's priority was to make Montana a safe place for incoming immigrants, especially the Irish. If he could do it without shedding blood, so much the better. Such was the case when Meagher dispersed those 400 hostile Indians at Fort Benton. Munson described the scene with Meagher standing next to Montana's howitzer and saying:

> If you do not end the fighting and leave the agency grounds by noon, I will order my men to start firing until every Indian is killed and the annuity goods restored to the government.[41]

      Meagher's effectiveness contrasted with Beidler's earlier performance. By using the howitzer as a prop of unknown potency supported by "his men," Meagher convinced a vastly superior number of armed warriors to disengage. Munson remembered the warriors dispersing by noon. Howie said the last one left by nightfall. In either case, Meagher retained control of the field without shedding blood.

Ground Blizzard (Barbara Van Cleve, 1989)

7. Storm

On December 10, 1865, a big storm settled over all of western Montana. It began with a nighttime blizzard that darkened through mid-morning and lasted another eight days with wind blasting snow off the ground and temperatures dropping to 30 below zero. Under clear skies, the flash of sun on snow blinded a person. If stung by wind at those temperatures, the same person's exposed flesh turned frostbitten in five minutes. The well-remembered storm marked the start of two years of intensified conflict in the territory.

Virginia City experienced severe cold and snow. Sheltered inside his residence and the Executive Office, Meagher worked through the weather to complete his December 14 letter to the Bureau of Indian Affairs. He conveyed those impressions he had of the treaty signing. In Helena, Munson and Howie found themselves dealing with the aftermath of a deadly card game. Twelve days earlier an Irishman named James Daniels stabbed and killed Andrew Gartley. The next day, Howie with a man name Charley Farmer and an extra horse rode six miles up the gulch to find the prisoner already arrested. They brought him to Helena's jail and placed him under the watchful eyes, alternately of Edgerton County Sheriff Robert Hereford and Helena's Town Constable John Featherstun.[42] Howie and Beidler gathered witnesses for Daniels' trial scheduled Monday, December 11.

The opening day of the trial cleared to bright sun and the temperature plummeted. Some witnesses showed, but Munson decided to postpone Daniels' trial for a week from Tuesday. On Wednesday, the temperature was 30 degrees below zero.[43] Munson had been sick and was "not very well yet" on December 19 as he empanelled the jury. As the Prosecutor charged Daniels with First Degree Murder, the weather began improving to moderately cold. The Defendant pleaded not guilty by reason of self-defense. After six days, the jury found Daniels guilty of Second Degree Murder. Munson fined him $1000 and sentenced him to three years, or 1095 days, of hard labor in Madison County's jail which served double-duty as the territory's thin-walled wooden prison at Virginia City. By this time Father Kuppens had arrived safely back at the active Saint Peters Mission on the Missouri and was certain Meagher had started a war.

A few days earlier, after the storm rushed over him, the priest had been fortunate to find shelter near the Old Saint Peters Mission on the Teton. There he was able to recover from being snow-blinded as he slogged his way back from a Piegan winter camp on the Missouri, 30 miles below Fort Benton. The priest had gone to teach at the camp after the treaty signing. He was surprised to find the usually friendly Piegan turned hostile against any connection with the white man, including missionaries. A friend advised the Jesuit, for his own good, to leave the area. He was returning west and upriver when he got blinded, lost and exposed in the cold and blowing snow. A passing miner had found him and taken him to shelter on the Teton.

While recovering, the blackrobe asked why the Piegan around the Old Mission also were sullen. He learned that two warriors, returning to camp from the Sun, reported seeing four other warriors being hanged. They had been left concealed outside as lookouts, when they saw a squad of armed men ride up, surprise and kill their companions. The four Indians' weapons had been laid aside while they ate dinner inside a log cabin belonging to John B. Morgan.[44] The Morgan cabin was near the Sun River Government Farm, then being called the New Agency. Morgan's Piegan wife was sister to one of the Indian guests. From their nearby cover, the two lookouts saw Morgan step outside his cabin, welcome the riders and invite them inside. The white men bound, dragged and placed onto the back of the same horse, each of the four Indians in succession. After hanging each from the same tree, the death squad stuffed each body down a hole chopped in the Sun's ice. A few days later, while passing through Sun River Crossing on his way back to the active mission, Kuppens heard of Morgan's boasting and learned that a man named Charlie Carson had led the squad.[45]

The Jesuits, with their particular familiarity for the area, recorded that Carson's squad was part of Meagher's Territorial Militia, suggesting Meagher's early involvement with the Sun River Rangers. Healy's rangers, or prairie men, began their activities in the weeks right after the treaty signing. According to Healy:

> . . . citizens had to take things into their own hands. Every man for himself in those days. We citizens understood the Injun. I do not take the view that all Injuns were bad Injuns. I myself have known Injuns that I could trust. But at the same time I do not take the view of many well-intentioned people of the East about them and how they should be treated. One or the other had to yield.[46]

Healy's biographer capturing these words observed:

The actions of the prairie men were not official. They were simply citizens who acted and had to act on their own in defense of their very lives and property.[47]

Ranger Captain Healy had experience serving as an enlisted man in the 2nd U.S. Army Dragoons during the Mormon War and had a reputation for honesty.[48] Johnny Grant, free trader and rancher at the mouth of the Little Blackfoot River, remembered him as a stranger walking onto his ranch and asking to borrow a horse. Healy returned a year later to pay for the horse. Also, Beidler had positive memories of Healy from the time they rode together as vigilantes during the fall of 1864. They captured the fugitive they were chasing, but then Indians attacked and wounded their man. Healy helped clean and comfort him before the man killed himself with his own pistol.[49] Several remember Healy as the bravest man they ever knew.[50] He never showed fear, except perhaps in Vaughn's account of the jumping mule. As a principle, Healy believed, "No man who is sober and not threatened will shoot another man in cold blood."[51] He first met Carson, said to be nephew of Kit Carson, that winter of 1865-1866 and considered him one of his best men. According to Healy, Carson was:

> ... a brave fellow who inherited his uncle's dislike for Indians, but strange to say he

had no love for Kit, frequently pronouncing him an old fraud.[52]

The Ranger squad's activity at Morgan's coincides with the "immediate hanging" of four horse thieves, claimed with no detail by white settlers. The four lynched Indians were part of a larger party of Piegan. Weeks earlier they found a way inside the Sun River Government Farm, after loitering for some time at a distance. At the time Healy's brother, Joe Healy, judged it best to invite them inside and feed them. He made them hand over their guns before offering them a meal. That hospitable approach worked. Without touching any property, the Piegan finished eating and left peacefully.[53] It was also during those early weeks of December that a war party of Bloods re-crossed the Missouri from the south near Fort Benton and caused quite a stir.

The Bloods were trailing horses north. One warrior traded a purse of gold dust to a Métis for a blanket. After they passed through a Piegan camp, word came from that camp to Fort Benton that those Bloods killed three white men on the Yellowstone. Another Métis in the Piegan camp reported more murder-related evidence. He saw a second purse filled with gold and a white man's revolver.[54] After some delay it became clear that the storm hid another incident.

About 80 miles northeast of Fort Benton, Hunecke and LeGree, two whiskey traders employed by Fort Benton merchants Carroll and

Steele, were returning from a Gros Ventre camp on the Milk River. On December 1, they had gone there with two young Gros Ventre helpers to retrieve horses. Coming south with four more Gros Ventre, including their own wives and two more helpers, they neared the Bear's Paw Mountains with the big storm bearing down on them. Hunecke told one of the boys to make the day's ride back to camp for sugar while he and the rest of the party built a cabin as temporary shelter. The storm forced the boy, Hunecke's brother-in-law, to wait in camp on the Milk for eight days. Finally able to travel the most direct route to Fort Benton, he was surprised to find Hunecke and LeGree and party were not there. The helper backtracked toward the Milk but encountered large numbers of Piegan "fairly swarming in that section in search of Gros Ventre horses and scalps." That forced him to stop. The helper returned to Fort Benton to find and guide a seven-man search party north after the New Year. At the camp on the Milk, they learned that before the traders even left camp a party of Piegan had been downriver stealing Crow and Gros Ventre horses. Eagle Rib, made chief by the treaty signing, had been the leader of the horse-stealers. The Crow and Gros Ventre killed nine of Eagle Rib's party who were seen following the same route toward Fort Benton behind the whiskey traders. Another Gros Ventre warrior found one of LeGree's horses shot near the Sweet Grass Hills. On their way back to Fort Benton, the searchers encountered some trappers on the Marias. The trappers told of a party of passing Piegan trailing about the same number of horses as belonged to the whiskey traders when they left the Milk.[55]

By early January 1866, information of the numerous incidents caused the non-Indians of Fort Benton to form a vigilance committee. Gough Steele and Henry Kennedy served as its local officers. Hiram Upham, Deputy to Upson, wrote to Upson, enroute to Washington City, telling him the local vigilantes were sending Berkin to get the territory's howitzer from Meagher. He said that Healy and Beidler were leaving the same day for the Sun intent upon "obtaining possession of the Sun River Farm." Upham made no mention of Howie. He arrived at Fort Benton a week later noting in his diary he purchased a pistol.

Dearborn Station (After 1866)

8. Irregulars

Descriptions of war at varying levels of intensity make little difference to a person doing the killing or the dying. Irregular warfare is as old as human beings, and Indians mastered it. Non-Indians became proficient during the Civil War, especially in Missouri and Kansas. Montana's space offered a prime theater for this kind of violent combat beyond control of government. Irregular wars end in three ways: some leaders discern causes on their own side and find ways to eliminate or offset those causes; hearts carrying the embers of the conflict for one side or the other finally die or disappear after a long time; or sometimes a powerful enough force arrives to isolate the fighters from each other or from their weapons long enough to cool passions. All three responses were at work along the Mullan Road. Some Indians and Métis murdered Little Dog and his son Fringe, because the Piegan Chief had the courage to try the first course, but embers lingered in hearts on both sides long after a stronger force arrived. While Meagher requested help from the U.S. Army, Upham in his July 25, 1866, letter convinced the nation's Commissioner of Indian Affairs to discourage the President from seeking ratification of the Upson Treaty. While making no effort to convey the Indian point of view, Upham reported:

> The Bloods, Blackfeet and most of the North Piegans are at open war with the whites, as well as with all other tribes of Indians. They live for the most part in the British possessions, and only come here to receive their annuity goods or to commit some depredations. Many of them have never been here at all. These Indians have plenty of horses, and living in a country where buffalo and other game are abundant, they are very independent. They openly and defiantly declare that they will kill every white man they find, and, as practice has demonstrated, they carry their threat into execution whenever an opportunity presents itself.
>
> There are about three hundred and fifty or

four hundred lodges of Lower Piegans, who live on the headwaters of Milk River and the Marias. Two head chiefs, the Little Dog and Big Lake, have for several years controlled these Indians. This camp of Indians is in the habit of coming to the post to trade. I am fully satisfied that all the chiefs and headmen of this tribe are in favor of a lasting peace towards the government. There are, however, many young men in the camp who are continually on the warpath against other Indians, and who, in the course of their excursions, are continually meeting with whites. In such cases a collision generally occurs, thus keeping up hostilities between the whites and the young warriors, while the chiefs and old men are trying to keep peace.

In June last the Little Dog, head chief of the Piegans, came in from camp and turned over to me twelve head of horses which he had taken from the warriors, they having stolen them from the whites. A party of warriors followed him, and when about four miles from here on his return to camp, he and his son were both murdered. They were killed because they were suspected of being too friendly with the whites.

Upham's Annual Report failed to mention many other murders, including of Indians, Fort

Benton's vigilantes and the Sun River Rangers along the Mullan Road. Upham also neglected to communicate that Meagher had mobilized a Territorial Militia to fight in support of the Sun River Rangers. Nor did he correct his earlier statements that Little Dog's son was stealing horses, and his earlier inflammatory suggestion that older heads of Indian families were participating in the breakdown.

On February 4, 1866, after reading copies of Upham's two earlier reports to Upson, Meagher signed a blank commissioning form with "Sidney Edgerton, Commander-in-Chief of the Militia Forces of Montana Territory in the United States of America" printed across its face. By signing that form, he commissioned Howie as a Colonel, Commanding the Second Regiment of the Territorial Volunteers.[56] Four days later Sanders "resigned his Commission as Quartermaster Colonel" leaving Meagher with no staff.[57] In his own hand Meagher directed Howie to Fort Benton:

> Take charge of those who volunteered and mount an expedition to relieve the citizens of Fort Benton from their state of siege, which they have been experiencing for several weeks. Go into the Piegan camp and demand horses and other property which had been stolen from Fort Benton's residents, and demand the Piegan turn over Eagle Bird (sic.) and the son of Little Dog. After careful enquiry and full

deliberation of their case, execute them by hanging in the presence of the Indian camp.

    The big motivator for Meagher was a letter placed into his hands by U.S. Marshal George Pinney. It paraphrased Upham's January 9 and February 2 reports to Upson. Beidler had carried the take-it-or-leave-it petition from Fort Benton to Howie in Helena; Howie carried it to Pinney in Virginia City. Signed by citizens of Fort Benton acting as a Grand Jury, the letter restated Upham's litany of grievances against the Piegan, Blood and Sisika Blackfeet.[58] After summarizing all the depredations from their point of view, Chouteau County's vigilantes said they intended, " . . . to exterminate their tormentors if necessary to achieve peace."[59]

    After receiving Meagher's direction, Howie had trouble finding horses to mount all the willing men he located in Virginia City. Acting as his own Quartermaster, Meagher called local merchants together and asked them for supplies. Few were offered. After a "council of war" in Virginia City, Howie rode to Helena and decided to send north as many as 50 men. In Helena he found Carson waiting with more news and letters. Whites along the Sun had been driven into Fort Benton. Among them, Morgan opted to take his family to Saint Peters Mission, where the priests, apprehensive about drawing hostile attention to their peaceful purposes, decided to shelter them. The Jesuits recorded:

Morgan was desperate to obtain shelter for them, on the plea of general insecurity of the country about and because he had to go to Helena on most urgent business.[60]

One of the letters that Carson carried came from James Hill and was addressed to Howie as a friend. Over the signatures of merchants Carroll and Steele, Hill wrote:

> If the Governor doesn't think he has the power or the means to mount an expedition, let the people take it in hand as they have done before and they would well pay themselves by the plunder they would take. Of 500 men each one would get at least 50 head of horses, which could be sold for twenty dollars per head, say nothing of the robes, peltries, etc. I think that $1000 would pay most anyone for two months work. Are Indian murders of miners on the Yellowstone not worse than attacking a stage with short shotguns, an offense for which whites are justly hung?
>
> Are Indians better than white men or should they be punished by death? If this is the case we should fight them as they fight, kill where you can and when you can and anyway you can. If all the men that want to fight have not horses, the first fight will furnish plenty. When Indians are once set afoot, they are whipped.[61]

This directive established Montana's Second Volunteer Militia with a recruiting office in Helena's federal courtroom. In addition to Howie, as Colonel, its other officers consisted of John Featherstun as Major; A.Z. "Quill" Lawrence, Robert Hereford, Charles J.D. Curtis and Joseph Cowbell as Captains; and Edwin Bell and A.J. Wilson as First Lieutenants. There was no staff and no one stepped in to replace Sanders as Quartermaster.[62] Howie finally decided to send ten men north. He assigned Quill Lawrence, another of his law enforcement assistants, to lead the detail. Howie advised General Meagher of the actions being taken and had Beidler carry the letter to Virginia City through another winter storm. The next morning Berkin, with his mule-drawn Diamond R Freight wagons, arrived in Helena from Fort Benton.[63] He brought with him the territory's howitzer, which he had already transported from Virginia City to Fort Benton in January.[64] At Sun River Government Farm he pre-positioned two cases of shot and shell, each round with powder included.[65] On February 16, some King and Gillette freight wagons arrived in Helena from Virginia City. They carried the 40 Springfield rifle-muskets Meagher signed to receive in October. Of these, 39 were complete stands of arms. Included with the shipment were more than seven cases of .58 caliber cartridges and percussion caps.

When Lawrence's detail rode north, at least four .58 caliber Springfields and one case of ammunition went north as well. Three of the muzzle-loaders later showed up at Fort Benton's Blackfeet Indian Agency, and at least one was destroyed in the fire at Sun River Government Farm. Of the nine volunteers riding north with Lawrence and Carson, one was Charles Curtis, a Catholic army veteran born in Ireland.[66] On the day the 11-man detail left, another 21-man detachment, working to survey and construct a road, left Helena for the Musselshell River. They were led by U.S. Army Captain R.W. Andrews.[67]

The day after both groups cleared town, Howie raised enough gold dust around Helena to pay King and Gillette Freight Company's ordinance transport bill of $162.50. He had enough dust leftover to pay for storing the unused ordinance. On February 19, Berkin's faster mule-drawn wagons with the howitzer overtook Andrews' oxen-drawn wagons. On February 20, news arrived in Helena that three Indians had been killed between the Belt Mountains and Fort Benton.[68] On March 1, Healy received a letter from Meagher granting him permission to trade with Montana's Blackfeet, Gros Ventre and Crow tribes.[69]

On March 17, Meagher told Howie to move the undistributed ammunition and stand of arms into the new Tutt and Donnell stone building on Helena's Bridge Street.[70] Another month passed before Berkin got back to Helena on April 17. He brought news of a March 3 skirmish, during which he lost an ox to a Piegan war party. He and six men pursued and killed five of the Piegan. Berkin had been on the road back to Helena for three days before Andrews' crew got into a fight with more Piegan attackers. One of the remaining 15 crewmembers was wounded. All the work cattle were killed. This forced Andrews to abandon the howitzer and the wagons.[71] After making his arrival report, Berkin loaded up the rest of the arms and ammunition stored on Bridge Street and departed for Virginia City with Beidler by his side on April 25.[72]

That same day, a war party of Piegans and Bloods continued a string of murderous incidents. Three days earlier after a frantic warning by an Indian woman, that war party attacked two of the men working at the Sun River Farm.[73] Then they attacked the active Mission and killed James Fitzgerald as he was herding in the field. Giorda described to Meagher the general situation:

> All the horses and cattle of Mr. Morgan are either stolen or butchered. Eighteen head of horses are gone. Mr. Kennedy's band is partly stolen, partly butchered, and partly wounded. The entire road to Benton from Clark's (sic.) on down is lined with war parties... I must leave today to go and see and perhaps remove the Mission and my brethren. We hope that as we were of necessity obliged by violence to retire for the moment that the property and claims of the Mission and missionaries will be protected by law and secured.[74]

The Jesuit hoped to move the mission personnel to the new mission below Bird Tail Rock. On the way they met several groups of "Indians and Whites stirred up for trouble."[75] After spending only one night under the Bird Tail, he decided to keep everyone moving west toward the Hell Gate River and Saint Ignatius Mission. While they were seeking refuge, details of Carson's death unfolded.

On April 25, the day Indians ended Carson's life, he and his fellow volunteers had barricaded themselves inside Dearborn Station expecting to fight off a war party of Piegan, Blackfeet and Bloods led by Bull's Head. Bull's Head's party had been raiding along the Mullan Road. Carson failed to realize the raiders had surrounded Dearborn Station when he walked over the top of a hill to recover horses that had drifted. As he aimed at one of the Indians throwing lariats over horses, he was shot and killed by a bullet coming through his Hawken rifle.[76] The war party didn't mutilate Carson's body but took his weapon and his horse, celebrated with a victory dance and disappeared. Next day Carson's friends and acquaintances buried him in the Dearborn Crossing Cemetery.[77]

After that incident the Dearborn Crossing area became a dreaded place, especially around Deadman's Coulee, named for a Mr. Lowe who died alone. In addition to Carson and Lowe, the Blackfeet separately killed James Chambers and old man Thebeau.[78] On the Teton, they killed

Paul Virmette. Understandably, through the rest of 1866 non-Indians occupied Sun River Crossing and 28-Mile Springs about half the time.

On May 15, Curtis rode back into Helena "with the boys." He turned them right around and escorted Meagher's wagon train to Fort Benton in order to meet the incoming Acting First Lady, Elizabeth Meagher. With the Sun in spring flood, wagon freighters, including the first oxen-train from Virginia City, were backed-up across from Sun River Crossing. They were all waiting for Healy. He had gone to Fort Benton for repair materials to fix his ferry's broken rope. It was shortly after that on May 27, that Healy's friend Little Dog and his son were killed.[79]

Meagher had been requesting regular army support from Camp Cooke, 108 river miles down from Fort Benton. The 13th Infantry tried to partly satisfied those requests with a forward detachment led by Captain Charles Webb and Lieutenant Martin Hogan. Their details, based out of the recently attacked and abandoned Saint Peters Mission, began patrolling the Mullan Road. These regular soldiers were armed with revolvers and .58 caliber Springfields as they carried mail back and forth to Helena. On nearly every trip they were forced to defend themselves.[80]

By then, in Montana, there existed a single M1865 first Allin conversion Springfield breech-loader. It belonged to a Gallatin Valley rancher named Nelson Story. He called it his needle-gun.[81] Though the modified weapon did not have the long needle of the type used in Europe, the single-shot breechloader did use a firing pin. Back in the states, the Springfield Armory had already improved on that first modification and was making 25,000 M1866 second Allin conversion Springfield breech-loaders. Their barrels were sleeved down to .50 caliber and they used center-fired copper cartridges instead of rim-fired..

Daniels' Demise

9. Disorder

Daniels' trial, conducted in Helena during the big storm, ended with legal disorder. As an Associate Justice on the Territory's Supreme Court, District Judge Munson tried to comply with Chief Justice Hosmer's vision upholding the fifth and eighth amendments of the U.S. Constitution.[82] Daniels entered jail January 1 and left February 23 after having served only 54 days.[83] Inadequate territorial prison facilities, severe weather, the probability of a strong case for self-defense and a petition for pardon from

32 of Helena's citizens influenced Meagher to reprieve the sentence, pending review by the U.S. President. The nuanced distinction between a pardon not permitted by law as a power of the Territory's Acting Governor and a reprieve pending action by the President was lost on people. Hearing Daniels was out of jail, Munson went to Virginia City with an order to have him re-arrested. Some have characterized Munson's mood with the word "furious." The word "frantic" would be more appropriate. Munson needed to forestall Daniels being lynched upon returning Helena. Munson may have been a Yale-trained lawyer, but in Helena he had been working and living in close quarters with the deadliest of Virginia City's 1863-1864 vigilantes. They were Howie, his peregrine assistants Beidler and Berkin, and long-time fugitive-chasing associates Hereford and Featherstun. By 1866, they had all migrated north and co-located in the Dunphy Block near Munson's federal courtroom or a few feet up the street. Munson not only shared offices with the men who had been Montana's leading extra-legal executioners, he played cards and enjoyed dinner with them. All had figured as prominent real-life heroes in Dimsdale's serialized book. As a practical matter, each of them had directly experienced Daniels' surly and unpleasant attitude.

Munson was no bleeding heart and no friend of Daniels, but his priority was to help advance the supremacy of common law while building the credibility of the territory's court system. Munson missed corralling Daniels. The reprieved prisoner arrived in Helena at nine o'clock on the night of March 2. He intended to confront one of his accusers.[84] The unlovable Irishman soon found it advisable to seek protection from Featherstun. That proved unwise. The town's Constable left him alone for a few minutes to go out to get a sense of the mood of the community. He was gone but a few minutes when three men visited Daniels. By ten o'clock he was 300 yards above the jail and 10 feet above the ground, hanging lifeless on a rope from a Ponderosa pine tree on the east side of Dry Gulch.

Dimsdale had communicated twice by letter with Howie about Daniels' release. The first message arrived the night of February 24, a day-and-a-half after Daniels got out of jail. A second Dimsdale letter got to Howie on February 25, the day Howie answered both.[85] Before Dimsdale died of consumption on September 22, Howie visited the author twice. The first time was July 15 and the last was the night of his death.[86] Dimsdale's serialized story had been published on August 25, 1865, six months before Daniels' hanging. Yet, Daniels' hanging was another of the vigilante executions included when the story was published as Montana's first book. Before it was published December 1, new material had been added for the 268-page book. The additions included an explanation of Daniels' hanging as the "last criminal, executed by the

Vigilantes (sic.)." Dimsdale, or his mystery editor, wrote this about Daniels' return to Helena:

> He had drawn his knife, and concealed it in his sleeve, with the intent of stabbing Hugh O'Neil in the back, after the fight between Orem and Marley at the Challenge Saloon. He said he 'would cut the heart out of the ----!'

This was the reason given in *The Vigilantes of Montana* for the lynching:

> Daniels renewed his threats when liberated, and was hanged; not because he was pardoned, but because he was unfit to live in the community.[87]

Langford wrote that Daniels' execution was not condoned by Virginia City's vigilance committee, of which he was a member nor did he think it had been condoned by the Helena vigilance committee. He considered the hanging "as the unauthorized act of certain irresponsible members at Helena."[88] It was unlikely that Daniels' lynching was in keeping with the standards and intentions of Meagher or Munson or even Howie. Deeper combinations of dynamics were gaining traction in the territory. Other happenings were bringing even the hardest core vigilantes into working relationships with the courts and with Meagher. Irregular warfare along the Mullan Road had become far more important. There were other demanding developments.

On August 29, a two and one-half ton load of gold dust arrived at Fort Benton from Confederate Gulch.[89] It didn't travel by the less-used Graham Wagon Road but by the Mullan Road. Beidler worked as a guard on the huge shipment and remembered the owners amassing their fortune in gold dust at a bank on Helena's Bridge Street:

> . . . we started from Helena to Benton with the dust loaded on three two-mule wagons, the dust in three safes, and fourteen men armed and on horseback . . . we camped the first night in Prickly Pear Canyon . . . the next night we camped at the Dearborn. Had no trouble till we got to Bull's Head (Coulee), 12 miles this side of Benton. While riding on a walk, my horse broke his right forward leg just below the knee through no apparent cause—no holes, rocks, or anything else to cause it, and how it was done none of us could find out. It just snapped off. We shot him there and I rode on in the wagon to Benton. While we were there, we fixed the safes ready for shipping them down the river in Mackinaw boats, no steamers being there. We fastened ten-gallon casks with long ropes to each safe in case the boats might upset, where the casks could act as buoys and the safes could be located. They got through to

the states all right. I got eleven ounces for my trip.[90]

Every day in August that year Fort Benton bid farewell to three Montana-made Mackinaw boats, each carrying an average of 15 persons down the river. Raw danger made the larger number of passengers advisable. In 1863, Sioux massacred eighteen people in one Fort Benton-built boat. From that group, one woman and two children were killed in a graphically brutal way.[91] Earlier in the summer of 1866 three men attempted the down river trip in a smaller boat. They were found massacred by Sioux.[92] By June, these kinds of harsh incidents involving the Sioux had started to become in people's minds Red Cloud's War. Virginia City's newspaper readers first learned of Red Cloud, the formidable Sioux Chief, when he came into a military post for the first time in 20 years of war. U.S. Army officers seemed hopeful there could finally be peace with his 1700 lodges.[93] That did not happen. As 1866 progressed, several dozen soldiers and emigrants along the Bozeman Trail were killed, and the rate of their being killed increased. During one July week, 24 died.[94] If people didn't start for Montana Territory as refugees from a war somewhere else, when they finally reached the shacks of Virginia City they found a refuge from the anxiety of traveling the Bozeman Trail. However, anxiety never seemed to overshadow optimism. One example was the 26 wagons drawn by hundreds of oxen in a single train. They were bringing machinery that used a new design for processing gold ore. They were headed for the Oro Cache Mine, high in the mountains, eight and a half miles up Alder Creek from Virginia City. The trip was risky. A process using Chilean rollers instead of stamps to crush ore was risky. Negotiating the steep, high and narrow road to the mine and mill site was risky. The potential for a fall off in gold production from the mine was risky. Yet, a fellow named Benjamin Franklin Christenot, using gold from the Oro Cache lode, convinced Philadelphia backers to take the risk. The slow-moving oxen pulled their enormous loads to Virginia City by October 1866, and the unusual machinery was installed and working by the following June.[95]

Toward the end of the summer of 1866, Meagher signed a second hand-receipt for another 40 stand of arms from the Niobrara Wagon Road Company. The second batch of ordinance consisted of obsolete muzzle-loading .577 caliber Enfields and 5,000 cartridges, at a time when the territory seemed to enjoy an overabundance of privately held guns and ammunition.[96]

On December 14, there was a big gunfight near Confederate Gulch. Five Irish miners died. Their names were Dennis Murphy, John Hastert, Thomas Cheevers, Patrick Osborn and Michael McLaughlin. When they were shot to death, another miner named John Flaherty was wounded. Nine German miners did the shooting. Each group of men believed the other to be claim-jumpers. After the surprise deadly fusillade, a hundred heavily armed Diamond City vigilantes surrounded the killers still barricaded in the same port-holed log cabin from which they'd done the shooting.[97] Someone sent for Howie. He rode from Helena with Beidler, Berkin, Lawrence and another hundred armed men. The friends of the killed men allowed themselves to be peacefully disarmed before the killers would agree to emerge from their bunker and be arrested for trial. Two hundred armed men formed their escort back into Helena.

While this was happening, Kuppens swam the Missouri and arrived "while the survivors of the two parties were still shooting at each other." He brought the five dead Catholics into town and, with their interments on December 16 and 17 inaugurated Helena's first Catholic Cemetery. The men were buried on the rocky bench above the Hanging Tree.

How both groups of grown men could passionately claim the same ground will probably never be fully answered. The Prosecutor's claim of "pure cold-blooded assassination" was supported by the testimony of Flaherty and Michael Lynch. Key testimony for the Defense came from the Cave Gulch Mining District Recorder R.L. McGonigal and another witness W.J. Clarke. Both witnessed the shooters previously working the disputed claims. There was great applause when the jury delivered a verdict of "not guilty."[98]

Enduring feelings, perhaps still being held from the War of Rebellion, surfaced during that winter of 1866-1867. On February 16, 1867, William McGlothlin, a 25-year old single man, was found dead. His body lay on the lonely road that crossed the hill from Virginia City's busy Wallace Street and descended into the willows and miners' shanties near the original point of discovery along Alder Creek. He was face down in the snow with a bullet in the back of his head. His Navy colt still filled his holster. Two months later, three black men thought to be his murderers were released for lack of evidence.[99] That action by the Madison County Grand Jury seemed remarkable, given that so many southern sympathizers and confederate veterans, including men who rode with Bloody Bill Anderson and William Quantrill, were living in the area. Most were trying to restart their lives. Some refused to change.[100] The murder went unsolved though a letter in the victim's pocket indicated that McGlothlin was one of a few adult male survivors of Quantrill's bloody raid on Lawrence, Kansas.[101]

One of Quantrill's men, John Byrd, mined in Alder Gulch at the time of the shooting but soon moved north to continue mining at Canyon Ferry on the Missouri near Helena.[102] Sanders' friend Creighton, a Union Army veteran and staunch abolitionist, followed the former confederate raider north and purchased four wagons and four mule teams from him. That such a transaction could happen between a passionate abolitionist and one of Quantrill's men, formerly a slave owner, testifies to the deep changes being forged in Montana. The same was true of the Indians. Though the Piegan and Gros Ventre kept fighting, the Gros Ventre and Crow looked past their differences and made peace.

Three other unpredictable events caused profound consequences: electricity being generated at Virginia City brought the capital city into telegraph connectivity with the states; Lakota Sioux, Cheyenne and Arapaho fighters massacred 81 regular U.S. soldiers on the Bozeman Trail; and Sanders, with help from his stay-at-home uncle, persuaded fellow Unionist Republicans in Congress to erase the work of Montana's second and third territorial legislatures.[103]

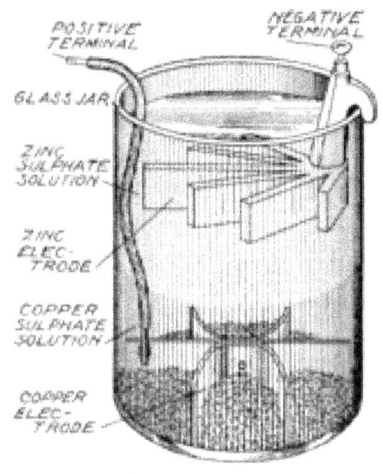

Fig. 64. Gravity Cell

A Single Primary Battery Jar

10. Electricity

Montana's first generated electricity happened after Creighton contracted with his older brother at Western Union to extend that company's telegraph line north from Salt Lake City. Creighton raised the required capital around Alder Gulch by selling script later to be exchanged for telegrams. In July 1866, his crews started construction on the Virginia City end of the line and then they left for Salt Lake City. In September, they returned with seventeen freight wagons of excess materials to be stored for a subsequent line extension to Helena. Other wagons loaded with wire and insulators were spaced along the 422-mile stagecoach road behind them, awaiting the hole-diggers, pole-crews, and linemen moving north at 8 to 20 miles a day. By September 17 at Virginia City, the last wire was hung on the last pole located at the street corner in front of Creighton and Ohle's stone-built store. Inside, at the end of the wire, was a box of glass jars interconnected by wires. Maintaining the tray of battery jars was the responsibility of the "lightning gobbler," Ireland-born Hughes, the same who had been a friend of Ives and one of the six discoverers of gold in Alder Gulch.[104] Inside each glass jar, he'd spread a copper strip on the bottom, hung a zinc claw-foot from the side, and poured in two rainwater solutions, copper sulfate followed by lighter zinc sulphate.[105] This turned each jar into a 1.1-volt cell in an expandable battery. Once the telegraph instruments were installed, practice signals went to Salt Lake City.[106] The day of the first practice signal, October 27, 1866, marks the first usage of electricity in Montana.

All the gold found in Montana has paled in value compared to the worth of electricity. If Hughes wasn't talkative, his "take it aisy" spoke volumes in that it predicted the real benefit of harnessed lightning.[107] What seems most amazing is that people who would appreciate owning their own gold mine little thought at all to owning and controlling their own source of electricity. Such was the case in 1866. It took the first telegraph message arriving in Virginia City from the states on November 2, for *The Montana Post* to announce, "The subtle force of electricity has again triumphed as the great even in our Territorial history." Operator Levi Wild deciphered this incoming message from the electric sounder's chatter: [108]

> Salt Lake, Nov. 2, 1866. Citizens of Montana: Allow me to greet you. It gives me pleasure to connect your city by lightning. Men of so much enterprise should not be forgotten. Your brave governor will send the first message free to A. Johnson, President of the United States. E. Creighton.

Montana Territorial Governor Green Clay Smith who had arrived October 3 answered:

> Virginia City, M.T., Nov. 2, 1866, 1 1-2 o'clock P.M. To Andrew Johnson, President of the United States, Washington City, DC: Montana sends greetings. We are this day brought in hourly communication with the United States and the world. God save the Union. Green Clay Smith, Governor of Montana.

At ten dollars for ten words, Smith's message cost over $40. That was cheap compared to the one-way stage fare to Salt Lake City at $120 or Omaha at $305. These fares were in addition to the cost of personal time, taking three and a half to sixteen days just to Salt Lake City and doubled for the return trip.[109] Later in the winter Patrick Largey, one of Creighton's wagon bosses on the Bozeman Trail, rode to

Helena to sell more script. Customers were plentiful since without the telegraph letters needed to be shuttled by horseback or stage between Virginia City and Helena and Fort Benton and the Gallatin Valley. Worldwide news received by telegraph at Virginia City was delayed until it came to Helena in Virginia City's newspapers for reprinting. Creighton and Largey hoped their crews would complete an extension to Helena in October 1867.[110]

Their planned telegraph line would go down the Ruby River, up White Tail Deer Creek, through Boulder and over into Prickly Pear Creek through Jefferson City. From 10-Mile Station on Prickly Pear Creek, it would cut west through the hills to Dry Gulch, down to Broadway and crossing Last Chance Gulch onto a tall mast over the telegraph office to the rear of the stagelines' offices. The line extension would use the same number 12 wire, the same rubber insulators and the same cut green aspen trees as the line from Salt Lake City.[111] During the summer of 1868, Largey would extend the line from Helena to Fort Benton through Deadman's Coulee. On August 1, 1867, the first of 20 men in several crews began sinking holes north of Nevada City and driving teams with cut poles to set. It took about 60 days for crews to stretch the 139 stored bales of wire all the way to Last Chance Gulch. Then Helena got "it's streak of lightning."[112]

As Helena's extension progressed, people in Virginia City could follow it more closely than the people in Helena. They were getting telegraphed reports from the field telegraph wagon at the end of the line. By October 3, the line reached Redferns Station. By October 5, it was at Jefferson River Bridge.[113] By October 8, it was 58 miles from Helena. By October 10, two teams and 20 men were stringing line at the rate of 27 miles a day. They would set poles, string out the wire and distribute the insulators, and use a 50-pound ladder to attach the insulators and carry the wire to the pole top. One man saw them working and said, "The men are putting up the line on a trot." The first telegraph operator for Helena, S.A. Wiley, stepped off the stagecoach from Salt Lake the evening of October 11. On Saturday afternoon October 12, Helena like Virginia City was in communication with the world:[114]

> The Company generously gave the Public the opportunity of telegraphic communication between the two places (Helena and Virginia City), gratis, and the opportunity was occupied to an extent probably unparalleled in the history of telegraphy.[115]

The "Company" was the Rocky Mountain Telegraph Company formed by Creighton and Largey. It handed the line off to Wiley, Western Union's first Helena operator.[116] In Virginia City Western Union erected a new office building on Van Buren Street.[117]

One Stand of Arms:
.58 Caliber Springfield Rifle-Musket With Sling, Cartridge, Tin Inserts, Cartridges, Musket Tool, Waist Belt and Cap Pouch

11. Fetterman

The terrifying attacks by Red Cloud's Sioux, Cheyenne and Arapaho warriors continued. In the heart of Crow country where the Big Horn River pours out of the Pryor Mountains, 100 men from the U.S. Army were building Fort C.F. Smith. It was intended to serve as the third of four planned patrolling bases north from Fort Laramie to protect travelers on the Bozeman Trail. During the winter of 1866-1867, Fort C.F. Smith was the most under-strength and isolated of the three completed installations. For longer than two months, beginning December 1, 1866, the soldiers stationed on the Big Horn River heard nothing from the outside world.[118] Nor did the outside world know anything concrete about Fort C.F. Smith's fate. The men inside were well-led and in high spirits but became more concerned about their situation after hearing rumors from the nearby Crow of aggressive Sioux, Cheyenne and Arapaho intentions. A Gallatin trader named John Richards arrived at the fort on February 2, 1867. He carried news from a December 15 telegram received in Virginia City that reported reinforcements were being requested at Forts Laramie and Reno.[119] On February 5 and 6, respectively, news arrived directly at Fort C.F. Smith carried by the Crow and by soldiers from Fort Phil Kearny. The news included bloody details from both sides of a recent battle, the Fetterman Massacre. On February 9, Richards left Fort C.F. Smith to go to Virginia City with the news for Meagher, advising him of a large buildup of hostiles near Fort C.F. Smith. The fort's commander specifically gave Richards the mission to return as soon as possible from Virginia City and the Gallatin with badly needed supplies. While this was happening by horse and mule, news from the Bozeman Trail reached Virginia City by telegraph and was immediately published in Virginia City's *The Montana Post*. Another account published on February 9 but written in Fort Laramie on December 27 reported:

On the 22nd a number of Indians came near the post, and Brevet Lieutenant Colonel W.J. Fetterman, Captain F.H. Brown, and Lieutenant G.H. Grummond, all of the 18th Infantry, gathered hastily eighty-nine men of Company C, Second Cavalry, and forty-five men of the 18th Infantry, and went after the Indians. The troops were gradually drawn on until a point four miles from the fort, when they were surrounded and slaughtered. Not a man escaped to tell the story of disaster. The bodies were stripped of every article of clothing, scalped and mutilated. Thirty bodies were found in a space not larger than a good-sized room. Nearly all the bodies were recovered and buried in the fort. Fort Phil Kearny was not captured, as would be inferred from the above. A sufficient number of troops have been sent from Laramie to insure its safety.[120]

When Gallatin trader Richards arrived from Fort C.F. Smith on March 15, he came accompanied by Mitch Boyer, the famous scout being paid twice his daily rate by the U.S. Army for making the critically important trip. Both men were part Indian and capable of moving more freely among the various tribes. They relayed descriptions of what the Crow and soldiers said happened outside of Fort Phil Kearny:

Two thousand seven hundred Indians were engaged; 900 did the fighting, while 1800 were lying concealed near the Fort to capture it if reinforcements had been sent to Fetterman. The Sioux lost in killed, Lone Bear and Iron Eye and six warriors. The Cheyenne lost in killed, Little Wolf and three warriors. About 150 were wounded.' Lying concealed on either side of the ravine, when they rose up and fired, the troops had advanced so far into the acute angle of the ambuscade, that they fired past them, and many of the Indians were shot with arrows from the opposite sides of the ravine.[121]

Raining arrows explained the chaotic minutes that doomed Fetterman and his men. They had to stand to load a paper cartridge and mini-ball and ram them down the barrel; if still alive or not wounded, take cover to fire at Indians who by then had taken cover; and stand again to reload, which gave warriors time to assault with hand weapons.[122] The two messengers reported Fort C.F. Smith having about 200 men. They said the Sioux had 1800 lodges each averaging three warriors under the command of Red Cloud, "the famous war chief of the recent massacre." They reported that no depredations had been committed because of severe weather and deep snow. They warned:

In anticipation of this summer's work, the

Sioux sent to the Bloods, Piegans and Gros Ventre the 'Peace pipe,' which they have accepted and joined the league against the whites. The northern bands were already camped on the left bank of the Missouri, with strength of something like 800 lodges. Their messengers to the Sioux camp said their tribes would soon cross the Missouri and camp near the Musselshell to 'begin a war of extermination.' Fort Commandant, Captain Nathaniel J. Kinney, did not expect to hold his position. 'If reinforcements do not soon arrive, the command will come to the Clark's Fork or the Yellowstone.'

Two days after the messengers from Fort C.F. Smith brought this information, news arrived from the states confirming that Sanders enjoyed a stranglehold on Montana's self-government.

U.S. Marshal Neil Howie[123]

12. Radicals

Sanders paid for his own travel to Washington City where he could influence Congress through his fellow radical Unionist Republicans. Word about the successful result of his efforts filtered into Montana during the first week in March. His fellow Union Leaguers expressed their jubilation with a formal resolution:

> Whereas the cause of Republican Union, unqualified suffrage and National Freedom, in Montana has heretofore had to contend with many obstacles, in consequence of the Territory being overrun by ex-rebels, and designing copperheads, who grasped the

reins of civil government and perverted all the powers of their high trusts to such base purposes only, as would insure their own aggrandizement and their continuance in office to rule over us; and ...

Whereas, Under these existing circumstances no honorable efforts on the part of our Union forces could of themselves be sufficient to correct public evils or inaugurate good government within our Territory, without the intervention of Congress to disarm the public enemies of the country, and place our civil contests on a fair and legitimate basis; therefore be it ...

Resolved, by the National Union League of Montana, in full council assembled, that we acknowledge our unfeigned joy and gratification at the reception of the late news from Washington, which announced that Congress has wiped out the bogus Legislature of Montana, annulled all their objectionable, odious and oppressive enactments, and so amended the Organic Act as to confer those privileges and that respect upon our honorable Judges which they so justly deserve.

Resolved, That we tender our earnest thanks to Congress—and especially to those friends in that body who have heard our petitions, and wrought out for the Union party of this Territory an epoch of success, and the certain means of an early, a complete and a glorious victory.

Resolved, That we recognize in Colonel W. F. Sanders and those others of our staunch Republicans of Montana, now in Washington who have so ably and so steadfastly presented our grievances before Congress, and have so untiringly labored for the consummation of these desirable ends, the true and tried friends, of the best interests of our Territory, and deserving the warmest thanks of all our good and loyal citizens.

By conveying his interpretation to the outside world about events transpiring inside Montana, Sanders nullified months of hard work by two legislatures. A few days later, on Saint Patrick's Day, Virginia City received a telegram from Pinney. He was also back in the states securing the appointment of the person that would replace him as U.S. Marshal. His message announced, "Neil Howie of Helena has been appointed United States Marshall (sic.) of Montana."[124] Five days later, from New York City, Sanders telegraphed the names of the new federal political appointees for Montana:

To: Editor Montana Post: W.F. Chadwick, District Attorney; James Tufts, Secretary of the Territory; Neil Howie, U.S. Marshal; J.X. Beidler, Collector of Customs. (Signed) W.F. Sanders.[125]

Sanders' clean sweep gained appointments for his chosen men to all the territory's paid positions. None of this surprised Meagher, who had already informed Hosmer of his intention to resign as Territory Secretary. Not everyone seemed as accepting.

Virginia City's other newspaper, *The Democrat*, which normally but inadequately tried to speak for the one third of territorial voters who were Northern Democrats and the one third who were Southern Democrats commented on both of Sanders' telegrams:

> The Democracy (sic.) of Montana are in a state of siege, and the besiegers at Washington are pitching hot shot, bombs and Greek fire among them by day and by night. They were only driven into their bomb-proofs by the annulling of the laws; but now comes another shot to blow up the garrison and smoke out the whole concern. There will be more 'thousands of dollars needed' now and more and more 'Legislative appropriations' required to bolster up certain parties and the trouble is, it is hard to divine what will come next. Those 'vipers and reptiles,' the enemies to Montana whose winter's effort was not worth a pinch of snuff,' are a desperate set of fellows, and the 'usurpation' of Congress is astonishing. It looks very much as though the scepter was sliding surely and rapidly out of the unterrified's (sic.) hands.

In making its assessment, *The Democrat* failed to allow for men sometimes changing. Howie, for example, had been a radical by necessity if not by choice. He was a hard man to categorize, because he kept his own counsel. Just as powerful rivers like the Missouri at Fort Benton run deep, the same hidden dynamics applied to men like the new U.S. Marshal.[126]

If the Missouri hid secrets born of changing flows among nature's forces, so did 40 year-old Howie. He had survived by trusting and shielding friends as they changed or failed to do so. In his diary he never condemned his friends or himself for the many times they were "tight" or "on a spree." Twice he judged Meagher as "drunk." His sparse entries convey strong friendship and respect for Pinney, upon whom he had been laying all hope of being appointed U.S. Marshal. In Howie's world, Sanders seemed more a man who needed to be obeyed or to be assisted as a favor. Those favors were usually difficult errands requiring long rides often in inclement weather. Though Howie kept his Masonic dues up to date, he labored over his decision to attend Sanders' Union League meetings among people Howie called "radicals." He ignored the Republican *The Montana Post's* patronizing attention and insensitivity. The newspaper would publish stories that included friendly innuendo for not stopping when in town, beneath a masthead that kept Pinney as U.S. Marshal and Beidler as Acting U.S. Marshal long after Howie's appointment. Howie ignored the newspaper's usual inflation of his own law enforcement and militia activities. His disposition, mannerisms and actions made other people, even Sanders, want and need him on their side, but he faced challenges.

Howie was the one who rode up the gulch to wrest Daniels from a group of Helena and Diamond City vigilantes. He had gained control on the proper argument that the bar room killer deserved due legal process. Howie's closest assistants, Beidler and Berkin, were heavily involved with the Helena and Diamond City vigilantes. When Daniels made the mistake of returning to confront a hostile witness, it was likely one, if not three, of Howie's four closest associates, Beidler, Berkin, Featherstun and Hereford, responsible for lynching Daniels. Howie worked within practical limits of having to bring along the men he knew and trusted. He did this while having to live with his reputation created by Dimsdale's book.

Fame of that kind, in the midst of hardened and strong-willed characters, invites trouble. The territory's flood of settlers had washed in a post-civil war flotsam of desperados, drunks, rebels, ruffians, whiskey traders and wolfers. They were a menagerie of potential killers. With this scale of challenging civilian work facing him, Howie was wise to leisurely monitor Meagher's requests for permission from General William T. Sherman to form a militia or to cause active military units to become better positioned along travel routes. When Meagher chose a veteran Confederate officer named Thomas Thoroughman to be overall field commander of Montana's Territorial Militia, it is understandable that Howie seemed less bothered than his supporters. The same was true for Meagher. He faced similar challenges.

On January 7, Meagher became Acting Governor again. That's when Governor Smith returned to the states to get his family in Lexington, Kentucky, and to visit Washington City to get more guns and ammunition released to the territory. Meagher had advised Smith, based on personal experience while commanding the Irish Brigade, that Sherman was a martinet. On that advice, Smith took his request directly to Sherman's boss General of the Army Ulysses S. Grant. While Meagher continued to exercise the lower level chain of command to Sherman, he could be certain that ordinance would eventually arrive in Montana. It might take a while longer for the necessary bureaucratic locks and balls and wheels to click and roll and paddle the guns and ammunition all the way to Fort Benton.

Row of Field-Stacked Rifle-Muskets

13. Adjutant

Sanders' messages from the states ended an era of good feeling in the territory. Those feelings hit their zenith at a March 18 Saint Patrick's Day celebration in Virginia City. The luxurious affair amounted to a splendid supper for a huge throng, lasted through the night and ended the next morning after everyone had breakfast. The venue's decorations included a portrait of George Washington with American and Irish flags draping on either side under a canopy of red, white and blue. Evergreens festooned the walls. At the opposite end of the hall, a second set of flags of both nations hung above Springfield and Enfield rifle-muskets, field-stacked around the territory's howitzer, returned to Virginia City from its abandonment on the Musselshell.[127]

Just after the Saint Patrick's party, a 25 year-old veteran named Sam Blythe rode into Virginia City. He'd just finished a hard winter in the Gallatin. Though an experienced printer, he couldn't get hired by *The Montana Post* or *The Democrat*. He ran into a hotel clerk, an old friend from their days in the 22nd Ohio, who staked him for food, found him a corral for his bed, and told him about another printer and friend, Martin Beem. From their days serving in the same company fighting at Shiloh, Blythe remembered Beem well:

> We were delighted to see each other. When the color bearer was shot and killed Martin picked up the flag and went forward. The Colonel made him a Lieutenant for his gallantry.[128]

After working just one half day driving oxen to tow a sled loaded with quartz, Blythe concluded that printing was a far better way to make money. He was happy to learn Beem had convinced the people at *The Montana Post* to change their minds.

Beem was more than a friend; he was a person to be respected. When he was 18 and couldn't enlist in his local unit at Alton, Illinois, because he appeared to be in fragile health, he went to Saint Louis and enlisted for three years as a Private in the 13th Missouri Volunteer

Infantry. On April 6, 1862, after 44,000 Confederates came yelling out of a morning dawn to surprise and nearly destroy General Grant's army above Pittsburgh Landing, the 13th Missouri made a surprise counter-attack at the onrushing Confederates. While they were still falling back, Beem saved a U.S. flag, later to be displayed in the trophy room at West Point, by wrapping it around his own body. As the center of the Union line was yielding, Beem further distinguished himself. He seized his unit's battle flag from the dead color-bearer and rushed toward the oncoming Confederates, thereby leading a turn in the tide of a pivotal strategic battle at a critical tactical moment. The 13th Missouri and adjoining units on either side held their regained positions long enough for Grant to establish his famous last line of defense. The next morning he maneuvered two armies to successfully attack from that line. Because of this Sherman, would not soon forget Beem.

The same general who considered Meagher "a stampeder" had personally thanked Beem for his gallantry at Shiloh. The Commander of the 13th Missouri, an aging West Pointer, promoted Sergeant Beem to 2nd Lieutenant for his actions. On May 29, 1862, the 13th Missouri became the 22nd Ohio. On October 21, 1863, Beem mustered out as a First Lieutenant.[129] He had been serving with that rank in the battles approaching Corinth, during which he was brevetted a Brigadier General.[130] During that time, he rose from a sick bed near Ioka, tied himself to a horse and fought through a two-day battle.[131] In Arkansas, he mustered out of the 22nd Ohio and two days later began serving as the Adjutant, responsible for organizing the 4th Arkansas Mounted Infantry consisting of five companies of loyal razorbacks. He fought with them until they were ordered to disband June 2, 1864.[132] From there Beem drifted West.

In the 33 months after being discharged from the 4th Arkansas, he had been recuperating from the war and traveling through the West Indies, Mexico, California and Oregon. On July 27, 1866, while he was still traveling, the U.S. Senate confirmed upon him the permanent rank of Captain by brevet.[133] On his way back to the states from the West Coast, he passed through Montana, where Meagher engaged him as Montana's Acting Territorial Secretary and then made him Montana's first Adjutant General. With Beem's capable staff assistance, Meagher moved quickly to execute his and Smith's plan for a more robust militia.

Even before the first big War Meeting in Virginia City's Court House on April 8, Meagher made Beem a Captain and the Adjutant responsible for all organization and recruitment.[134] To Command forces in the field Meagher settled on General Thomas Thoroughman, a popular attorney from Missouri. For expertise building bridges across the Madison River and Gallatin River and laying out defensive patrolling bases on both sides of the passes from the Gallatin into the Yellowstone, he chose Lieutenant Colonel Walter W. DeLacy, the Territory's map-maker and Madison County's Surveyor to be Engineer-in-Chief. In Captain Isaac Evans, Meagher found a field-experienced supply and commissary officer willing to serve as Assistant Quartermaster for forces in the field.

During that first War Meeting, all except Beem were in the Gallatin with Meagher, determining "the true conditions of affairs there."[135] The morning after the War Meeting, Beem started taking names of 50 to 60 volunteers in the Territory's Executive Offices. Curtis, the Union Army veteran, occasional stage actor, and owner of a Helena junk shop and auction house who had ridden to Fort Benton with Lawrence's detail, was in the Gallatin taking names of 50 to 60 more men.[136]

Major W.M. Clinton, the regular army officer responsible for most U.S. Army forces in Montana, agreed with Meagher's assessment of the seriousness of the Indian threat. On April 17, as Camp Cooke's Commander, Clinton responded to a direct plea from Meagher. He wrote to say he had no authority to reassign his command in its entirety, nor could he divide his force. The U.S. 13th Infantry already had 850 soldiers in Montana, 600 of them penned inside Camp Cooke. Even with this strength, Clinton expressed grave concern:

> Under the present circumstances, I do not feel like spreading my command and being whipped in detail, as was done at Fort Phil

Kearny. With my present force, I have no fear of the result of any encounter I may have with any force of Indians that may come against me, but to divide it I'm not so certain of the result. From the number of warriors the Sioux have, armed as they are said to be, you will see at once the propriety of keeping my command well in hand.[137]

On April 24 with the regular army option not available, Meagher called for 600 volunteers to enlist for three months. He appointed all the necessary officers, making Howie a Colonel to serve as his Aid-de-Camp in Helena.[138] Howie never acknowledged his new assignment, even by making an entry in his diary.[139] Meagher's decision to raise volunteers followed news of Blackfeet warriors, posing as Crow, killing John Bozeman and wounding Tom Cover. The two men had been attempting an ill-advised trade development trip to Fort C.F. Smith, Fort Phil Kearny and Fort Reno. According to first reports, Cover had been able to fire "fourteen rounds (sic.) from his Spencer carbine," swim the Yellowstone and walk 40 miles back to Bozeman City.[140] The messenger bringing news of Bozeman's death carried a petition signed by nearly 300 in the Gallatin asking Meagher for military assistance. On April 25, the capital's second big War Meeting resolved to begin recruiting volunteers onto a war footing.

At that big meeting, Meagher gave "his

personal assurance that 'to the victors should belong the spoils.'" The next morning Virginia City "resembled more the stirring times of '61, than anything seen since."[141] Some rounds were fired from the territorial howitzer and a recruiting flag was flying. Two hundred fifty horses were tendered for service. S.R. Kirby of Bannack donated as many as 74 guns, of unknown types and caliber, for use by the militia. Men were using wheelbarrows to move these, ammunition, and the 40 Enfields and 36 Springfields along the streets. Over the Jefferson House door hung a huge sign: "Headquarters Montana Militia." Clerks inside were helping volunteers complete their enlistment contracts.

On April 27, Meagher and Hosmer tried one more time for success. They jointly telegraphed for federal permission to raise a militia. That's the day *The Montana Post* reported on Lowe's body being found next to his wagon west of Dearborn Crossing. He had been killed by Indians. His two rifles, a sixteen shooter and 50 to 100 cartridges were gone, but his body, riddled with seven bullet holes, had not been scalped or mutilated in any way.[142] Another report told of Kennedy, the Wolf Creek rancher with his wife and child and two other men, being saved from the same fate by one of Kennedy's hired Métis who told the Indians they couldn't kill the Kennedy family without first killing him. That one man's courage caused the war party to leave.[143]

On April 28 and 29, Meagher published his

General Orders setting forth the first concepts for organizing and operating Montana's Militia.[144] Chief of Staff, Colonel Francis C. Deimling, coordinated the staff effort. 1st Aide-De-Camp, Lieutenant Colonel John Hearn wrote the General Orders, and Adjutant General Beem wrote General Order 1:[145]

Headquarters Territorial Militia,
Executive Office, M.T. April 28, '67.
(General Orders.)

I. Francis C. Deimling is hereby appointed and commissioned as Chief of Staff, and John D. Hearn 1st Aid-de-Camp.

II. Martin Beem, having been appointed Adjutant and Inspector General of the Territorial Militia, with the rank of Colonel, he will have the chief and general direction of the organization of all troops now being raised for the defense of the Territory – he will see them properly equipped and otherwise supplied and dispatched in the best possible condition, and without delay, to the field.

III. Hamilton Cummings, having been appointed and commissioned Quartermaster and Commissary General, with the rank of Colonel, will have exclusively the authority to issue subsistence, ordinance and transportation to the several Companies, and enter into contracts for the various articles and stores which may be required under these heads.

He will give the proper vouchers for whatever he receives. To the end that this two-fold department shall work the more effectively, the Quartermaster and Commissary General is hereby authorized and directed to appoint two Assistant Quartermaster and Commissary Generals – one for the troops raised in Edgerton County, another for the troops on service in the field.

IV. Thomas Thoroughman on reporting himself to the Undersigned at Bozeman City will be appointed to the command of all the troops in the field and on active duty, with the rank of Brigadier General. He will have the disposition of these troops and the initiation and control of all movements it may be necessary to undertake -- and he, as well as all the officers herein mentioned, will be respected and obeyed accordingly.

V. Neil Howie has been directed to take, with the rank of Colonel, chief and general direction of the troops raised in Edgerton County. John Featherstun, Charles Curtis, J.X. Beidler and James L. Fisk, have been appointed his assistants, as recruiting officers, with the rank of Captain.

VI. Granville Stuart, Walter B. Dance, and William L. Irwin, have been appointed recruiting officers for Deer Lodge County, with the rank of Captain.

VII. On the arrival of the several

companies at Bozeman City, the commanding officers will report in person to General Thomas Thoroughman, who will under the authority set forth in Article IV. assign them their respective posts and duties as well as enforce whatever special regulations the circumstances may warrant.

VIII. The sincere and hearty thanks of the Undersigned and officers co-operating with him, are eminently due, and are hereby tendered, to the merchants and other businessmen of Virginia City for their prompt liberality in furnishing gratuitously a very considerable amount of supplies for the use of the troops taking the field. The historian of the Territory, when he comes to write of these days, its danger, efforts and sacrifices, will not forget them.

By order of
THOMAS FRANCIS MEAGHER
Acting Governor and Commander in Chief, Montana Militia.

John D. Hearn, Lieutenant Colonel and Aid-de-Camp

Adjutant General's Office
Territorial Militia, Virginia City, M.T
April 29, 1867.
(General Order No. 1)

In compliance with the foregoing order I have this day assumed the duties of Adjutant and Inspector General of the volunteer forces now being raised for the defense of the Territory.

To expedite the organization of companies, the following instructions are herewith published:

I. Companies will be composed of one Captain, one First Lieutenant, one Second Lieutenant and 50 men – including one Orderly Sergeant, four duty Sergeants and four Corporals.

II. When the above number are recruited, the commissioned officers will be elected by the men, and the non-commissioned officers appointed by the Captain who will immediately notify these Headquarters of such organization, giving the name of the officers elected, so that commissions may be issued and the proper instructions transmitted.

III. Company commanders will make requisitions without delay upon Hamilton Cummings Quartermaster General, at this place, for all supplies of clothing, camp and garrison equipage, subsistence and quartermaster stores, ordnance and ordnance stores that may be required.

IV. Blank muster rolls can be obtained upon application at these Headquarters. When these printed blanks are not used, company muster rolls must specify the names of the officers and men, residence within the Territory, post office address in the States, where enlisted, when, and length of time.

The utmost dispatch in the recruiting and formation of companies is essential, so that they may be equipped at once and sent, with the least possible delay to the defense of the threatened portion of the Territory.

By order,
    MARTIN BEEM
    Adjutant and Inspector General.

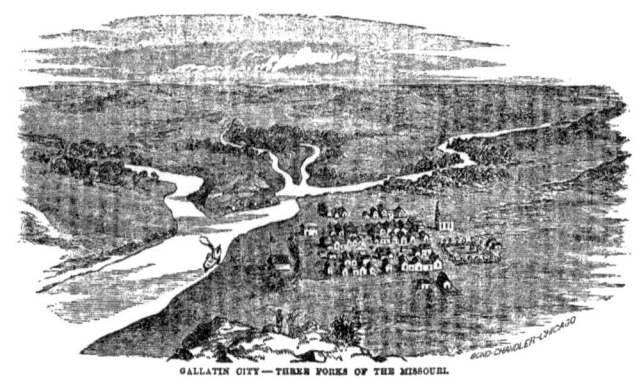

Gallatin City

14. Gallatin

The 1855 Judith River treaty gave to the Blackfeet all the land west of the Milk's mouth and north of the Missouri and the Musselshell, clear to the continental divide. The 1851 Treaty of Fort Laramie had given the Blackfeet more land in the south, including the three headwaters rivers comprising the Three Forks of the Missouri, as well as the Yellowstone down to the mouth of 25-Yard Creek. After 1855 those southern areas would be recognized as common hunting grounds for the tribes traditionally using them. The Blackfeet gained the Sun, Teton and Marias and areas north of a west-east line drawn between the Hell Gate and the western most source of the Musselshell.[146] The new arrangement didn't mean much to the Sioux. They were not represented, because the treaty had been signed before they found themselves pushed up the Missouri and Yellowstone.[147] Nor did it mean anything to the non-Indians after the fall of 1863 when they began farming the rich soil of the Gallatin Valley on the rebound from dashed gold-mining dreams. On February 2, 1865, when the first legislature at Bannack authorized eight operational counties for the territory, it attached a ninth county to Gallatin County for judicial and administrative purposes. Big Horn County was filled with Sioux, Cheyenne, Arapaho, Assiniboine and Crow, non-voting residents with an attitude. The combined Gallatin and Big Horn Counties equal in size to half the territory were first administered from Gallatin City, a tiny place between the Madison and Gallatin and within a few hundred feet of the Missouri's Three Forks. The combined county's non-Indians included soldiers barricaded in forts, would-be miners, merchants and settlers headed for the Gallatin Valley and survivors already on the Gallatin trying to stay alive. Those survivors, ignorant and insensitive to the treaties of 1851 and 1855, and as self-righteous as settlers usually are or must be, continued to feel threatened. They were already persevering through the inconvenience of forming and positioning a self-defense militia in some of the passes out of the Yellowstone. Sioux had killed at least one of those defenders.

By late April 1867, the citizens of Gallatin Valley had a War Meeting at Elkananah Morse's Store, located on the post road between Gallatin

City and Bozeman City. The date of the meeting remains uncertain, because the recording secretary's minutes dated April 29, 1867, were published after the killing of John Bozeman in an issue of *The Montana Post* dated April 27. The meeting at Elk Morse's Store further organized the local protection effort.[148]

The Gallatin's citizens resolved to allocate responsibility among themselves for defense of the passages from the Yellowstone, as follows:

> Bozeman and Bridger's Passes would form a First District, guarded by pickets drawn from Bozeman and Noble precincts, Flathead and Ross's Passes would be the Second District, guarded by pickets from the East and West Gallatin precincts, and Sixteen Mile Creek Pass would form a Third District, picketed by guards from Gallatin City and Jefferson precincts. They decided to require each district to fund having four pickets on each patrol, beginning May 1.
>
> A final motion passed directing one man to survey the mountains between Bozeman City and Sixteen Mile Creek to determine picketing requirements and a system of signals between patrols.
>
> The precincts of Gallatin County then organized themselves into military companies for mutual protection, and petitioned Meagher to use his influence to

provide aid from the rest the territory and the federal government.[149]

On April 29, Meagher and others from Virginia City responded to news of the meeting at Morse's Store by riding to the Gallatin to make another assessment of the situation.[150] In Helena that day, Howie received the territory's two General Orders by stagecoach. The next morning in Helena a recruiting office began working out of the building that housed the federal courtroom. Curtis, also serving Helena as recruiting officer in charge, circulated this information:[151]

> The men will go on the same conditions as those enlisted in Virginia City, to take all the scalps and ponies they can lay their hands on, more particularly the former. It will be a crying shame on both our patriotism and manhood if we let your little one horse town of Virginia beat us in the race for booty and topknots.

Curtis may have been trying mightily to make this a race between towns, but the 80 men first sworn into service by the end of April, as later estimated by U.S. Army Inspector General James Hardie, were all from Virginia City.[152] That's where the horses were.

On April 29, as 108 horses arrived in the capital, recruiting progressed favorably. There was already enough donated coffee in hand to supply 500 men for two months.[153] The next morning, Virginia City's first company was sworn in for three months unless earlier discharged or relieved by federal troops. The men in that company elected George Hynson as their Captain and Thomas Baume as their 1st Lieutenant. They fell into formation as prepared for the field as could be expected under the circumstances.[154] Few of the horses had ever been ridden or handled. Witnesses observed:

> The boys each took hold with a will and when they rode out of town their mounts looked like old cavalry horses, able for efficient duty once in the field.[155]

After selecting those first horses for immediate use, the Quartermaster traded the remaining for larger and better animals broken for riding. The merchants of Virginia City and Nevada City liberally contributed supplies and money. This contrasted sharply with Helena level of support.

Helena's supply effort didn't start until its first War Meeting at nine o'clock in the morning on Thursday May 2. From *The Montana Post* description, the Helena gathering seems to have been subdued:

> Though the courtroom was crowded, there appears to be an absence of anything like enthusiasm, and if we were to judge based on the amount of interest we'd predict failure.[156]

Fisk, the accomplished leader of three expeditions across Sioux dominated territory, provided more detailed information to the *Rocky Mountain Gazette*. He reported that the gentlemen of a committee "went to work with a will" calling on the merchants of the city. By two o'clock in the afternoon they had secured enough, with the exception of horses, to outfit the first 100 men. There was a feeling that the lack of horses could be overcome as soon as Howie received vouchers from Meagher "as security therefore." The committee felt men could be supplied and equipped as rapidly as they could be mustered. A few prominent citizens seemed inclined to do all in their power cheerfully, "but many of the merchants doubt, hesitate, quibble and refuse point blank to do anything for the movement." Only 25 horses were pledged:

> The difficulty of procuring more (horses) will be the greatest obstacle to raising forces at this point. If the full number of animals could be readily brought into Helena, the necessary quota of men would be forthcoming without delay.

Although only a few horses had been acquired, participants had been able to gather enough commissary stores, camp equipage, saddles and bridles for 300 men. With horses remaining scarce, the gathering still hoped that by May 6th there would be enough steeds to mount and send 100 men to the Gallatin. During this process, Helena exhibited a determination to have a second battalion or second regiment of its own.

This early indication that Meagher's General Orders were being ignored became real as two men, Reed and Lyons, announced they were forming "Company A of the Helena Battalion." Helena seemed to have a different attitude by and about its volunteers. Fisk criticized several fellow citizens for their lack of better sense:

> . . . loafing among squads and groups of men on the street corners and elsewhere throwing cold water upon the whole thing.[157]

By May 6 in Virginia City, while Helena's militia leaders hoped for a convergence of men and materials, Captain Jerry Lewis with a full company of men waited for the horses that had already been purchased and were on hand:

> This company is composed of splendid material, and Helena will have to put an A number one company in the field or yield the laurels. Captain Foster's Company of 25 Scouts is also ready and awaiting horses to leave May 4, and General Thoroughman is ready to leave May 4.[158]

There was less support for Captain John Slater, a

Virginia City attorney actively advertising for 30 more men to fill his company of 50 scalp-hunters:

> Time of service not to exceed three months. Provisions promised from the time of muster. Those not having arms and horses will be supplied. All the plunder taken will be the property of the captors. A bounty of $10 will be paid for each scalp taken from hostile Indians by members of this company. Those who have fought Indians as soldiers or mountaineers preferred.[159]

Although the last 35 of 200 mounted and armed men did leave for the Gallatin on May 4, Slater's scalp-hunting company never left town. Thoroughman had led with 75 officers and men, including the volunteers from the Gallatin; Captain George Hynson followed with 50 officers and men of Virginia City's Company A; Captain Gerald Lewis rode behind them with another 50-man company; and Captain Reuben Foster brought up the rear with a 35-man Scout Company. This main force would have brought along the territory's howitzer and remaining shot, shell and canister. They carried a flag presented to Hynson's "Virginia City Rangers" by Mrs. Hosmer, Mrs. Bartlett and Mrs. McMath.[160]

Saddling a Bronco the First Pull at Latigo

15. Helena

Helena's Company A, 65 men from Deer Lodge and Helena, were ready to ride on May 6. They still lacked 40 horses. Howie thought it better not to field a unit that was too small and chose not to swear the men into service. He discharged the formation and discouraged all of the men "from any further attendance at headquarters."[161]

In the meantime, there was another War Meeting in Virginia City to discuss a new telegram from Washington City. The participants of the meeting considered the telegram to be reassuring, because it seemed to place financial and material support for the military mobilization on a "better basis." The telegram overcame their lingering doubts about obtaining or providing supplies with the use of vouchers. As recruiting continued in Virginia City, the Quartermaster purchased another 240 good horses and 30 saddles and bridles. He expected 70 more sets of tack to arrive in three days but faced a growing problem of too few guns. From the field on May 6, Meagher advised Beem:

> The Virginia troops will be posted for the defense of the Bridger and Bozeman passes, the Helena troops at the Flathead pass eighteen miles to the left. Company A, Captain Hynson's Company, came in this morning in excellent condition, in the best of spirits, and is under the most excellent discipline. They are in barracks for the present, with the very beautiful flag presented by the ladies, flying from their quarters. On to-morrow General Thoroughman, Colonel DeLacy and myself and escort go on a reconnaissance to Bridger's pass in order to establish the picket line and posts in that direction, the day after to Bozeman's pass for the same purpose. On Friday the troops will move out, take position, and set to work. By all accounts, we have from ten days to a fortnight to prepare after that we will have to keep a keen lookout. A party of five miners who came in here yesterday from Fort Smith, having avoided the road the entire journey by crossing on mountain

trails, tell me the Sioux have sworn to break through here and that the Crows are as bad as the Sioux. Between the Bridger and Bozeman passes General Thoroughman will build a stockade Fort. (signed) T.F. Meagher
Cover's Ranch, May 6.[162]

On May 7 at Bozeman City, Thoroughman took command of all forces in the field, and on May 8 in Virginia City, Beem issued General Order 2:

Authority having been received by the Governor, from Lieutenant General Sherman to raise a sufficient force for the protection of the Territory during the present Indian invasion and to this end one thousand (1,000) volunteers are required immediately.

The following is the quota assigned to the different counties of the Territory:

Madison County   400
Edgerton County   400
Deer Lodge County 100
Jefferson County   100

Recruiting officers heretofore appointed are earnestly enjoined to work vigorously to fill the quota in their respective counties. Those desiring to recruit companies can receive authority upon application at this office. Companies of volunteers will be accepted from counties not mentioned above. Troops will be subsisted from date of muster. All requisitions upon the Quartermaster General at Virginia City will be promptly filled.

    By order of the Commander in Chief
    MARTIN BEEM
    Adjutant General[163]

    Two days later on May 10 in Helena, Howie noted in his diary:

Received a letter from General Meagher approving me of my appointment of Brigadier General with Command of Edgerton, Jefferson, Deer Lodge and Meagher County.[164]

That night, a Mr. Barnard arrived in Helena from Bozeman City "with dispatches from General Meagher to Brigadier General Howie, desiring him to forward immediately all the troops at his command." Barnard had come through the Gallatin Valley from Fort C.F. Smith. He and others in his party told about the soldiers in the fort being in jeopardy from starvation and from Indian attacks. They reported, "There are 150 men there, but they hardly dare go outside."[165]

    May 10 was the day Meagher started for Virginia City, carrying the latest dire reports about conditions at Fort C.F. Smith. He had no knowledge of Howie having a problem getting horses and men into the field. The general's focus was a need for more weapons.¹⁶⁶ Beyond guns and ammunition, there was also a great need for saddles. In Virginia City, there were plenty of horses though the normal cost of an $80 mount was climbing toward $201.¹⁶⁷

Willing volunteers were snubbing, haltering, breaking, branding and shoeing the horses being issued to them. They were grabbing the purchased saddles, bridles, ammunition and arming themselves with every available breech-loading weapon. Two companies of men, as soon as they were equipped, were ready to move to the Gallatin within 48 hours. By May 9, Captain Campbell's Company had nearly enough guns to leave, as did another company being formed by Captain Deasey. Guns, the main challenge facing them riled *The Montana Post*:

> Let every man who has a gun he can spare sell it to the Quartermaster. That pay is as sure as greenbacks are and this holding back for a big price is so utterly disgraceful that it is with shame that we record it. Judge Hosmer, yesterday received a telegram from General Sherman, which is undoubtedly authority for the organizing and supporting of the troops. Do not wait for another massacre to spur you to activity. Many of our best men are in the field, and others are ready to go and finish this uncertainty at once. Let it be done and be over. Bring out your guns to day.¹⁶⁸

In the capital, only 30 to 40 guns remained on hand with fewer than 200 rounds of ammunition for each. Less than half of those weapons were suitable for cavalry service. If scarcity was at work around Alder Gulch, avarice was definitely in play, because good prices were being paid. Rifles and carbines, selling two weeks earlier for $10 to $40, were now fetching $75 to $100. *The Montana Post* scolded:

> Holders of them are very indifferent about selling them. Now this is all wrong. Persons having guns at all fit for service demand for them the most outrageously exorbitant figures.[169]

In another column the newspaper screamed:

> Sell your surplus guns and let the boys go who are impatiently waiting. This delay is dangerous, costly and discreditable.[170]

Scrounging for guns had become central to mobilization activity in Virginia City, while scouring for horses had become equally important around Helena. After May 7, all were aware of another fruitless War Meeting. By May 11, everyone realized Howie was actively seeking horses. Helena seemed incapable of generating enough mounts for the men of even one company. The problem came fully into the open by May 18.[171] After reporting about Howie discharging everyone on May 6, *The Montana*

Post apologized:

> Thus has this important matter fell to the ground: but it must be said from no fault of those who had the management of it, every exertion had been made by Colonel Neil Howie and the other gentlemen associated with him to secure riding stock, but without avail.

Excuses and apologies carried no weight at all. The same newspaper published Thoroughman's first report from the field to Meagher. The good-natured Gallatin Commander was begging for more men:

> I have had no reports from Helena, not one word from Colonel Howie, or Captain Beidler. Nothing from Virginia—do not know that another man is coming. Do get them in motion as soon as possible, at both Virginia and Helena, and then point them down this way, for I can assure you they will be needed very soon.[172]

Thoroughman penned this May 11 report from the west side of the two most direct passes from the Yellowstone into the Gallatin Valley. He was located east of Bozeman City in a defensive patrolling base he called "Fort (sic.) Elizabeth Meagher," in honor of the territory's Acting First Lady.[173] In his letter, Thoroughman pleaded:

We must actually have more men, and those we have must be supplied in the way of commissaries, for they are absolutely out of everything, even potatoes and flour. I have failed up to now to get even a single beef, but have some hopes of getting one today, but they have no sugar, no coffee, no salt, and no candles. I have really used the right word "nothing;" even flour and potatoes.[174]

Though scarcely supplied, the men still were able to enjoy the best things in life that were free. They patrolled and worked under snow-capped mountains and shared camaraderie with their messmates around campfires. One man in Hynson's Company wrote that among his 49 comrades there were at least one veteran from every corps in Grant's Army, one from every corps in Lee's Army, and two "colored troops" to boot.[175] Finally, in Helena there was movement.

On May 16, the men of Captain Lyons' Company mounted their cayuses and paraded through town behind Howie, Beidler, Lyons and Cummings. The Quartermaster had come up from Virginia City to help Howie with procurement. Hereford was among the officers leading and drew a comment from the newspaper:

By the way we don't know what office this individual holds—but on the present occasion he looked fierce enough to be M (Major), G (General). The boys made a very creditable appearance, although from the diversity of uniform, it had somewhat the resemblance of Falstaff's celebrated Regiment.[176]

The unit made its first attempt at departing after the parade, when someone else observed:

> Captain Lyons' Company numbering 50 men started for the Front on Friday morning last. This is all the men, which at present can be sent from here. As the necessary equipment can be found, more will be forwarded.[177]

That report proved premature. A day later there was another departure attempt followed by another on May 18. All the while, a myriad of responsibilities created chaos in Howie's normally orderly existence. On May 11, he wrote in his diary:

> Snowing and raining early, aroused in bed by the soldiers, got up and got them some bread. Storming all day. Very unpleasant.[178]

On May 19, with Helena's entire first company still in town, Howie wrote:

> Weather a little more pleasant today, all hands busy getting things ready for the

troops. Street very muddy, on a march and at 1 o'clock, a good many of them tight, some men missing, think Beidler and Hereford rode out a short distance with them.

That was a false start, as well. It wasn't until May 20 that Helena's first unit finally cleared town. A bystander recorded the scene:

> The boys labored under both natural and physical disadvantages on leaving town. The day was dismal-like and stormy, the mud-deep Cayuses unbroken and they themselves apparently as unbroken as their Cayuses; but for all the drawbacks, they managed to get off in pretty good shape.[179]

They were led by Captain H.H. Lyons, assisted by First Lieutenant Robert Hughes, and totaled 58 officers and enlisted.

During those weeks that Helena was sending its first company, Virginia City's 25-man Scout Company under Captain Foster, having departed on May 4, returned home for final equipping. When they left again for the Gallatin on May 12 *The Montana Post* noted:

> The material of this company is splendid, they are excellently mounted and their fine appearance elicited the most flattering comments from all. The company formed

in line in front of the Governor's residence, to be presented with a beautiful guidon by 'Mrs. General Meagher.' Captain Foster returned eloquent thanks with a few words, and the boys gave three rousing cheers for the fair donor. Amid the huzzas of the spectators they wheeled into columns and started for the Gallatin.

Foster's Scouts included Captain Foster, First Lieutenant E.U. Driggs and Private Christ Yunson.[180] On May 15 when the company arrived in the Gallatin, a member of Hynson's Company thinking they were Company B under Driggs observed:

> I believe if all the companies come in like this one we will have a well-drilled army before they are drilled. Each man seems to know his place and duty and therefore they (sic.) appear all that the most rigid disciplinarian could desire. Tomorrow they will also move to the front. I furthermore have to inform you that the late Captain G.W. Hynson is now Colonel G.W. Hynson commanding First Regiment, Montana Militia.[181]

A week later Meagher was back in the Gallatin while Thoroughman was at Virginia City seeing his children off to the states and reporting to the townsfolk about the field situation. Cummings had gotten back from Helena, and

Colonel William H. Lewis, acting as Sherman's eyes and ears, had been in Virginia City for three days. Beem, Hull and Carpenter were the other militia staff present in the capital. Publicly, Cummings reported that all merchants in Helena were generous and that he was confident Helena would do nobly:

> A finely mounted and equipped company, composed of splendid material under Captain Lyons, is now on their way to the front. Another full company is ready, and still a third is full.[182]

As Cummings was giving this report, Curtis was riding out of Helena at the head of a 30-man Scout Company that included Lieutenant Joseph Williams and Private John Sullivan.[183] Helena's local press reported they were:

> . . . as fine looking a body of men as could be found anywhere. Their appointments in every particular were first class. We feel confident they will give a good account of themselves, once at the scene of active operations.[184]

From the field Meagher anticipated the arrival of these new Helena troops in his May 25 dispatch:

> We arrived here after a delightful ride Wednesday evening (May 22), and found Colonel DeLacy's supply train had left for

C.F. Smith. They crossed the Yellowstone on Thursday evening (May 23). This morning, Friday May 25, the first detachment arrived from Helena under the command of Captain Lyons. Lieutenant Colonel Beidler having reported the evening previous (May 24). The Helena troops look splendidly and are as fine a material for good soldiers, as one would wish to see. They are well mounted with few exceptions and well equipped for service. Accompanied by Colonels Hynson and Hearn, and Major Boise (sic.), I met them a few miles from here and had the gratification of presenting them with a handsome guidon, a gift from the lady so highly honored by the Montana Militia in naming the first fort. They are now encamped a mile and a half from here (Bozeman City), preparatory to their moving out to the newly established line, 14 miles from here and 7 miles this side of the Yellowstone, there to entrench and hold a very strong position commanding both Bridger's and Bozeman's Passes, and completely covering the valley.

Captain Curtis' Company of Scouts are on their way here. When they arrive the commands of Captains Curtis and Foster will be consolidated and placed under command of the former. They will be sent to patrol the road forward of the

Yellowstone and keep it securely open for DeLacy's return. The bridges over the Gallatin and the Madison are completed, affording free communication at all stages between this place and Virginia.

Two men from the Virginia Scouts have been missing for two days. It is feared the Indians have captured them. I want everything needed to secure the efficiency and comfort of the soldiers, with a sufficiency of stores to last two months, forwarded to this place at once, as on Monday next (June 3), we will take armed possession of Fort Smith to have and to hold 'until relieved by the regulars.'

The Fort Smith mentioned in Meagher's dispatch was not Fort C.F. Smith on the Big Horn but rather a new forward patrolling base on the Yellowstone at the mouth of the Shields. Meagher planned to name it in honor of Governor Green Clay Smith.

Meagher had changed places with Thoroughman, while the latter was in Virginia City. When the former confederate officer returned to the field, one of the volunteers riding out on a patrol beyond Bozeman Pass captured some observations about Thoroughman riding close by with a contingent going to the new base:

This genial, enterprising, energetic gentleman proved to us by his substantial good sense and indomitable determination and activity, to be just the right man in the right place. We Gallatians had lots of faith in him, and believed 'Mr. Ingin' would find in fighting him the 'Big White Chief,' unlike Uncle Sam's regulars, is no woman. What ever he is, he is certainly a thorough man in all respects. Thus favorably impressed, we separated.[185]

Running Cayuses in Montana Territory 1867

16. Quartermaster

In a time when regular army soldiers were getting paid $16.00 per month, the officers and enlisted men volunteering for Montana's Militia did not expect to be paid.[186] After being sworn in at muster, they did expect to be armed, mounted, fed and sheltered, all activities that were the responsibility of the Quartermaster and Commissary of Subsistence Officer. Meagher anticipated the requirement for a robust logistics capability before that April 8 War Meeting in Virginia City, which he did not attend. At the time he was on his way back from the Gallatin.

The meeting's Resolutions Committee, with Meagher listed as a member, formulated the motion to telegraph Washington City for permission to raise one regiment of volunteers.

The same resolution thanked Kirby for his early tender of arms and ammunition and directed the opening of an armory at Virginia City to receive arms. After the War Meeting approved that resolution, it created a three-member committee and assigned it the task of locating an armory. Meagher was made Chairman. The other two members were Virginia City attorney Hamilton Cummings and Virginia City Assistant Post-Master A.M.S. Carpenter. They soon became the territorial Quartermaster and Subsistence Officer and the Chief Ordnance Officer, respectively.[187] Cummings aggressively used his procurement authority.

    The territory's procurement system operated on a general assurance from the U.S. War Department that after a "real crisis" the federal government would reimburse the territory and vendors for countersigned territorial vouchers. With this in mind, officers working for the Quartermaster had vendors sign a voucher itemizing the equipment, livestock, goods or services being provided and return it to Cummings. Cummings held the signed vouchers for the Governor's approving signature.[188] The first mounted militia volunteers were able to ride out of Virginia City rapidly, because Cummings was operating within a solicitation for sealed bids due May 10 requesting:

> 300 horses not older than three years and of sound body and limb, 300 saddles and

bridles, new or used, but fit for service, and 3000 pounds of bacon.

Carpenter, the Ordnance Officer, addressed responsibilities that included horse tack, weapons and ammunition by locating "an indifferent cabin" for temporary storage. He worked up solicitations for bid proposals due May 13 and May 20.[189] Bidders were to provide 500 saddles and bridles, including serviceable used, 200 pairs of spurs, 3000 pounds of cordage for lariats, 300 cavalry carbines or rifles and 50,000 rounds of fixed ammunition. Breech-loading cavalry carbines or rifles were preferable to surplus Civil War .58 caliber and .577 caliber muzzle-loading rifle-muskets, but improved weapons and sufficient ammunition for them remained scarce.

On May 10, Cummings left for Helena to help Howie with his supply problems. Before leaving, he transferred his Commissary of Subsistence responsibilities to Creighton.[190] The merchant telegraph-builder had been near Canyon Ferry on the Missouri between Helena and Diamond City purchasing four wagons and mule teams on May 1.[191] He drove one of the teams himself back to Virginia City past his 600 cattle grazing along the Missouri and by way of the Gallatin. After checking into Planters House, he set about publishing this solicitation:[192]

Office Territorial Militia, Virginia City, M.T. May 11, 1867. Proposals will be received at this office until Thursday, 12 M, May 15, 1867, for the following commissary stores: 30,000 pounds flour; 9,000 pounds of bacon, 15,000 pounds of beef-net to be delivered on the field, 2,000 pounds of green Coffee, 3,600 pounds of Sugar, 3,600 pounds of beans, 1,000 pounds of salt, 1,000 pounds of soup, 350 pounds of candles, 5,800 pounds of potatoes. Bids will be received for any or the whole amount of the above articles. The Commissary General reserves the right to reject any or all bids.

John Creighton, Colonel and Commissary Gen' Montana Militia.[193]

In the same issue as Creighton's solicitation *The Montana Post* admonished:

The full authority received from General Sherman, and the information from General Thoroughman and General Meagher call for immediate and earnest action in the matter. The movement must be carried out with vigor or become a farce. The hour has gone by for delay and supineness. Let what is to be done, be done at once. Our Generals say the danger is imminent and the war department authorizes the movement. The highest judicials assure those furnishing stores that the question of pay is beyond dispute. The men are ready to go. Let us see vigor action and energy in the matter, or eternal infamy and disgrace will cluster around the memory of the whole affair.[194]

As Cummings rolled and bumped his way toward Helena by stagecoach, behind and around him raced, bucked and collided 100 of the unbroken horses purchased in Virginia City. They ran north, freshly marked with an "M.M." for Montana Militia, driven by men riding under Nelson.[195] Once he reached Helena, Cummings familiarized Fisk with the territory's procurement procedures and appointed him Acting Quartermaster General for the district comprising Deer Lodge, Edgerton, Meagher and Jefferson Counties.[196] He departed from his General Orders' authority to recruit two Assistant Quartermasters. He was probably diplomatically deferring to local merchants who were insisting on a Helena Battalion. From them Cummings procured more horse tack for Virginia City. On his May 22 return trip, he brought 100 saddles and bridles. They were purchased from Last Chance Gulch merchants as part of $60,000 worth of contracts for supplies, horses and equipment. As soon as Cummings got back from Helena, Carpenter set out for Fort Benton.

Aside from the inadequate response to solicitations for arms and ammunition, the territory had received a letter from the Arsenal Commander at Saint Louis. His letter released ordnance for Montana Territory. He said the ordnance would include one complete battery of 12-pound howitzers with ammunition and 2500 stand of .58 caliber Springfield rifle-muskets with 750,000 cartridges. The letter contained no details to identify the steamboat or its expected date of arrival. The shipment would land at Camp Cooke below Fort Benton.[197] Carpenter immediately boarded a stagecoach for the first leg of the 265-mile journey to Fort Benton. From there he planned to continue down river to where the shipment was expected.[198]

After Cummings got back to Virginia City, he learned that Creighton had requested and been given an honorable discharge for business reasons. The telegraph builder intended to extend the Salt Lake City telegraph line to Helena.[199] He had been replaced by Colonel J.J. Hull who was already working another food solicitation.[200] Cummings found out about the May 19 stagecoach from Salt Lake City that brought Sherman's man, Lewis, to town.

Lewis had been briefed by Beem and was impressed enough by the situation, mobilization and deployment that he had telegraphed Sherman for federal permission to muster 400 volunteers. Sherman told him to muster 800. On May 24, one of Sherman's field commanders, General C.C. Augur, followed up with another telegraphed message:

> . . . organize and muster in eight hundred (800) for two months . . . They will be paid by the United States. A paymaster will be sent out for that purpose.[201]

Due to a lack of an appropriation by Congress, pay for Montana's Militia never materialized.

Cummings soon realized that the same stagecoach bringing Sherman's man from Utah had returned Sanders from the states. Lewis and Sanders had checked into Planters House on the same night. The territory's former Quartermaster, though he had resigned his militia commission, still felt comfortable using the rank of "Colonel" when he signed the guest register. He had explained around town that his arrival with Sherman's eyes and ears was "pure coincidence."[202] He described leaving his family continuing upriver on the steamboat, Abeona, while he took the faster overland route to Virginia City. He said he needed to supervise moving their house from outside of town to a location in town on Idaho Street.[203]

Having attended to that pressing chore, Sanders opened his campaign for election to be Montana's single non-voting delegate at Congress. For his first speech, he stood above Content's Corner near where Beem and Meagher had the Executive Offices. His intent was to justify his reasons for working to nullify the accomplishments of the last two Territorial Legislatures. Sanders also attended to business.

With Cummings back in town, he was able to rent to the Quartermaster his family's first Virginia City home, a log cabin across from the Planters House which had been serving as his law office. Cummings agreed to pay Sanders

$150 per month, retroactive to the beginning of May.[204] He also found time to enjoy his friends.

The night of May 23, Sanders gathered 20 Virginia City donors of funds he had used to purchase a gold watch in New York City. Together they presented the gift to Creighton as their token of appreciation:

> One of Charles Frodsbam's superb chronometer watches, selected by Colonel Sanders at Tiffany & Co., New York, and the finest watch in their establishment.

The heavy gold watch case bore an engraved scene of a telegraph party erecting a line, with high mountains in the background. Its inscription said, "To John A. Creighton, from his friends of Virginia, Montana." [205]

His friends shared an understanding that Creighton and Sanders had been the real openers of the ball in 1863.[206] They knew that Creighton would be returning to a promising future in Omaha after he and Largey completed the line to Helena. As Creighton received his gold watch and Carpenter passed through Helena, Cummings was preparing another solicitation:

> 200 pairs of pants, 400 pair of blankets, 40 axes complete, 75 spades, 75 pick-axes, 50 camp kettles, 50 mess pans, 4 large tarpaulins, 300 pounds of horse shoes, 100 pounds of mule shoes, 100 pounds of horseshoe nails, 1000 pounds of lariat

rope, 100,000 pounds of oats, 300,000 pounds of barley, 235 tons of hay, delivered as Quartermaster directs.[207]

These supplies were needed in the field by 166 troops including Curtis' 31-man combined Scout Company and DeLacy's 42-man relief detail, escorting ten supply wagons working their way down the Yellowstone to Fort C.F. Smith.[208] There would soon be more volunteers to supply, when Gallatin Valley farmers finished their spring planting and returned to service.[209]

John X. Beidler Holding Henry Rifle

17. Messenger

Beidler wore a lot of titles, not all good. Once asked to describe his occupation, he cryptically wrote, "Messenger."[210] Long before that day when he signed into Montana's organization for pioneers, 200 miners from his favorite haunt, Confederate Gulch, warned him:

> We will give you no more time to prepare for death than the many men you have murdered . . . we shall live to see you buried beside the poor Chinamen you have murdered.[211]

Beidler was a stern face of the law and an excellent messenger in a place where law-enforcers and messengers needed guts. It's just as truthful to say he lacked the attributes necessary for being a military officer. On May 14, Beidler, already working as Territorial U.S. Customs Inspector, was commissioned by Howie to be a Lieutenant Colonel "in the regiment to be raised in this section." On May 20, Howie "Deputized J.X. Beidler, Deputy U.S. Marshall (sic.)."[212] On the same day that he made Beidler his Deputy, Howie sent him to the Gallatin with Lyons' "Company A, Edgerton County Battalion," as the ranking officer from Helena. He was:

> ... to take charge of the troops moving to the front. The colonel will probably remain with the command during the period it is in the field and, if the opportunity occurs, will make it lively for any of the Lo family who may be lying around loose.

Helena's *Tri-Weekly* made a big story out of Beidler's commissioning and assignment:

> An appointment worthily bestowed ... Go in for glory 'X'-two crutches and a wooden leg. We understand that this gentleman will command the first body of troops that will move to the scene of hostilities. We have heard of no other appointments.[213]

With that flurry of flattery the newspaper took the opportunity to apologize for its earlier remarks about Hereford, left in Helena to form the next unit:

> By the way in speaking of Captain Hereford, in an item last week on the first parade of Company A, we unintentionally committed an error. At that time we were not aware that the gentleman had a military title; we have since learned our mistake and herewith make the correction. We have only to add that no disrespect was intended to be the case on Mr. Hereford by the mention of his name in the article in question.[214]

Though the Lieutenant Colonel and Lyons' Company left Helena together, Beidler arrived in the Gallatin a day earlier. Meagher was commanding in the field at the time, because Thoroughman was in Virginia City making his public report.[215] No one has described what happened between Meagher and Beidler, but words must have been exchanged about Beidler reporting as the leader of an unsanctioned regiment or battalion. Reflecting the probable tenor of his conversation with Meagher, Beidler unexpectedly rode alone to Virginia City. Upon his arrival, *The Montana Post,* relied on Beidler to shed some light on his sudden change of assignment:

In Town, X the Unknown, but knowing, whose face wears a wreath of perpetual smiles, but who's heart is hardened by 'custom.' X, who never weakened before, has conducted his warriors to the Gallatin and finding a 'Lion' in the way, left the Lyon possession of the field, and in obedience to instructions, reported to Colonel (sic.) Howie for duty. We understand he will leave to day on an important mission, and wherever his duties or inclinations may lead, he will have the best wishes of a legion of friends, which cannot be 'confiscated.' It was our 'duty' to say this much, but will 'tax' your patience no further, unless you "collect" the boys and put us under 'bond.'[216]

Beneath this light-hearted explanation it seems obvious that when Lyons refused to take orders from Beidler, Meagher agreed. Beidler told *The Montana Post* he was in Virginia City following instructions to report to Howie.

As Beidler arrived from the Gallatin on May 28, Howie and Sanders were arriving from Helena on the same stagecoach. All three men checked into Virginia City's Planters House.[217] Their simultaneous arrival from two different locations was remarkable, since there was not yet telegraph connectivity from Virginia City to Bozeman City or to Helena. When asked, Howie told *The Montana Post* he was in town on military business.

Beem, after conferencing with Cummings about Helena's rogue regiment or battalion, exercised his responsibilities as Adjutant General. It was his responsibility and rank to insist that Howie get his organization into line. Beem seems to have enlisted Sanders help bringing Howie to the capital for a conference. Sanders would have appreciated the essence of Beem's situation from his own previous work for the Adjutant of the 64th Ohio Volunteer Infantry. Meagher knew to send Beidler to Virginia City to meet Howie, because Beem had been able through the daily dispatch rider to advise Meagher that he was bringing Howie to Virginia City.[218]

On May 25, Sanders boarded a stagecoach and traveled the 124 miles to Helena.[219] His morning newspaper carried first word of DeLacy's relief expedition to Fort C.F. Smith.[220] It was Sanders' practice to send messages ahead on earlier coaches, and that night he "was warmly greeted by friends."[221] It was time well used as a campaign stop. He left a filing with Munson's Court to admit a new attorney, Wylie Scribner, incoming on the Abeona. The trip afforded him the opportunity to meet George Wright, Upson's replacement as the new Blackfeet Indian Agent. Wright, as the latest Meagher critic, had ridden to Helena with three .58 caliber Springfields and a case of 1,000 cartridges and 1,200 percussion caps.[222] He had publicized discovering them at the Fort Benton Blackfeet Indian Agency and had offered them to Howie for use by the militia.[223]

After spending two days in Helena, Sanders climbed back on a coach to Virginia City, "after a brief sojourn in our midst on professional business."[224] Howie climbed aboard with him. Given the limited time in Sanders' schedule and that he was planning a trip to Fort Benton, his round-trip to Helena was extraordinary. It had to be related to a meeting called by Beem for Howie and Beidler.

Howie's inner circle of trusted colleagues, in place since forming the territory's 2nd Volunteer Militia in February 1866, had not been authorized as part of the territory's 3rd Volunteer Militia command structure.[225] Beem had the knowledge, courage and personal presence to prevail on Howie with standard military operating procedure. Their Virginia City conference must have ended on a positive note, because later correspondence shows the two men communicated in a mutually respectful way. Howie's new problem was how to deal with Beidler.

On May 30, Beidler left on the same stagecoach for Helena with Howie.[226] Howie made no diary entries between May 20 when he deputized Beidler and June 10 when he restarted his diary noting that he was deputizing Berkin. On June 13, Constable John Featherstun arrived home in Helena from a six-week trip to Denver, looking hardy.[227] Howie announced he intended to form another Helena Company to be ready to march by June 15. Helena's newspaper sounded its support:

> We would say to those wishing to immortalize themselves either by getting scalps or being scalped . . . should call on Captain Hereford at the headquarters on Broadway.[228]

Howie mentioned none of this in his restarted diary, but on June 14 he did write:

> Mr. Geo. M. Pinney, Lady, Boy & Girl arrived from Benton (Humbley's (sic.) Coach) about 5 PM. Took a ride about that time with J.X.Beidler & Capt. Hereford up to the big ditch, to see the water come in for the first time.[229]

As the three vigilantes turned lawmen talked, they watched the big canal's water. After flowing seventeen miles from 10-Mile Creek through a 146-foot tunnel through solid rock and a 266-foot flume over Grizzly Gulch, it poured down Davis and Spencer Streets to sluice Helena Hill Districts' claims, below Broadway and between Dry Gulch and Last Chance Gulch. During their visit they agreed about who would command the next Helena Company. It became obvious to everyone after a few days that Beidler had been further demoted. The Helena *Tri-Weekly's* strained light-heartedness seemed sarcastic:

> X. Beidler and John Featherstun have been promoted to pole of Captain Robert Hereford; the first as H.O.J. (Hand of Justice) with the rank of Brigadier-General and the latter as A.H.O.J. (Assistant Hand of Justice) with the same rank. We understand Captain Robert takes exceptions to the word 'pole,' as not being en militarie—he says it should be 'staff.' Both gentlemen are now in the active discharge of their duties.[230]

Howie had placed Hereford in charge of raising and equipping the next Helena Company, and Beidler, assisted by Featherstun, was supposed to help him. Two nights later, Howie met with an accident:

> He said he was preparing to retire for the night and had taken off his belt and revolver, which he held in his right hand, while he closed the room door with his left. In the act of doing so, the pistol unaccountably went off, the ball passing through the wrist of his left hand, inflicting a very painful flesh wound. Nothing serious will result, and the General will, with care, be able to attend to his regular duties in three or four days.[231]

Three or four days stretched into 25 days of not being able to write through the critical period spanning Meagher's mysterious death. Howie's last diary entry, before apparently shooting himself, noted:

> I, this day, appointed Elk Morse, Special Deputy Marshal, to serve subpoenas at Salmon River, Idaho Territory...[232]

Morse, in the Gallatin Valley, was another of Howie's old vigilante friends. He, along with Baume, had been part of the original vigilantes who captured Ives. His new special traveling responsibility stemmed from the Territorial Supreme Court's intention to schedule some of Munson's Court proceedings in Diamond City. Those would deal with cases from Meagher County and Musselshell County, which one of the nullified legislatures had formed from parts of Gallatin County.

The decision to continue judicial operations as though the two latest counties would eventually be reauthorized happened on June 12 at a meeting of the Territorial Supreme Court. The three judges organized themselves into three districts, assigned themselves and established the dates their respective district courts would be meeting. Judge Munson's Third District, which was Howie's own, would:

> ... embrace the counties of Edgerton, Jefferson and Chouteau, and all that portion of territory previously designated as Meagher and Muscleshell (sic.) counties,

before congress annulled the two preceding legislatures.

Munson's first regular Court term in Helena would start July 1. His Court in Diamond City would start the second Monday in August. The Diamond City term would handle all cases from that portion of Montana designated as Meagher and Musselshell counties.[233] This insured that the law enforcement responsibilities of both Howie and Hereford would be fixed in Helena for at least several weeks beginning July 1, 1867. The August 12 court date in Diamond City insured there needed to be active advance preparation by Deputies Beidler and Berkin, the federal law enforcement officers most associated with Meagher and Musselshell Counties. With a little more leeway in late June and early July, Beidler and Berkin would be available to help Hereford meet his pressing requirement for guns and ammunition. There were others assigned that mission, as well.

On June 18, Curtis had detailed Sergeant Sullivan and eleven other men from Helena to Fort Benton. They rode north with extra teams to "bring up" the six complete carriages of the Mountain Howitzer Battery.[234] When that news broke, on the day before Meagher disappeared, Hereford said he intended to:

> . . . put his men in camp at an early day, to await the arrival of the ordnance stores now on their way from Benton.[235]

Virginia City's 1867 First Class Post Office, A.M.S. Carpenter, Clerk

18. Professor

Much happened in Carpenter's life between May 23, 1867, when he left Virginia City by stagecoach and June 29, 1867, when he checked into Virginia City's Planters House with a woman. Back in the states, he had experienced serious differences with his mother over a woman, but he had seemed to have been a single man during his first winter of 1866-1867 in Virginia City.[236] One source indicates that Carpenter married a woman named Carrie Watson in New York on June 8, 1870.[237] His wife, whoever she was, was known in Virginia City. A letter he wrote from the U.S. West Coast years later to Sanders, then an attorney for Northern Pacific Railroad, requested a free rail pass "for you-know-who," then visiting with her family in the East.[238] The identity of the woman entering Planters House with Carpenter on June 29 remains a mystery.[239]

During his month in Fort Benton as Chief Ordnance Officer, Carpenter watched Clinton move six companies of the U.S. 13th Infantry over the levee and to Camp Reynolds on the Sun.[240] Three of Clinton's companies didn't leave Fort Benton until June 14.[241] Carpenter may have mistaken the ordnance support for those regular units as the ordnance shipment Montana had been told to expect. Carpenter was most likely the source of the bad information received by Meagher on June 10 in Virginia City. He was motivated, smart and reliable, but he had no military experience.

Carpenter was an elocution professor before he immigrated to Montana in 1866. Virginia City had just become a First Class Post Office, and he came to assist Sanders' close friend, Virginia City Postmaster Dr. James Gibson. Gibson ran the pharmacy in the back of the Stuart and Dance General Store. As Assistant Postmaster in February 1867, Carpenter went out of his way to try and communicate with the mother of the murdered McGlothlin by writing to his mother's sister in answer to a letter found in the dead man's pocket.[242]

Carpenter was reading the law, hoping to join the Madison County Bar when Meagher gave him an opportunity to remain an educator.[243] On March 4, Meagher appointed Carpenter to be Montana Territory's fourth Superintendent of Public Instruction. Neither man realized that two days earlier Congress had nullified the actions of two previous legislatures.[244] This change of statutory authority caused Unionist Republicans to question whether Meagher could make the appointment under the Bannack Statutes that required one year's residence. Meagher stood by his appointment of Carpenter, but Carpenter faced a long battle before he finally got paid the position's $253.33 salary. While not being paid but acting as Superintendent, Carpenter made an effort to collect information and report on the condition of Montana's schools. Eventually he won a lawsuit against the territory for back compensation, and by an act approved January 12, 1872, the Territorial Legislature finally paid him $241.12.[245]

In the month before realizing he had an important sounding job with no pay, Carpenter helped advance a local effort to bring a Harvard Geology Professor to Montana. The idea was to have him assess and publicize the territory's mineral riches.[246] On May 23 when Carpenter boarded the stage to Fort Benton, he knew he would not be getting paid for the education job. This caused his militia responsibilities to pale in his mind compared to his immediate need to make a living. Shortly after he arrived in Fort Benton, a solicitation had surfaced. It was "signed by a number of the most respectable men of Fort Benton." It petitioned Meagher to appoint Dr. L. Tibbets to be the Probate Judge of Chouteau County. [247] Nine days later, Carpenter appeared for the first time as an attorney and became involved in the first Chouteau County lawsuit of 1867. He represented the crew of the steamboat Ben Johnson (sic.)[248] against their Captain William Massie who was representing himself before Judge Tibbets. The plaintiffs wanted to leave their jobs as deckhands to go in search of gold. Massie won. He proved:

> ... that the men had shipped for the round trip, and the Judge rendered a verdict against them.[249]

After losing his first case, Carpenter greeted Governor Smith on June 20. He and his family were returning from the states on the steamboat Octavia. Carpenter continued hanging around Fort Benton. On June 22, U.S. Army Captain R.S. LaMotte witnessed Smith signing a letter of introduction for Carpenter giving him authority to arrange transportation for all the territory's arms and ammunition.[250] By then, Sullivan and his eleven men and six teams had arrived, but the only steamboats at Fort Benton were the Octavia and the Guidon. The Gallatin had been making shuttle runs back and forth to Camp Cooke and was expected to bring up the arms and ammunition on one of those runs. The ordnance would eventually have to pass through

Camp Reynolds for inventory onto a hand receipt. Carpenter continued waiting and, in Fort Benton, waiting was exciting.

On June 23 as the Octavia prepared to leave for the states, there was a big brawl. That brawl led to another court case involving Carpenter and another street fight involving the governor. A discharged fireman from the Guidon had brandished a Bowie knife and forced another man, Nat Piles, to defend himself with a derringer. The two had been playing cards in Moses Saloon. The knife-wielder accused the derringer-waver of stealing $200. Chouteau County Sheriff William Hamilton arrested both and arraigned them for trial. With no Justice of the Peace in town, there was an informal court held in the back room of Bill's Saloon. The proceedings amounted to considerable arguing. Carpenter appeared for the fireman with the Bowie knife, and the same Morgan, who watched the Sun River Rangers bind the four Piegans and lynch them by his home on the Sun, represented Piles. Eventually, someone with sufficient presence or sobriety dismissed the parties and Piles started for the Octavia. Carpenter's man, still waving the Bowie knife, went after him. Piles was able to disappear into the Octavia leaving the fireman still wanting to fight anyone upon whom he could lay his hands. The closest candidate happened to be Governor Smith, sitting on the front deck of the Octavia. After more knife-flourishing and rude insults associated with dogs, Smith became aroused enough to find a club and to strike the threatening man three or four times. The governor dropped Carpenter's client to the ground with the approval of about 200 spectators. As they dispersed they were muttering that the beating "served him right."[251]

That day, Smith and his family left Fort Benton for Helena leaving Carpenter to wait fruitlessly for three more days. During this interlude, Carpenter managed to arrange commercial transportation. The commercial transport consisted of wagons from a train waiting on behalf of Virginia City sawmill owner W.M. Couch. Couch had been expecting two large consignments of freight on two different steamboats. One of his loads had become stranded on the J.H. Trover II, hard aground 45 miles below the mouth of the Musselshell. That cargo's prospects worsened with the river dropping.[252] With the territory's ordnance expected July 1 on the Gallatin, Couch released some of his wagons. After accomplishing that arrangement, Carpenter decided to go back to Virginia City. It was clear from *The Montana Post* that Meagher was coming north. Carpenter reasonably expected he'd be at Fort Benton and Camp Reynolds to sign the necessary hand receipt. On June 27, Carpenter and his female companion boarded the stagecoach for Virginia City. Passing through Sun River Crossing, he was able to update Meagher.

On July 1, the Gallatin arrived from Camp Cooke with a load of government freight. Instead of being ordnance, the freight consisted of mules that were offloaded at the mouth of the Marias. If, as reported, the Gallatin waited overnight before returning downriver, it waited below at the Marias. [253]

When Meagher rode into the river port late that morning of July 1, there were no guns or ammunition on the levee. One person who said he greeted Meagher and visited with him would have been the best possible source of information about the ordnance at Camp Cooke. He was qualified, having once formed an Artillery Battery in Ohio. As his steamboat, the Abeona, offloaded 40 tons of cargo at Camp Cooke, he had plenty of opportunity to view that cantonment. He and another man walked a few miles to catch up with the Gallatin, to hitch a faster ride to Fort Benton. From the Marias, he had ridden into Fort Benton on one of the off-loaded mules. Sanders was that man. Yet, in his recollections of his day in Fort Benton with Meagher, he mentioned nothing about passing information concerning Montana's ordnance to Meagher. He only mentioned something about Meagher being in town, waiting for "one hundred thirty muskets." This peculiarity in recollecting July 1, 1867, leaves one certainty: Sanders carefully crafted his foundational chronicle of Meagher's last day.

Alexander K. McClure

19. Chroniclers

On June 5 in Virginia City, Sanders received a letter from Tufts, the Territory's new Secretary, saying that he expected to arrive at Fort Benton about June 11.[254] Two days later Sanders left Virginia City for the river port to meet his family.[255] He arrived at Fort Benton by June 9 in time to report about the steamboat Gallatin conducting an excursion to the falls of the Missouri.[256] While the Republican candidate was en-route, *The Montana Post* published some remarks by an early Democratic opponent, Major John Bruce. Bruce accused Sanders of being one of those "bummers" infesting Washington City and working to increase federal Judge's salaries to $6,000, an amount he considered too much. Bruce criticized the Territorial Code Commission under Sanders "who spent $9,500 for nothing," and Howie who spent $12,000 to pursue criminals he didn't catch.[257]

After a short time in Fort Benton, Sanders hitched a ride downriver on the Yorktown, and on June 16 he met the Abeona carrying his family upriver. After spending two weeks riding with them toward Camp Cooke, he decided to speed ahead. When the Abeona docked at Camp Cooke, he walked 3 miles to ride on the Gallatin "to engage passage in a coach to Virginia City.[258]

On the morning of July 1 while Sanders was riding a mule into Fort Benton, his filing to admit Scribner to practice law in Montana gained approval in Judge Munson's Court.[259] As had been anticipated since mid-June, Munson also ordered:

> . . . all issues of fact arising in cases originating in what has heretofore been called Meagher county, and triable with witnesses be transferred for trial to Diamond City, at the August term of Court to be held there.

As another matter of judicial housekeeping, Munson had orders for Hereford:

... the Sheriff of Edgerton County summon 24 lawful citizens of said county to be in at attendance on this court on Friday, July 5th at 9 o'clock a.m. to act as trial jurors for the term.[260]

To make sure he was being heard, Hereford re-announced his intention to arm 100 men as soon as guns and ammunition arrived from Fort Benton.[261]

With Sanders busy at Fort Benton, a fellow Republican of national stature was traveling south from Virginia City, eight miles up Alder Creek to Union City. He was Alexander K. McClure, the new manager from Philadelphia for the Christenot Mill used for crushing the ore of the Oro Cache Mine. McClure was an influential, national-level Republican power broker. He had received the rank of Colonel, as an honorary title, from the Governor of Pennsylvania for serving in that state's cabinet. In addition, McClure was a publisher and nationally known writer. After arriving in Virginia City on June 22, he wrote and mailed two letters to the *New York Tribune*. They related some of his experiences in Utah and the last leg of his trip to Montana. Two years later he would republish these and other letters written over the next six months in Montana, in a book titled *Three Thousand Miles Through the Rockies.*

The writer arrived in Union City in time to capture his first impressions of the patriotically named mountain community and on the Fourth of July, 1867. In an honest passage he recorded:

A few days ago he (the Mountain King) blew his cold breath upon the son of the forest, and 'Lo' and his dusky bride visited me. The lord of the wilderness came from his summer of idleness, or worse, to beg for bread, while his menial partner led the pack-pony, and packed herself what the pony could not bear. He shook his head mournfully as the shrill song of the steam-whistle called the pale-faces to their daily toil; for it told the story of a new supremacy. 'Buffalo, moose elk, deer, antelope, sheep—all gone—all gone! Injin starve!' was his sorrowful ejaculation. 'White man everywhere—everywhere! Injin must die!' he added as he looked out over the expansive valleys two thousand feet below us, and saw them spangled with cities and farms. He was one of the few remaining noble specimens of his race—tall, proud in his bearing, straight as his unerring arrows, his blanket gathered gracefully about him, waving feathers in his hair declaring the honors he had won in his tribe. His well-worn Kentucky rifle lay carelessly across his arm, and he stood for some moments in painful reflection, as he seemed to comprehend the sad destiny of himself and his brethren. 'White man at war, --Injin must die, --must die!' was his parting expression, as he walked off, in broken pride, toward the capital, to share in the bounty of the Great Father. While her lord was thus tarrying to contemplate the inexorable laws of progress and mourn over the fast-receding sun of their existence, the tender helpmate ransacked the rubbish about the cabins for worthless rags; and, guiltless of sentiment and indifferent to fate, she plodded on in her favorite pursuit. They were Bannocks, and friendly, civilized by General Conner, who taught the path of peace as his batteries and battalions swept half their warriors to their graves.[262]

That day McClure traveled down the face of Old Baldy Mountain to Virginia City and checked into the Planters House.[263] For the next week he mailed his Union City letter; wrote for *The Montana Post* on the efficiency of the Christenot Mill; experienced the community's response to news of Meagher's death; and mailed another letter datelined Virginia City July 9, 1867, for the *New York Tribune*. Sanders and his family had arrived in Virginia City at eleven o'clock the previous night and went directly to Dr. Gibson's house.[264] Sanders, on July 9, was the first person in Virginia City able to relay the details of Meagher's death.

To compose his July 9 letter from Virginia City, McClure did not rely on direct observation but on his reading of Dimsdale's book about the vigilantes and upon an anonymous interviewee for updated information about Beidler. Though

McClure once knew Beidler in Pennsylvania, he would not be able to write about him from updated personal contact for another four months. Of his earlier encounters, McClure wrote:

> . . . Some twelve years ago I was accustomed to meeting on the streets of Chambersburg, Pa. (sic.), a young man named John X. Beidler. His frugal wants were supplied by the manufacture of brooms, and finally he mixed the best of cocktails and juleps at a neighboring summer resort. He was as amiable and unoffending a lad as the community could furnish, and his jolly, genial humor made him a favorite with all who knew him. Although he had attained his majority, he was scarcely 5 feet six inches (sic.) in height and far below the average of men in physical power.
>
> He finally wandered west in search of fortune . . . This diminutive man, without family or property to defend, has himself arrested scores of the most powerful villains, and has executed in open day, an equal number under the direction of that wonderful unseen power that has surrounded the hasty scaffold. So expert is he with his faithful pistol that the most scientific of rogues have repeatedly attempted in vain to get 'the drop' on him . .

. His career has, indeed, been most remarkable, and his escape unharmed, through his innumerable conflicts with the worst of men seems almost wholly miraculous. He has recently been appointed Collector of Customs for the port of Helena, but while there is a thief, a defaulter, a murderer or a savage to disturb the peace of Montana, he will remain the most efficient messenger of justice known in the mountain gold-regions.

By the time McClure completed this portrait for the *New York Tribune*, all of Montana knew Meagher had disappeared. On July 3 two days after that disappearance, Beidler emerged from the shadows. He told a newspaper he had been unable to cross the Missouri's high water at Canyon Ferry but was forced to cross higher up using the Indian Creek Ferry. He was traveling to Helena by way of Confederate Gulch and Diamond City. McClure and his interviewee did not realize Beidler had been appointed a Deputy U.S. Marshal. Neither they nor the newspapers suggested he spend time solving Meagher's disappearance. The governance of Montana and the command of Montana's Militia continued; both had been handed-off by Meagher to Smith.

On August 10, Republicans at Montana's Union Territorial Convention devised a plan to have McClure join Sanders in his campaign to be Montana's non-voting delegate to Congress. Their scheduled stops, some covered by

McClure's letters, began at Sterling on August 15 and ended August 31 in Virginia City. The night of August 31, Sanders' campaign ended in Virginia City with a torchlight parade, when he gave a speech as did McClure and Secretary Tufts. It was a wild night. The Sanders family opened their home to revelers on the street, who later went to McClure's temporary residence to serenade him. The election proved grim. The people of Montana gave every seat in both houses of the Legislature to the Democrats. In his race to be the Territory's single non-voting delegate to Congress, Sanders lost by an embarrassing margin to Democrat James M. Cavanaugh.[265]

An unexpected geologic fault hid the Oro Cache Mine's gold seam, and in early January 1868 McClure returned to Pennsylvania on board a mid-winter stagecoach. More than 37 years later he wrote an eulogy for Sanders' death on July 5, 1905:

> I visited Montana in 1867, and when I arrived at Virginia my attention was speedily called to a resolution that had been adopted by the Republican territorial convention that had met only a few days before and nominated Col. Sanders for Congress. The resolution invited me to join Col. Sanders' campaign and I was very glad to accept the invitation. I had not met him until then, but I was with him from that time until the close of the contest, on the

stump every day and reached every community in the territory.²⁶⁶

More than 40 years ago, when I was in daily intercourse with Col. Sanders in Montana in a public letter given to the New York Tribune, I wrote of Col. Sanders with the freshness of personal association, and make the following quotation from it: 'Col. Wilbur Fisk Sanders was one of the first permanent settlers of Montana. He had previously served with marked gallantry in the Union Army until health compelled him to abandon a calling that enlisted his whole heart and was an inviting theater for his manly courage.'²⁶⁷

In 1861 when the call was made for troops for the Civil War, Col. Sanders was among the first to volunteer, and was First Lieutenant and Adjutant of the 64th Ohio Infantry, and on the staff of Gen. Forsythe. Before the close of his second year of service, his health was so broken that he was compelled to leave the service, and was honorably discharged.

Although he had been compelled to retire from the army on account of ill health in 1862, the first Congress after his death passed a bill giving to Mrs. Harriet P. Sanders, his widow, a permanent pension of $50 per month.²⁶⁸

Mrs. Sanders did receive a pension for being the widow of a Civil War invalid, and according to McClure, Congress made that happen as a special effort on behalf of one of its previous members. Pension records show "Sanders, Wilbur F." was an invalid, and his service was as "Adjutant, 64th Ohio Infantry." Sanders filed as the invalid on May 9, 1905, two months before his death. His widow filed for her benefit as an invalid's widow on June 19, 1906. If Sanders was wounded during the Civil War, why was such unique action by Congress required to qualify him for a pension already generously provided by Congress to invalids and their widows?[269]

Packaged .58 Caliber Rifle-Musket Ammunition

20. Handoff

In Sterling, the town midway between Virginia City and Bozeman City, Captain Neil Campbell and his officers had been able to organize a company of 25 men. On May 30, they received the last of their needed horses, saddles and arms.[270] In mid-afternoon of June 5, they rode out of Sterling well mounted and equipped for service.[271] That night, after riding 40 miles, they reported at Bozeman City.[272]

In Virginia City, Captain Nelson formed another company. By the time he had 32 men in quarters, Nelson decided it was better for discipline and cohesion to organize and train outside of town.[273] The recruiting office stayed on Jackson Street but after a man was sworn to service, he was sent to a camp at the upper edge of town for drill and instruction. The camp had excellent facilities for stabling and exercising horses. It came to be named Camp Cummings in honor of the Quartermaster on June 4.[274] By June 8, Madison County Sheriff A.J. Snider, a man with awareness of criminal activity and knowledge of horses, started inspecting every animal before purchase.[275] On June 9, Nelson's Company drew up in front of spectators at the Executive Office. Cummings presented a flag, Beem presented a guidon from Mrs. Meagher and Meagher gave a flowery speech. The troops cheered Meagher's words:

> The Territory was threatened—they had volunteered in its defense, and while he congratulated them as volunteers, they should remember that in this voluntary acceptance, they had not only assumed the privileges and hardships, the perils of a soldier's life, and it might be of a soldier's death. They had voluntarily accepted discipline essential to their efficiency. He presented the flag, feeling assured they would acquit themselves as becomes American Volunteers, with honor to themselves, to the flag and this fair young Territory, and win the gratitude and honorable esteem of its people. He said their cause was a noble one—for the protection, the development and the honor of our mountain home, the fairest, richest

and youngest born of all the states to be. They should guard it with their zealous care, be faithful and stead fast in their duties, and a grateful people would give them their heartiest support and joyous welcome home.

The troops gave three cheers for each donor, wheeled into columns with the colors flying and passed through Virginia City before returning to Camp Cummings.[276]

On June 13, because of reports that Sioux and Crow war parties were starting toward the Gallatin, Meagher ordered the entire Montana Militia to shift its position to the Yellowstone by advancing to a place he intended to call Fort (Green Clay) Smith.[277] The move was to happen as soon as medical stores could be forwarded. On the Yellowstone that same day, officers already in the field voted to name their new camp after Thoroughman's daughter, Ida:

> At a meeting of the officers, field and staff, of the Montana Militia, the following resolutions were unanimously adopted: 'It having been deemed necessary to move our camp from Camp Elizabeth Meagher to our present position on the Yellowstone,
>
> Resolved, that we have implicit confidence in the integrity and valor of our commanding General Thomas Thoroughman.

Resolved, that our present encampment be here after known by the name of his beloved daughter, Ida Thoroughman.

Resolved, that a copy of these resolutions be forwarded to his daughter, Ida Thoroughman, and to *The Montana Post*, *Gazette*, *Herald* and *Democrat* for publication.

(Signed):
Henry N. Blake, Col. and. A.A.G.[278]
Major John Kingsly[279]
Robert Hughes, Capt, Co. A.
Frank Davis, Capt. and A.D.C.
James Dunlevy, Surgeon,[280]
Captain Ruben Foster,
Captain Neil Campbell[281]

On June 15, though still short of his 80-man goal, Nelson led Company D out of Virginia City for the Yellowstone. The company's strength was 50 men including three officers. On the same day Company D departed, Meagher started north from Virginia City:

> . . . to personally superintend the transportation of ordinance stores from Fort Benton to Helena.[282]

On June 10, at the Territorial Executive Offices he had received a long-awaited letter reportedly advising:

... the arms mentioned recently as being transferred to the Territory of Montana, consisting of a 12-pounder battery complete and 2500 stand of arms, have arrived at Fort Benton.

Though failing to identify the individual in Fort Benton who wrote and mailed the letter, *The Montana Post* added:

> A sufficient number of these, to provide for the wants of the militia, will be brought forward at once, and the difficulty heretofore experienced in this particular will be obviated.[283]

Realizing that neither Smith nor Tufts would arrive before the July 1 deadline imposed by Congress for apportioning the territory into legislative districts, Meagher did it. As Acting Governor he exercised discretion and initiative and apportioned the Council and Representative districts.[284] He had not anticipated doing this. *The Montana Post* commented about Meagher's necessary actions on its front-page:

> (Meagher's decision) will probably be accepted as a fair basis of representation by all parties. It appears to us however, that the apportionment of Representatives of the fourth and fifth districts is not strictly just...admitting the difficulty of making an apportionment that will give

universal satisfaction, where the number of (Council) Representatives is limited to thirteen for the entire Territory.[285]

At issue was Meagher's proclamation causing the Fourth Council District, comprising Meagher and Chouteau counties, to lose one Council delegate.[286] He reapportioned the 26 Representatives in the House by giving Edgerton County four members in the House, as opposed to the previous three, which had allowed three for Chouteau.[287]

With the reapportionment task behind him, Meagher left Virginia City for the last time and reached Helena on Wednesday afternoon, June 18. He arrived intending to "spend a few days."[288] In Helena, he commissioned Pinney as a Captain and appointed him Aid-de-Camp, or principle order-writer, for the incoming Commander-in-Chief. This meant Hearn and Davis were no longer serving. Thoroughman in the meantime rode to Virginia City June 19. He found another new company forming. As the returning field commander, he reported, "All Quiet on the Yellowstone." Another company of 52 men and officers, led by Captain A.F. Weston, rode in from the Salmon River country of Idaho. They quartered on the edge of town, waiting for their horses to be shod before continuing to the field. *The Montana Post* reported that they partook in the urban delights:

The boys came in through the 'heavy wet' of Thursday morning, and the Quartermaster issued a ration of whiskey to dry up the fountains of distress. Some of them took a little more consolation than was prudent and behaved disorderly . . . but as the night came on the tarantula juice lost its grip and all went on quietly.

After avoiding jail and reaching their barracks they sobered and elected their officers: Captain A.F. Weston, First Lieutenant Thomas Burns and Second Lieutenant Charles H. Hosted.[289]

By June 21, all mobilized Montana Militia except for Meagher, Thoroughman, Cummings, Hull, Carpenter, Sullivan and his 11-man ordinance detail, and Helena's five officers including Pinney, Fisk, Hereford, Beidler and Featherstun, were operating from Camp Ida Thoroughman.[290] Nelson was supervising the construction walls for their stockade at the mouth of the Shields, known as 25-Yard Creek. The fort was in a large meadow outside the range of any rifles that might be fired from the nearest bluffs. No word had been heard from DeLacy's 42-man detachment escorting supplies to relieve Fort C.F. Smith. Campbell's Company patrolled down the Yellowstone. Curtis, with a detail of ten men, scouted Flathead Pass, and other patrols reconnoitered in all directions. Beem served as ranking officer in the field. He reported to Thoroughman: "Officers and men are cheerfully performing all duties assigned."

As Adjutant General, he took the opportunity to make adjustments in the organization. Based on his decisions, from June 21, 1867, the Montana Militia would be called the First Regiment of Montana Cavalry. Its structure consisted of Captain (Brevet Colonel) Hynson's Company A; Captain Hughes' Company B; Captain Evans' Company C; Captain Curtis' Company D; Captain Campbell's Company E; and Captain Nelson's Company F.[291] On that first day of the First Montana Cavalry, Meagher started north from Helena on his fateful journey to Fort Benton, plainly restating his intention:

> . . . to personally superintend the transportation of the ordnance stores from that point to Helena.[292]

Meagher was traveling north three days behind Sullivan's ordnance detail. If not alone, he would have had with him no more than one officer. That officer might have been Pinney as his Aide-de-Camp. Because Meagher preferred the Buffalo steaks at Dearborn Station, he probably stayed there overnight. The Sun had been at flood stage recently and had sunk Bollard's ferry along with two wagons of a Diamond R train. It was not until June 23 that the Sun at Sun River Crossing was down to "a very fine boating stage."[293] Calmer water allowed Smith's southbound express coach to cross the Sun after June 23. Meagher and Smith met on the Mullan Road south of the Sun, most likely at

Rock Creek Station, the changing-over halfway station between Sun River Crossing and Helena.²⁹⁴ Both men were surprised by the encounter.

Meagher had just reapportioned the territory, expecting Smith, like Tufts, to arrive after July 1. Smith had just authorized Carpenter, waiting in Fort Benton, to receive and transport the territory's ordnance when it arrived. As experienced field officers, they executed a field change-of-command ending Meagher's time as Acting Governor and Commander-in-Chief of the Montana Militia. Smith asked him, as a favor, to continue the mission of transferring the ordnance to the territory.²⁹⁵ If Pinney was with Meagher as his Aide-de-Camp, he returned to Helena where he immediately started writing orders for Smith. The Huntley Express Coach brought Governor Smith and his family into Helena the night of June 26.²⁹⁶ The only Militia Officer recorded as arriving in Helena the same night was Beidler. He arrived at nearly the same time as the Smiths, coming from Fort Benton on Wells Fargo's Express Coach.²⁹⁷

Beidler had surfaced unexpectedly in Fort Benton on June 23. He had in his custody several men from Diamond City he had apprehended on the 150-mile Graham Wagon Road from Confederate Gulch to Fort Benton.²⁹⁸ Beidler and his prisoners came in on horseback and somehow crossed the Missouri's high water to Fort Benton. Possibly, they used the Baker

Street Ferry.[299] In answering the Fort Benton newspaper correspondent's questions, Beidler said his prisoners had absconded from Diamond City with $4,000 or $5,000. The correspondent seemed impressed that Beidler brought any men to jail while they were still alive:

> One of the men had started to draw his pistol, but "X got the drop on him and he had to surrender at discretion.[300]

The incident seemed strange because Diamond City, as the seat of Meagher County, had its own jail.[301] As the seat of Chouteau County, Fort Benton also had a its own dilapidated jail. [302] Beidler would have to eventually escort his prisoners to Diamond City's jail so they could stand trial. That Beidler waited to move his prisoners south suggests he had more pressing business. Once he placed his Diamond City prisoners into the Fort Benton jail and found a place for the horses, Beidler boarded the Wells Fargo Express to Helena. On the way, the Deputy U.S. Marshal would have passed Meagher during the changeover at Rock Creek Station or as the general rode north alone through herds of wandering buffalo.

From Smith, Meagher had learned that the letter he received in Virginia City on June 10 was wrong. The ammunition and guns were not on the levee at Fort Benton. Whether or not he felt ill, as some have suggested, he chose to spend the time at the Healys.[303] While there, he could receive new information on the status of the arrival of the ordnance. As it happened, Carpenter, in possession of the latest information, passed through Sun River Crossing, and arrived in Virginia City on June 29.[304]

On the evening of June 30, a blacksmith working for Huntley's Stage Line reported seeing Meagher enjoying dinner and "laughing and joking" at the Healys. None of the territorial staff was available to attend. Pinney was in Helena as Smith's Aide-de-Camp; Cummings was bringing his wife, daughter and son back to Virginia City from Fort Benton; Hull was preparing and serving as Grand Master for the June 24 laying of a cornerstone for Virginia City's Masonic Temple; and Carpenter, Beem and DeLacy were elsewhere fully occupied with their military duties.[305]

Sanders, the principle chronicler of July 1 events in Fort Benton, recalled "Captain William Boyce" riding into Fort Benton with Meagher that morning. Boyce, spelled as "Major Boise," appears in Meagher's May 25 dispatch from the field. Major Boyce may have ridden to Sun River Crossing to join Meagher, because Beem or Thoroughman had decided to send their own Aide-de-Camp to assist with the weapons. Although he claimed there were members of the General Staff of the Montana Militia with Meagher when he rode into Fort Benton, Sanders did not identify any of those individuals. If he mistakenly considered some militia officers from Helena as part of the Territorial Staff, those possibilities were limited. Howie and Hereford were supporting Judge Munson's Court; Assistant Quartermaster Fisk, a newspaperman important to Sanders' campaign might have gone up to get the guns and ammunition for Hereford's Company; Berkin could have brought up a Diamond R Fast Freight for hauling, but he would be driving a wagon; and Featherstun would have been riding as Beidler's A.H.O.J. (Assistant Hand of Justice).

    Beidler was the one Helena militia officer most likely to be entering Fort Benton with Meagher. He had prisoners to pick up for transport south to Diamond City. As Hereford's H.O.J. (Hand of Justice), he was to expedite ordnance for the new Helena Company

Evening Edition, March 15, 1902
Butte Inter Mountain

21. Telltale

Sanders waited 35 years to publish his recollections of July 1, 1867. They first appeared in 1902 in a Butte newspaper two days before Saint Patrick's Day. Three years before his own demise Sanders wrote:

> Early in June 1867, I left my home at Virginia City for Fort Benton to meet my family then on their way from the East to Montana via the Missouri River on the steamer Abeona. Remaining some ten days at Fort Benton in daily expectation of their arrival I accepted the invitation of the captain of a Pittsburgh boat, the

"Yorktown," to go down the river and meet them. Momentarily expecting to see the boat I sat on the deck for two days, when at Spread Eagle Bar, near Fort Union, I was transferred to the returning steamer, which was nearly three weeks thereafter reaching Fort Benton.

A little below the mouth of the Marias, impatient at the slow progress of our steamer, in the company of Walter Trumbull I stepped ashore and walking four or five miles across a bend boarded the Gallatin, Captain Sam Howe, a boat which he had discerned in the distance then doing service on the upper Missouri and which was reputed to be able to navigate a light dew.

Having boarded the Gallatin we proceeded to the mouth of the Marias where Captain Howe discharged a cargo of mules and we availed ourselves of his offer and had a mule back ride to Fort Benton. About 12 or 1 o'clock I discerned upon the tableland, whence the road descended into town, a number of horsemen in military apparel and upon their arrival we greeted General Thomas Francis Meagher and his military staff. He advised us that he was on his way to Camp Cooke after a hundred and thirty muskets (sic.), which the general government had proffered to the territorial authorities for use in the Indian war in which we were then engaged. The day was intensely hot and the general and his staff had made a swift and dusty ride from Sun river, where Messrs. Carroll and Stull (sic.) had a camp, and were founding that flourishing town, and near which Major Clinton was marking out the site of Fort Shaw, so named in honor of Col. Robert Shaw of the Fifty-fourth Massachusetts regiment, who at Fort Wagner had been buried 'with his niggers.'

I do not recall all the members of the general's staff nor their number, but one of them was Captain William Boyce, afterward a resident of Butte. The afternoon was delightfully spent in social visits through the business portions of the town and General Meagher seemed at his best in a conversational way, but he resolutely and undeviatingly declined that form of hospitality with which Fort Benton then abounded.

As he was my dear neighbor at Virginia City and a most genial and interesting companion I spent most of the afternoon with him, introducing him to so many of the citizens and sojourners in that unique and thrifty seaport as he had not theretofore known.

The Fort in that early time was only 20 years old and although past its prime it was in very good form. Major T. H. Eastman had it in charge for the fur company then carrying on the trade, then about equally divided between the Indians and whites on this frontier. Major Eastman was a most intelligent gentleman and his abounding hospitality well maintained the repute of the remote trading posts of the West. His dinners were veritable feasts of Lucullus and scarce a day passed that a choice lot of merry guests did not surround his hospitable board. During the afternoon he invited General Meagher to dine with him at 6 o'clock, which invitation the general accepted.

Six or seven steamboats from St. Louis or beyond were tied to the riverbanks and among them was a somewhat cheap and rude old craft named the G.A. Thompson. It was a freight boat but had cabins for perhaps a dozen persons. The pilot or mate of the boat was an Irish-American by the name of Dolan (sic.), I think, and when during the afternoon I had introduced him to the general, he doubtingly interrogated me as to whether this was the famous Thomas Francis Meagher, renowned in the Irish Rebellion of 1848, and upon my assurance that it was, he could not conceal his delight at meeting so distinguished a person who evidently was his idol, and he showed the general much deference and attention and wasted on him no inconsiderable blarney. Ascertaining the general's errand he invited him to become his guest on his voyage the next morning down the river as far as Camp Cooke.

General Meagher returned from the fort about dusk, in company with some other gentlemen whose names I do not now recall. I was seated in front of the store of I.C. (sic.) Baker and Company when my attention was arrested by abnormally loud conversation, and as the party came nearer I saw that it came from General Meagher.

As the party came to the place where I was, and I had listened a moment, it was apparent that he was deranged. He was loudly demanding a revolver to defend himself against the citizens of Fort Benton, who, in his disturbed mental condition, he declared, were hostile to him, and several who then joined us sought to allay his fears and by all the means in our power to restore to sanity his disturbed mental condition.

His nautical friend, whose host he was to be (sic.) the ensuing morning, suggested that he go to his stateroom on the boat, and thither three or four of us accompanied him. He was still insistent that the people of Fort Benton were hostile to him and was importunate for a revolver. He was induced to retire to his berth, which was on the starboard side of the boat next the bank, and in the hope that he would sleep we all went on shore, seeking to allay his anxiety by the promise of getting him a revolver.

As he had removed his outer garments and lain down in his berth, we did not apprehend there would be further trouble, thinking the temporary aberration the result of the hot and exhausting ride of the morning, which sleep would speedily correct. It was a great shock to all his friends, but we were all confident of his immediate recovery.

I do not stop here to speculate on the cause of his hallucination that the people of Fort Benton were hostile to him, but I have always thought that a contention between the Blackfoot Indian agent, George Wright, and the general as superintendent of Indian affairs, wherein the general directed the release of all intoxicating liquors in the country which the agent had assumed to seize, was in his mind. This controversy had assumed an epistolary form in the newspapers, as General Meagher's controversies were exceedingly wont to do. I only attribute it to this for lack of other causes, but General Meagher had no more loyal friends than those in Fort Benton who solicitously surrounded him there in his last hours.

I cannot say that any one remained in the stateroom with him, for nothing was farther from our thoughts than the denouement then impending. After a brief consultation on the lower deck, I went to the office of the Indian agent, opposite the G. A. Thompson and perhaps fifty yards distant, where I wrote a letter for the outgoing mail to Helena, which left at 11 o'clock. Perhaps I had been in the office 30 minutes when I heard Capt. James Gorman, the stage agent of C. C. Huntley, excitedly exclaim: "General Meagher is drowned!"

I dropped my pen and hastened out the door and rushed across the gangplank and across the lower deck of the steamboat. There was a colored man, one of the men connected with the boat—the barber I believe—who replying to my interrogation, said a man had let himself down from the upper to the lower deck and jumped into the river and gone down stream. I immediately returned to the land and ran down the riverbank, repeating the alarm until I reached one of those lower steamers, the Guidon, I believe, where I went across the boat to the riverside to watch for the general.

Boats were instantly lowered and manned, and many anxious eyes were peering into the darkness at the swift rolling waters of the great river, that never seemed so wicked as then. It gave back no wished-for sight or sound. The search was kept up all night, and for two or three days thereafter. Loaves of bread were cast on the turbid waters in obedience to a belief that they would cause a drowned body to rise to the surface of a stream. A cannon was brought into requisition for the same purpose, but the mighty river defied all our solicitudes and kept its treasure well. I turned from the steamer as I saw the boats go down the river in darkness to fulfill the sad duty of advising Mrs. Meagher of the overwhelming calamity, which had befallen her and us all. She lived on the same street near me in Virginia City, and it seemed to me to be my sad duty to tell her the sad story. I enclosed my letter to Dr. James Gibson, the postmaster at Virginia City, an accomplished gentleman and a fast friend of Mrs. Meagher, confiding to his discretion the manner in which he should break the melancholy news.

As there was no telegraph, the news of the event went by mail that night. No person, so far as I know, save the colored man, saw General Meagher go into the river, and he related to me the circumstances as I have told. The next day some members of the general's staff said to me that we must report that he fell from the boat accidentally and must not mention the mental aberration nor attribute it to that. I said to them I had written to Mrs. Meagher the exact facts as they had been related to me, and could see no imputation upon the general nor cause for humiliation to his friends if his eager devotion to his duties in hand had brought him to so great an affliction. Some of them seemed to think otherwise, and in the proclamation by Governor Green Clay Smith announcing his death it was, I believe, alleged to have been caused 'by accident.'

I can well appreciate the affection, which General Meagher inspired among his race and his countrymen. His form was manly, his manners cordial, his demeanor gracious, his conversation instructive, his wit kindly, his impulses generous, and I agree with Horace Greely (sic.), who once said to me that General Meagher was one of the finest conversationalists and extemporaneous speakers he had ever known.

It is to be regretted that so much is said and written of General Meagher and the manner of his death that is not so. Those who were with him on that last day of his life will join me I know in denying that his death could be attributed to any convivial habit. I was with him most of the afternoon, and he was as resolutely abstemious as the most devout anchorite, and it is cruelly unjust to repeat such an accusation.

The river was searched for his remains down to the mouth of the Marias, but the search was in vain. Somewhere in the stream his manly form sleeps in as serene repose as it would in classic Arlington, but the jealous waters guard their secret well, and the rushing waves from unfound springs seem destined forever to be his monument and his grave."[306]

By July 3 in Virginia City, Carpenter and his lady friend learned of Meagher's death. Realizing no one else had been authorized to sign a hand receipt on behalf of the Territory, they checked out of Planters House and went north to Camp Reynolds, arriving by July 7. There he inventoried the cargos carried by Sullivan's detail on the six prairie carriages and Couch's train, before signing this hand receipt:

I hereby acknowledge to be received of the

United States by the hand of Brevet Brigadier General F.D. Callender of the U.S. Army the following arms, ordinance and supplies: (lists entire shipment totaling $6,294.00) Includes a six 12-pounder battery, stand of 2500 .58 caliber arms and accoutrements, 750,000 rounds, 300 rounds for each howitzer for 12-pound howitzers, 125 arms chests, 982 boxes and packing. Which are received on account of the quota of arms due the territory of Montana under the act of April 1808 for arming the whole of the militia and for which I have signed triplicate receipts at Camp Reynolds this 7 of July 1867. (Signed) A.M.S. Carpenter Major and Chief of Ordnance, Montana Militia.[307]

To this was attached an inventory list, incomplete because it listed 1125 fewer howitzer rounds :

12 tarpaulin (6 x 10)
6 vent covers
225 12-pd mountain howitzer shells, fixed
 "   "   "   "   " , spherical
 "   "   "   "   " , cannister
2,500 caliber .58 Springfield rifled-muskets
250   Ball Screws
2,500 Screw Drivers
250   Spring Vises
500   Tumbler Punches
1,250 Wipers

2,500 Bayonet Scabbards
2,500 Cap Punches and Picks
2,500 Cartridge Boxes and Plates
2,500 Gun Straps
2,500 Waste Belts and Plates
750,000 Caliber .58 Elong Ball Cartridges
125 Arms Chests (20 rifles per chest)
982 Packing Boxes

    Carpenter and his 'lady' did not return to Virginia City until August 17. On that night, they checked into Planters House again. A week later, *The Montana Post* announced Carpenter's nomination on a non-partisan citizens ticket for election as the Sixth District's single delegate from Chouteau County to the Legislature's Council.[308] Carpenter's name failed to appear on Chouteau County's September election ballot.

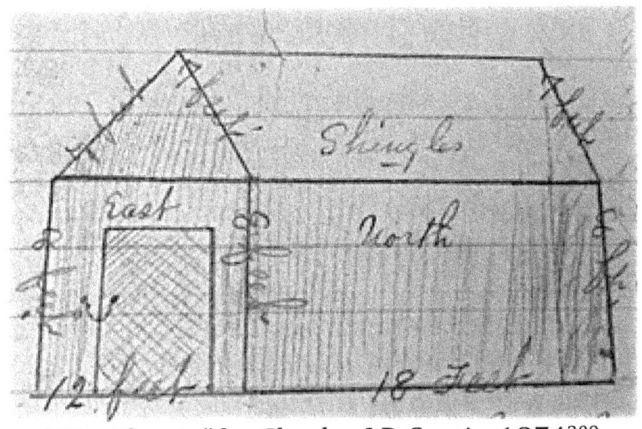

"The Shanty" by Charles J.D.Curtis, 1874[309]

22. Shanty

Montana's Territorial 3rd Volunteer Militia started April 1, 1867, when Acting Governor Meagher, with the help of Montana's First Adjutant General, sent the first volunteers to the Gallatin Valley. It ended July 31 when the last of their three-month enlistments expired. Over those four intervening months, service strength rose to 200 enlisted and 50 officers.[310] Casualties, not counting one man who was lynched by Vigilantes after being properly mustered out of Captain Foster's Company, were: one officer missing, one enlisted wounded, one enlisted killed in non-combat, two enlisted wounded in non-combat, one enlisted died from sickness and three Indians killed.[311] All strategic, operational and tactical missions had been accomplished, including restoration of public confidence, relief of Fort C.F. Smith and the receipt, transport and storage of federal ordnance transferred to Montana. The guns anticipated by Meagher finally arrived aboard the Gallatin at Fort Benton on July 6, accompanied by "an immense amount of ammunition."[312]

The Ida Stockman brought up some of Couch's cargo from the Trover on June 28, and the Amaranth brought another 25,698 pounds directly from Saint Louis on June 29.[313] Couch stayed with his train through the July 4 holiday. That celebration, included a speech by Sanders from the deck of the Antelope and a big Squaw Dance followed by a bad windstorm on July 5. As soon as the territorial cargo could be transloaded, heavily laden wagons trundled in groups toward Helena and Virginia City. Wagon transport took time. By the time Carpenter and LaMotte signed the completed hand receipt, some wagons were already two days on the road. After three weeks, *The Montana Post* reported the first ordinance arriving at Virginia City:

> Five hundred stand of arms and the necessary ammunition have been received in this city and placed in the armory and magazine. We understand the artillery is also on the way here from Helena. Over 100 of the militia at the front have not heretofore been armed. They will now be armed and equipped and rendered efficient for such service as may be required. It is

gratifying to know that the necessary weapons can be had immediately. The call in the spring developed the very unpleasant fact that it would have been almost impossible to have procured arms and ammunition for 500 men in as many weeks.[314]

Eventually, all arms, ammunition, accoutrements, pack saddles, limbers, caissons and accessories associated with both the rifle-muskets and the howitzers were apportioned between Virginia City and Helena. [315] The capital got 1,500 rifle-muskets and four M1841 mountain howitzers in two sections on prairie carriages. They were parked and stored around and in a small cabin. The smaller portion of ordnance, as much as 20 tons consisting of an artillery section on two prairie carriages, a thousand rifle-muskets in 50 boxes, 300,000 rounds of ammunition in 300 boxes, and 46 cases of accoutrements, remained on Couch's wagons parked in the Allen Corral on Rodney Street. A longer-term solution for Helena had already been placed in motion. On July 4, Smith had ordered Howie to:

> . . . oversee construction of a powder magazine to store the ordinance coming in from Fort Benton.[316]

In 1874, U.S. Marshal William Wheeler, the man who had replaced Howie in 1869, had some questions about the details of that storage arrangement. The questions came through by way of a dispatch from Captain Andrew Dusold, a detective working to stop whiskey trading with the Indians.[317] Curtis answered:

> A few friends, Neil Howie, George Pinney, James Fisk, J.X. Beidler, Charles Curtis and some others, pooled $150 to $175 in gold dust to construct a house.

Curtis said he and Howie chose the building site on the hill west of Clore Street. The group of donors decided to make Howie:

> ... 'a Special Committee of One' to purchase 1800 feet of lumber and sufficient nails, contract and pay the carpenters, and take possession of the structure once completed.

The 12-foot wide by 18-foot long dimensions of the building had 8-foot high doubled walls, an extra-wide entrance in its east end and no floors or windows. They called their powder magazine and arsenal 'the shanty'. It was constructed while they were away on the Yellowstone preparing for winter operations, after earlier forays had ended well.

DeLacy's military escort arrived at Fort C.F. Smith with army scout Mitch Boyer and ten wagons filled with John Richards' supplies and their own provisions. The first report of that mission surfaced in *The Montana Post* on July 13, when Lieutenant William Hazlett, one of the 42 relief escort men from Hynson's Virginia City Company came ahead of the returning party to get more provisions and move the Yellowstone ferry farther downriver to enable returning wagons to cross the swollen Boulder. He reported the expedition, consisting of 10 wagons and 55 men, including Boyer, Richards and wagon drivers, had already been on the road 41 days. They'd seen both Sioux and Crow Indians but none had tried to attack the train:

> This is accounted for by the strength of the escort and the fact of the train belonged principally to John Richards, who is half-Sioux and who kept in front the greater part of the time and communicated with the Indians.

Crow Chief Blackfoot had left a large part of his band below the Clark's Fork and traveled with the detachment to Fort C. F. Smith. He and his men returned upriver in a hostile mood after the fort refused them provisions. Two days before the relief wagons arrived, 17 Sioux came in close to the fort and stole 16 horses trying to entice the soldiers into following them. The soldiers didn't take the bait. The fort had reports of 18 bands of Sioux, with 30 warriors in each, coming up the north side of the Yellowstone. When DeLacy and his men appeared across the Big

Horn from the fort, the river was at flood stage as were all the other streams on their return trip.

The tiny Montana relief column of militiamen soon learned that another train of 40 government supply wagons, escorted by 600 regulars, had just entered the fort from the south, off-loaded and returned to Fort Phil Kearny with 500 of the escort troops still accompanying. According to Hazlett, Fort C.F. Smith had been left with 100 men added to the 180 already barricaded there. He reported the fort had one piece of artillery and 70 horses. The relief detail's volunteers were disappointed when the fort's temporary commander, replacing the officer who left with the departing government train, refused to give them permission to enter his premises or even to cross the river on the ferry with the wagons. They were assured of his gratitude for the spirit shown bringing down the supplies, because the men in the fort had been existing on nothing but corn for some time. Hazlett felt sure the Post Commander's poor hospitality was due to "fears of his men deserting and joining the militia."

Twenty immigrants traveling from Fort Phil Kearny with the regulars' relief column continued their journey with the militia's train up the Yellowstone to the Gallatin. On that return trip, DeLacy's Relief Detachment built rafts to cross the Stillwater and Clark's Fork but were forced to stop at the Boulder though nearly out of provisions.[318]

In contrast to Hazlett's theory, there was another reason why the Commander of Fort C.F. Smith was so unwelcoming to the volunteers. In truth, it was the appearance of the Montana Militia. They were scary looking enough to worry the fort's acting commander, Major Thomas Burrows. The diary of another regular army officer, First Lieutenant George Templeton, contains this observation:

> They are a hard set and although they have a colonel, a captain and two lieutenants, they don't mind any of them, but do just about as they please. The major did not allow any of them to come on this side of the river.[319]

These impressions recorded by a lower ranking regular officer match the observations of a young recruit in the Montana Militia. Ohio-born Thomas H. LaForge, then 17-years old, had enlisted from Gallatin County while he was working at the top of Bozeman Pass. He remembers John Evans and a man, partially remembered years later, named Griggs recruiting him. That would have been First Lieutenant E.U. Driggs, second-in-command of Captain Foster's Scout Company. Part of Foster's Company left for the Gallatin by May 4. The rest didn't clear Virginia City until May 17. LaForge's parents tried changing the young recruit's mind, but he kept to his 90-day commitment. In his book, *Memoirs of a White Crow Indian*, LeForge recalled going to a training camp on the Gallatin side of the pass:

> Our company mutinied a day or two after my induction into the militia. We were being held there with only our own personal arms, without clothing or other military accoutrement, without any horses, without provision for shelter, with scant food, except for a little wild game. The specific act of our insubordination was our refusal to leave the temporary camp and go to the Yellowstone, where hostile Indians were plentiful. [320]

This was the scarcity described on May 7 by Thoroughman when he wrote to Meagher, "The men have nothing." Without remembering there had been a lapse of two week's time before the rest of Foster's Scout Company, including Private Christian "Chris" Yunson, arrived, LaForge told of a later act of insubordination:

> Governor Meagher ordered the entire company to be arrested, and brought to him, up where the Northern Pacific tunnel now goes through the mountain's top. When we arrived there we found companies from Virginia City and Bannack drawn up to receive us. We were headed so as to go between them, but our leading ones turned aside so as to go behind them. Governor Meagher stood up and began a

lecturing speech to us. Some of the men in other companies handed guns to men in our companies. A man named Chris, a tough but good-hearted mormon leveled a rifle at the governor and told him we had heard enough. The untamed militiamen of the other companies cheered him, cheered his associate culprits, and shouted, 'We are with you, boys!' The governor had to yield the point. The matter was soon settled in a manner acceptable to all. Not long afterward we were on our way to the Yellowstone in search of marauding Indians, or anything else that might stir up excitement.

This incident atop Bozeman Pass happened after Meagher sent his May 24 dispatch reporting the departure of DeLacy's escort and his own intention to combine the Helena Scout Company under Curtis with the Virginia City Scout Company under Foster, with Curtis commanding. That dispatch conveyed Meagher's intent to move all companies forward to a new base of operations on the Shields.

Enough Saddled Horses for a 10-man Squad

23. Volunteers

By itself, the nearly 50 tons of wood, metal, leather and powder comprising the territory's ordnance couldn't kill people. It needed joining with horses and volunteers. A military volunteer is a human being who enlists in military service by free will, not for money as a mercenary or legionnaire. Military volunteers were a cross-section of people, good and bad, Indian and non-Indian, for whom they fought and worked. LaForge, having started as a young recruit, maintained an unvarnished, lifelong assessment of his fellow volunteers:

> This first (sic.) Montana militia was composed largely of ex-ruffians of the Missouri-Kansas border. As soldiers, they were utterly unruly.

He remembered working to build the new fort, a cottonwood stockade, storehouse and other structures on the Shields:

. . . headquarters of the three companies, while we skirmished along the Yellowstone and its tributaries.

As the fort was being built, a band of Flatheads on their way to the buffalo country east of the Bridger Mountains by way of Flathead Pass got into an altercation with a white rancher. "He was injured but not killed." Afterwards, Laforge rode with Campbell and some other men to intercept the Flatheads:

> We came upon them at the mouth of Brackett Creek. We demanded the man or men who had attacked the Gallatin rancher. Flathead Jack, an English-speaking Indian, responded for them. They designated the man, but they wanted to substitute another for the coming sacrifice, since the offending Indian was held to be an important one in the tribe. Some parlaying was done, but not for long. We seized the principal factor in the intrusion on white men's rights. In a jiffy he was hanged, or was strangled to death from the limb of a cottonwood tree. The other Indians were permitted to go their own way.

Newspapers carried a written report of the incident. They said it started when the owner of a stolen horse traced the thief to a Flathead Camp of about 50 persons, eighteen miles from Camp Thoroughman. When the rancher requested assistance, Campbell was ordered to take a squad and arrest the offender. After finding the chief cooperative but the suspect missing, Campbell's squad rode to a position from which to observe the Flathead camp all night. The next morning they rode back into the camp and again demanded the thief. This time they found the suspect. After a considerable resistance, they put a lariat around his neck and hanged him from a nearby tree:

> The boys run him up and told the chief he could save him if he said so, but the chief said he was 'bad Ingun—give him a heap of trouble—let him die.' and die he did.[321]

That report written July 4 opined:

> This was a masterstroke of policy, and will insure the future good behavior of all those 'friendlies' . . . reflecting . . . when said mortality has stolen a horse in this 'damned vigilante country.'[322]

At near the same time, there was another incident not mentioned by LaForge, because it happened miles away on the previous day. This second skirmish resulted in the wounding of an enlisted volunteer and the deaths of two more Indians. As Nelson passed with a messenger through the Gallatin Valley, the two men learned that a party of nine Indians had stolen a settler's horse. At Jack's Ranche, Nelson found out that the suspects were ahead of him a short distance. When he and his companions started to pursue them, they gained sight of two Indians nearing the summit of Bozeman Pass. When the Indians saw they were being chased, they rode for their lives for 30 miles over hills and valleys. The volunteers resolved "to catch the redskins or kill the horses." The Indians reached the Yellowstone ferry on exhausted and trembling horses covered by foam. They told the ferryman to take them across "quick," but the ferryman took his time. When the followers arrived, the ferryman and the messenger fired their rifles killing one of the Indians. The other ran for the trees and some swampy ground along the river. Nelson rode to Camp Thoroughman and raised 50 more men to help search for the fugitive. Once he was found, "they riddled him with bullets."

The militia casualty happened while one member of Company B was feeling with his hands and arms for the Indian under the water. For his troubles he received, from the Indian's pistol, a bullet in his face "shattering his jaw dreadfully." The newspaper report observed:

> He suffers a great deal but will recover. He's a brave young fellow and we would regret to lose him.[323]

These encounters with Indians weren't the reasons LaForge considered his companions to be ruffians. Among the illustrations he used to make that point, he described a man from

Company D using a Bowie knife to instantly kill a man from Company A. On July 27, twenty-five volunteers had been assigned to escort Smith from Bozeman City as soon as he arrived. Fifteen of the men were from Company A and five each were from two other companies. Baume, the officer in charge of the detail, was in Bozeman City, and the men were all camped outside of the town enjoying a fine summer evening. The men were cooking and eating by five-man messes. Two Company D men, Messler and Sullivan, were sparring and wrestling when another soldier, James Spencer from Company A, came up and tripped Messler. Then he kicked him while he was still down. This caused several of Messler's messmates to yell, "Hey, that's not fair play." One of those who objected was Yunson, sitting nearby and quietly eating his dinner.

Spencer, a 28-year old man from New York, approached Yunson and said, "May be you want to take it up." Yunson put down his plate, stood up and said, "I don't care if I do." At that response Spencer drew his loaded revolver and pointed it full-cocked at Yunson's head. Yunson told him repeatedly, some say four, some say six or seven times, to pull away his pistol, but Spencer refused. In a flash, while the cocked and loaded firearm was still at his head, Yunson drew a large knife from the sheath at his side and struck the man:

> The blade entered Spencer's body just below the ribs, on the right, passed under

the heart and entirely through his body, killing him instantly.

Spencer was buried with military honors that evening at Bozeman City. Yunson gave himself up and was taken under guard to Camp Thoroughman. He was court-martialed and acquitted. According to Laforge there was scant evidence.[324] Baume said all witnesses, including 15 from his own company and five from Yunson's, stood behind Yunson. Some men who did not witness the incident agitated for hanging Yunson, but others who were witnesses pled his case. Everyone agreed Yunson should not be publicly condemned unless convicted.

LaForge recalled the volunteers as ruffians for being tough on their officers. He remembered one officer named Captain Hart being shot by one of his own men and another company drowning its own captain:

> One company drowned its first captain. He showed some inclination to disciplinary action so the bold and un-terrified subordinates threw a rope around him and dragged him back and forth through the Shields River (sic.) until life was extinct.[325]

The story about Hart getting killed was partly wrong. In later years he kept a saloon on Last Chance Gulch. The story about the drowning requires some effort to narrow down the names of officers who might have been killed in this manner. Foster was a prime candidate for being eliminated by his own men. He initially led Laforge's company, about which Meagher reported in his May 24 dispatch:

> Two men, belonging to the Virginia Scouts, (Captain Foster) have been missing for two days. It is feared they have been captured by the Indians.[326]

Fortunately for Foster, he turned up two weeks later to sign the resolution naming the Shields camp after Ida Thoroughman. Besides Meagher himself, another top candidate for extinction by drowning would have been Captain H.H. Lyons, the first commander of Helena's Company A.

Lyons disappeared from public mention after chasing off Beidler. He was nowhere to be found by the time Camp Ida Thoroughman received its name. First Lieutenant Robert Hughes signed the resolution for the company from Helena in place of Lyons. Fortunately for Lyons, he resurfaced months later serving as Sergeant-of-Arms at the Unionist Convention. Captain William Deasey was a third excellent candidate for retribution by extinction. On Sunday morning June 30, he somewhat harshly quelled a disturbance among his whiskey drinking Virginia City recruits. The newspaper said Deasey:

. . . interfered to preserve the peace, when another of the recruits became suddenly unimpressed.

When the indignant recruit swung at his officer, Deasey hit him back. He struck hard enough to drop his man to the ground and to order transport for him to a temporary hospital. By then Deasey had used a pick handle to subdue the other belligerents and restore the harmony of his unit in their barracks.[327] It comes as some surprise that Deasey proved to be still alive on December 4, when he checked into Helena's International Hotel. Still, it seems that LaForge wasn't too far off regarding both incidents. As it turns out, Hart was in a deadly gunfight and another officer was dragged and drowned by his own men. Both incidents happened more than a month after Meagher disappeared. By then, nearly everyone including LaForge, had re-enlisted for another six months.

      This shouldn't translate into all the volunteers being ruffians and "border trash." This was a time when life was hard, and haircuts and showers were scarce. Though the Montana Militia had its share of hard looking men, they did get the job done. The truth is that Montana's militia accomplished its tactical mission of chasing down and killing Indians; its operational missions of receiving and transporting a huge tonnage of guns and ammunition and relieving Fort C.F. Smith; and its strategic mission of protecting and calming fellow citizens.

Historians often acquiesce or parrot Sherman's distanced and biased view that Meagher was a stampeder. This implies there was a non-existent serious threat. In fact Meagher was a necessary leader at a time when there was a serious threat to the Gallatin Valley from outraged, well-led and capable Indian forces on the Yellowstone.

Force protection measures were being taken by regular army officers on the Missouri and Yellowstone. Those precautions were professionally justified by an intelligence assessment from the most respected authority possible on the subject. On March 4, the aging Jim Bridger, still scouting for the U.S. Army, sat inside Fort C.F. Smith and wrote:

> Every person that knows anything of affairs in this country knows very well that the massacre at Fort Philip Kearny was planned weeks before and that the Sioux, Cheyenne and Arapahos had been collecting together, in preparation for it, on the Tongue River, where they numbered 2,200 lodges. The intention was to attack Fort Philip Kearny first, and if they were successful to then attack Fort C.F. Smith. At the present time the entire tribe of northern Sioux are collecting on the Powder River, below the mouth of Little Powder River, and their avowed intention is to make a vigorous and determined attack on each of the three posts, and all the trains that may come along the road.[328]

This seasoned assessment by Bridger was soon confirmed by estimates and actions of the U.S. Army. On March 23 a letter arrived in Virginia City from Fort Phil Kearny. The letter reported Indians, numbering about 11,000 warriors, camped on the Tongue about midway up the Bozeman Trail to Fort C.F. Smith. It totaled the numbers for each Sioux, Cheyenne and Arapaho force arrayed across that area and concluded:

> A small but respectable war is inevitable during the spring and summer.

Because Fort Phil Kearny at the southeastern end of the string of three vulnerable forts needed relief, the army planned a military expedition of 5,000 troops, comprised of the 2nd Cavalry, 12th, 18th, 19th, 20th and 27th Infantry.[329]

This news carried little assurance for anyone. It confirmed the potency of the threat, while making everyone realize that infantry stood no chance chasing over long distances on foot behind some of the world's finest light cavalry. That same perception resonated in Colorado Territory, where four days later Governor Hunt wrote to Sherman requesting authority, as in Montana, to organize mounted volunteers for a "campaign against the savages." He had concluded:

> . . . depredations from Indians on our eastern and western borders are of daily occurrence; the present military, being mostly infantry are essentially inadequate for the protection of the settlers and the great thoroughfares.

He could have added that other Indians were also at risk. On May 4, below Fort C.F. Smith along the Yellowstone 50 miles from the mouth of the Big Horn, a large band of Nez Pierce fought a major battle with a combined force of Sioux, Arapahos and Blackfoot proper. The Nez Pierce lost enough people to fill seven lodges. They were forced to move upriver for western Montana.[330] While passing, they relayed to non-Indians through their Flathead allies that only the Blackfoot proper were in the feared league with the Sioux, but the white man could be rest assured that the Gros Ventre and the Piegan still hated him.[331]

On June 1, Hunt ordered formation of 720 Colorado volunteers into six companies. He anticipated that 300 Utes would join his expedition.[332] The next day, Meagher rode into Virginia City and made his last report from the field:

> The supply train, when last heard from, was within a few miles of Boulder creek. Along the Yellowstone they found evidence of numerous Indian camps but recently vacated. A band of Nez Perce Indians (sic.)

who had been with the other Indians on the Big Horn river, report that there are now but a few small bands of Indians this side of Fort Smith. The Indian tribes are concentrated on the Dry Fork of the Powder River, between Forts Phil Kearny and Reno, to the number of 6,000 lodges, consisting of Sioux, Cheyenne, Arapahos, Crows, Gros Ventre and a few Comanche. They confirm the report that the Indians will endeavor to capture the three forts on the Bozeman route. Blackfoot, with his band of Crows, is destined for Fort Phil Kearny for a peace treaty. They say the troops at Fort (C.F.) Smith have all their horses in good condition, plenty of pork, coffee, and salt, but are destitute of flour, hard bread, tobacco, etc; and have been living for some time on corn. The bands on the Yellowstone left that stream and joined the main force, on seeing and hearing of the soldiers concentrating at Bozeman. There are now 135 soldiers for duty, with the train and in the pass, fourteen miles beyond Bozeman, exclusive of Captain Curtis' Company, which has by this time arrived.

Meagher spoke with the highest regard for the Helena troops and advised Virginia City to look well to her laurels. He was satisfied that the three-month militia was doing its job:

The families are returning to the Gallatin and prospectors are diverging out in various directions in search of new diggings.

Saying nothing of the tremendous loss of life among the Nez Pierce, he also relayed news of that band's horses being stolen by the Sioux. He said they were now traveling toward northwest Montana to find the Bannocks and, with them, to establish a treaty to defend against the Sioux. Then Meagher as an informed and experienced military leader made these conclusions:

> It is clearly demonstrated that the militia have done three important things—not the less so that the victory has been so far bloodless. They have driven the bands of lurking Indians from the confines of the valley; restored confidence to the settlers remaining, and thereby insured the return of many who had fled; and are sending relief to the beleaguered and destitute garrison on the Big Horn. The troops have been kindly treated by all the people of Gallatin.[333]

From the affected people's view, he and his volunteers had well represented and protected the non-Indian settlers of Montana. The remainder of June occupied Meagher, as he completed his civil and military responsibilities.

Bull Team

24. Settlers

Over the summer of 1867 more immigrants flooded Montana.[334] They brought determination and self-righteousness. While Meagher spent his last few days on the Sun with the Healys, *The Montana Post* printed a front-page article titled "Don't Like Him." The piece discussed Hunt's telegram to Secretary of War Stanton requesting authorization for Colorado to raise a militia like Montana's and Sherman's response:

> The Denver papers are severe on General Sherman, who in response to Governor

Hunt's telegram asking permission to raise troops when men are being slaughtered in all directions, replied that 'the facts indicated great carelessness on the part of the stage company,' and asked, 'where and against what Indians do you propose a campaign?' To which the *News* replies in an article headed 'Murderous Stupidity—'The question is an insult to Governor Hunt, an insult to the people of Colorado, and an acknowledgment that the man who asks it is not fit to command the department over which he has been placed. 'When should such a campaign be made? Now? 'Against what Indians?' Those who are every day making war on us. ***We have not the vocabulary severe enough to express our condemnation of General Sherman or to picture the contempt in which he will be held by our people. His conduct is obstinate, stupid and criminal. We can only suggest to the government that a man with ordinary common sense be placed over our department and that General Sherman be permitted to retire to the 'holy land.' The *Tribune* goes after him in the following style: 'And then we are not only threatened by the Indians, but we are over-lain by that self-conceited and rickety-headed General whose peculiar glory was in marching a great army over a country where there was no opposition. The government has no interest in her children, and has handed us over to that man whose tastes in every way, as well as his capacities, better fit him to take sides with the savages than to fight against them.'[335]

News telegraphed the next day to Virginia City brought this June 26 report from Saint Joseph, Missouri:

General Terry and General Sherman have each written a letter to the Governor of Dakota advising the postponement of the contemplated exploring expedition to the Black Hills. They say that country is still conceded to be within the Indian reservation, and say attempt to occupy it by the whites would be resisted by the Indians, and that in the present condition of affairs the government cannot promise protection. The telegraph line between Fort Laramie and South Pass, a distance of 175 miles, is in the hands of the Indians now, and has been for two weeks; Omaha dispatches report a general eruption of Indian hostilities along the Platte Route; General Augur has reached Fort Laramie from Fort Morgan; Captain Mix's Company, after scouring the headwaters of the Republican and Powder Rivers, in all directions for eight days, and going 150 miles to the south, returned to Fort Sedgwick on Saturday, having seen no Indians or any sign of them; Colonel Green, with five companies of Infantry, and one company of Cavalry, left Fort Phil Kearny on the fourth (June 4) with soldiers for Fort C.F. Smith, with which post communication was cut off. The Indians seem to have left the Platte Route, going North and West, ...and others South, the latter in a body. It was these who made the raid on the Smoky Hill route, and the Kansas and Pacific Railway on Saturday last.[336]

Also from Saint Joseph dated June 14:

The steamer Only Chance arrived this morning, making the trip in nine days and a quarter from Fort Benton. She brings one-half a million dollars in gold dust. No trouble from the Indians. Met twenty-three steamers upward bound.[337]

Those boats steaming upriver included now familiar names like the Gallatin, the Octavia, the Abeona and, of course, the G.A. Thompson, the vessel where Meagher was last seen the night of July 1. As tradesmen completed the ordnance shanty in Helena, the last militia three-month enlistment contract expired. Re-enlistment had gradually become an option. While later auditing the expenses submitted for Montana's 1867 Indian War, Hardie observed:

The men manifested great anxiety to be re-enlisted for a period to embrace the coming autumn and winter. Though the settlers had recovered from their alarm, they naturally encouraged the plan, and the governor, apparently convinced that the troubles threatening the settlement of the Territory by Indian invasion had not been brought to a termination, issued a proclamation on the 31st of July, calling for the service of 800 men for six months from the 1st of August, and inviting the old force to re-enlist.[338]

When reflecting objectively on the attitudes being held by non-Indian Montanans regarding their Indian co-residents, it's hard to accept the frequent claim that Montanans have always viewed themselves through the lenses of eastern writers. Regarding Indians, that statement could not be farther from the truth. As to the question of properly dealing with Indians, Montanans held views closest to the 'kill them all' end of the spectrum of national opinion. On July 20, *The Montana Post* published a *Sacramento Union* correspondent's coverage of a Commission that reported in Washington City about the Fetterman Massacre. The report blamed not the Indians but rather a U.S. policy failure to negotiate a military presence along the Bozeman Trail, the use of which was not even needed.[339] The Commission argued there already existed safe southern trails and the steamboat route through Fort Benton. It laid blame on traders, peddlers and military contractors for antagonizing the natives and inflating rumors of their savagery in order to profiteer from sales to isolated army posts and to plunder the treasury.

The same newspaper printed a verbatim copy of Sherman's June 21 General Order. Using that order, he attempted to set out a framework for dealing with the nomadic Indians in his Missouri Division, encompassing the entire Great Plains from the British Possessions to Mexico and from the Mississippi to the Rocky Mountains.[340] He reviewed the laws of Congress, including the one that placed care of the Indians on reservations in the hands of the Department of Interior and its Superintendents, Special Commissioners and Agents:

> When the Indians leave their reservations and go beyond the country committed to them, and there commit a crime, they fall under military control, or subject themselves to arrest and punishment by civil power.

Sherman explained that he divided his Division into three departments. The Department of Dakota was responsible for the north under General Terry, who commanded as large a portion of the regular army as could be spared. His General Order continued:

> As a great diversity of opinion and practice exists as to how far civil authority can apply, especially in cases such as have

recently prevailed, where Indians in small bands have infested the traveled roads and settlements, it is hereby made known that if each State and Territory will organize a battalion of mounted men, ready to be called into the service of the United States, it will be called for by the department commander, and used in connection with the regular troops, if an emergency should arise in his judgment, to make it necessary. In that event the regiment, or a part thereof, will be mustered in, according to the laws of Congress now existing—each man to provide his own horse, for which the allowance of forty cents a day will be stipulated; and the same pay, clothing, food, and allowances as are now or maybe hereafter provided by law. It must be clearly understood that it will require an appropriation by Congress to make the actual payment of everything except rations, forage and supplies needed by such volunteers, during the time they are in the service of the United States.

There had been telegraphed news of this order about the time Meagher and Smith executed their field change-of-command. Now the newspaper laid the entire proposition before the people of Montana, including the expected role of county sheriffs:

The civil authorities of the said States and

Territories should by their sheriffs of counties and by their deputies have small posses armed and prepared at all times, to pursue and hunt down the small horse-thieving bands of Indians, who by dispersing, avoid the military forces. When they make captures clearly within the county, or within their official jurisdiction, the thieves should be confined in the county jail and proceeded against according to law; but if traced to any Indian reservation, the case should be reported to the United States Marshal, by whom the property stolen should be demanded through the resident agent, and a demand made for the surrender of the thief or thieves. Sheriff's parties in pursuit of Indians who have committed thefts, will be justified in using their arms, unless promptly surrendered on demand...

The week previous to publishing this Sherman order verbatim, the same newspaper associated with Montana Territory's Unionist Republicans pronounced on its front page:[341]

The Indian Policy of this Government is the most stupendous humbug of this century, and we see but little prospect of a change for the better. Better it never will be while the faith of those who have power to change it is pinned to the skirts of that erratic, conceited genius, George Francis

Train; Indian-Agents, contractors and sutlers, through all their various ramifications of swindling influence; the *New York Tribune*, with its sickly sentimentality that leaps over the corpses of mutilated white victims to suck sorrow from the sore finger of a barbarian; or the *Salt Lake Telegraph*, the vindicator of every outrage against God and humanity that base passions can inspire. A pretty group of advocates, indeed—a fop, a philosopher, a Mormon and a mongrel crew, whose prototypes, we are told, were driven out of the Temple for making it 'a den of thieves.'

The Republican paper then offered sincere appreciation for Montana's Militia:

The war of this season among the contiguous tribes extending from the British Possessions to New Mexico commenced within forty miles of our settlements, where the great bulk of the Sioux, Cheyenne and Arapahos were concentrated. Immediate and determined local measures and a few hundred mountaineers thrown into the gap stayed the tide and it swept off to the south. Colorado, New Mexico, Arizona, Utah, Kansas, Nebraska and Dakota have each felt the shock... May the hideous spectacle of Fort Phil Kearny, the starving garrison of Fort Smith, the victims of the knife and torch over all this broad west, rise up in judgment against the instigators of such consummate folly. There has never been permitted an honest fair investigation of Indian difficulties in Congress since civilization crossed the Missouri.

On behalf of the volunteers the paper stated:

Our miners have left their employment to protect our borders. We have 350 good men and true on the Yellowstone. The Indians fled before them. They are returning. Sherman said we must protect ourselves until the regulars arrive, and we hope that the Montana Militia will be permitted to do it, not on the settler's door sill, but in the villages of the savage, the only place an Indian can be whipped. This is what they enlisted for, it is what they desire. Light-footed, light-hearted and heavy handed, turn them loose and they will do more to settle permanently these Indian troubles than all the heavy lumbering columns of cavalry between Fort Smith and Omaha. If it is merely 'dress parade' service that is required, in the name of men who would never have enlisted for that service, we beg that General Sherman will relieve them and permit the hard working, poor but patriotic men, who volunteered to fight Indians to return to their employment before the summer is ended. Regular soldiers have permanent employment. We do not wish to see our militia kept in the field while they could labor, and be mustered out without a cent in the teeth of a hard winter. In two weeks their numbers will be increased to 500 efficient men. They will have been properly armed with guns now at Benton and we hope they will either be unfettered or mustered out.

On the front page of the same paper were these thoughts:

The order of General Sherman . . . is an elaborate piece of non-sense, of as little practical use in assisting the people subject to the ravages of Indian warfare, as would be the reading of the riot act to a band of Sioux. It is piece and parcel after the style of McClellan's famous idea of 'exhausting the resources of statesmanship' after three and a half years of war. The Sheriff of Big Horn County will form his posse at once. The miners earning $6 per day will buy horses, arm and equip themselves immediately and be ready to march four months thereafter, if the commander of the military department, cut off from all communication, should in his infinite sagacity and unerring judgment, determine that an emergency had arisen, when the United States government could afford to accept them at 40 cents per day. But, in the meantime, if your homes are destroyed, your wives ravished, your children slain, your farms laid waste and every outrage that the fiendishness of the incarnate devils can inspire them to commit, is heaped upon the isolated districts, do not, under penalty of the displeasure of William Tecumseh, raise a hand or stir a foot against the injured red man. Your sheriffs will go out and arrest them with 'a small posse,' and put them in jail, or report them to one of those immaculate Indian Agents, the resident saints of the reservations. The magnanimous and generous delegation of power to the sheriff to 'use his arms if they do not promptly surrender' is worthy of special acknowledgement. Most potent commander, for whom the people of Denver are organizing an experimental army of grasshoppers on behalf of the highly favored sheriffs of Montana, we thank you. The experience of the last four months has shown that the Indian question is entirely above, either his comprehension, or, ability to settle. The people of the mountains are disgusted with him and anxiously await the good that is to come out of Nazareth. Who is the coming man, with comprehension to understand, a heart to sympathize with an outraged people, ability to plan and nerve to execute measures for their relief? Sherman is a failure.

The Democrats of Montana communicated their core feelings in their party's platform. It denounced the 'political tricksters' false and slanderous misrepresentations of the Territory of Montana to the Thirty-Ninth Congress, inducing the last session to annul the laws of the territory. Then the Democrats:

> ... endorsed the action of our late lamented Acting Executive in calling out and organizing the militia of the Territory to defend our homes against the invasion of hostile Indians, and also approved the action of our present Governor in his endorsement of the same and hereby express our appreciation of the self-sacrificing and patriotic spirit that prompted the noble response on the part of the officers and men who responded to the call of the Executive in the hour of danger, and hereby pledge them our support while in the field.

Popular support was holding for the militia as the best possible force against the Indians. Yet, people knew all was not well. They seemed not surprised when Smith suddenly reorganized the Montana Militia.

Governor Green Clay Smith and Staff: 1. J.J. Hull, 2. Martin Beem, 3. George W. Hynson, 4. Green Clay Smith, 5. Neil Howie, 6. Hamilton Cummings, 7. M.S. Carpenter (sic.).

25. Regiment

While impending change continued to build, volunteers were still reporting from the field "All quiet on the Yellowstone."[342] After they moved forward as ordered by Meagher, the men at Camp Thoroughman adopted a resolution to mourn the general's death by lowering the colors at half-mast for 30 days.[343] At the end of that period, Curtis brought in another message reporting the quiet:

No hostile Indians in the vicinity and the boys are anxious for a brush with the enemy.[344]

The number of volunteers enlisting kept rising despite abundant job offers from the Yellowstone at Emigrant Gulch, said to paying up to $6 a day in gold dust.[345] Whiskey drummers still peddled their bug juice around Indian encampments and troop concentrations.[346] In Virginia City every week, *The Montana Post* carried the same classified advertisement asking for information on George Ives.[347] Apparently, no one ever contacted his mother and sisters or even responded with advice to buy a copy of Dimsdale's *The Vigilantes of Montana* in which they could have learned that their loved one figured as a main character in a book. That was in the past. Feelings mounted in the present as incidents occurred.

The scalp of the first Indian killed while trying to evade Nelson and his companion turned out to have woven within its hair the brown tresses of a white woman.[348] A trader, Charley Smith who went downriver with DeLacy, had stayed at Fort C.F. Smith and now reported about how he had recovered one of his horses on the Yellowstone. With the help of the Crow Chief Blackfoot, he was able to recover his stock near Blackfoot's 70 or 75 lodges. Close to that Crow encampment, he spotted another camp of 80 lodges led by the Crow Chief Bear Tooth. The two chiefs posed quite a contrast. According to

Smith, Blackfoot seemed friendly and sensible, but worried:

> He deprecates war, and is doing what he can do to prevent his band from engaging in it, as he says they will be exterminated if they do.

Blackfoot seemed anxious that Bear Tooth might take the warpath, possibly inducing his own (Blackfoot's) band to join. "He (Blackfoot) will abandon them all together." Smith concluded that Bear Tooth, with the largest band and the most influence "has all the worst Indians." He believed Bear Tooth's band had been tampered with by Sioux, as well as influenced by a band of Blackfeet Confederation renegades consisting of Mountain Chief, his two sons and two nephews:

> (They) were expelled from their tribe for killing Little Dog and have been accepted into Bear Tooth's tribe of Crows.

The trader believed that Mountain Chief's renegades, while down on the Yellowstone, were the five Indians who killed Colonel Bozeman:

> They boast of it, and have his horses. They say they ate dinner with Bozeman and Cover; that they intended to kill them, and steal horses; that Cover was suspicious: left them eating, and went to saddle the horses; that while he was doing this, the same one

who killed Little Dog, their own chief, shot Bozeman twice and killed him.

While recovering his own horse, Smith saw in this Blackfeet band's herd thirteen other horses branded MM:

> These they refused to give up and said if the soldiers wanted them, let them come and try to take them.

Mountain Chief's men ". . . declare they will murder and steal whenever they have an opportunity." Smith also reported:

> The Sioux were having a sun dance down on some of the rivers and are ready for war.[349]

These reports helped to explain the "boys being anxious for a brush with the enemy" having to wait while the returning governor reorganized. All the fine public sentiment to the contrary, the reorganization was more welcomed than would be expected. *The Montana Post* admitted:

> The order of Governor Smith reorganizing the Montana Militia . . . was necessary. There were evils to correct, abuses to be remedied, and the order had to be evoked from a realm of chaos, or the movement rest under a dead weight that was crushing out its vitality and bringing it into

contempt. In doing this, it would have been almost an impossibility to avoid, in the details, creating dissatisfaction, and even doing injustice to some of the parties to whom the order applied. To what extent this has reached we are not aware; but to the general principles involved in this reorganization we give hearty endorsal (sic.), and believe they will meet the approval in the army and out. While making the command more efficient, (and) it will reduce the expenditures—two desideratum (sic.) to which, without doubt, even those who have felt aggrieved by the order will submit gracefully for the good of the cause.[350]

The hoped for smooth transition did not happen. Instead, some major rough patches during the reorganization changed the command structure intended by Smith with his second General Order No. 1:

General Order No. 1
Headquarters Montana Volunteer Forces,
Virginia City, July 14, 1867

I. In order to more perfect the organization and consolidation of the volunteer forces in the Territory of Montana, now in service, and being raised for the defense of the citizens of said Territory, the Companies raised and now in the field, and those being recruited in Virginia City and at Helena shall constitute the First Regiment of Montana Volunteers.

II. It is directed that Thomas Thoroughman take command of said forces in the field, with the rank of Colonel; George W. Hynson, with the rank of Lieutenant Colonel; Neil Howie with the rank of First Major, and J.H. Kingsley (sic.) with the rank of Second Major.

III. The Companies of said Regiment shall take rank as follows: Company A, Captain L.M. Lyda; Company B, Captain Robert Hughes; Company C, Captain Chas J.D. Curtis; Company D, Captain J.H. Evans; Company E, Captain Cornelius Campbell; Company F, Captain John A. Nelson; Company G, Captain A.F. Weston; Company ICaptain Robert Hereford; Company K, Captain William Deasey.

IV. Colonel Thoroughman will continue his headquarters in the Gallatin Valley, and protect the frontier from Indian invasions. He will send out from time to time such forces, as may be deemed necessary to chastise marauding and guerrilla bands of Indians. In order to expedite the movement, I have directed Major Howie, now at Helena, to take Command of Captain Hereford's company and one section of artillery, and move down the Muscleshell River one hundred miles, or thereabouts, and establish camp for the protection of the settlers and miners from hostile Indians in that direction. Major Howie will report regularly once a week to Colonel Thoroughman and to these headquarters.

V. Regular weekly reports must be made from the headquarters in the field to these headquarters of the number of men on duty; number sick; number absent with leave; number absent without leave; number of desertions and names; number of horses on hand; number of rations to the company, and amount of provender on hand; number of guns and kind and amount of ammunition.

VI. Orders have been given to Captain George M. Pinney, A.D.C. at Helena, to forward, upon arrival, one section of artillery to Colonel Thoroughman's headquarters.

VII. The following named officers constitute the staff of the Governor and Commander-in-Chief: Martin Beem, Adjutant and Inspector General, with the rank of Colonel; Hamilton Cummings, Quartermaster General, with the rank of Colonel; J.J. Hull, Commissary General, with the rank of Colonel; Walter W. DeLacy, Chief Engineer, with the rank of Major; George M. Pinney, Aid-de-Camp with the rank of Captain; James K. Duke, Aide-de-Camp, with the rank of Captain. They will be obeyed and respected accordingly.

VIII. The Quartermaster and Commissary Generals are alone empowered to make purchases and enter into contracts for Q.M. and C.S. stores for forces in the service and those being organized. All vouchers must be issued by the chiefs of the Departments. They may, however, in their discretion, authorize the purchase of such articles as may be necessary for the service, by assistants appointed by them, who shall be commissioned Captains and A.Q.M. and A.C.S. Such assistants will issue receipts to parties from whom purchases are made, and forward copies, together with duplicate bills, to these headquarters, on which vouchers will be issued. Said assistants, however, before entering on the discharge of their duties, will be required to enter into bonds with the United States, in the sum of ten thousand dollars, for the faithful performance of their duties. Said bond to be approve by the Commander-in-chief. Assistants heretofore, acting, will, without delay, make returns to these headquarters of the purchases and distributions made by them together with the receipt and bills.

IX. The Regulations of the army, under which the Volunteers of the Territory are being organized, designates the number and rank of officers belonging to a Regiment; therefore all commissions issued by the late Governor Meagher, other than those mentioned in this order, with their rank, will be held as complimentary, and no one will be called into service unless the emergency shall arise.

X. It is desirable that peace be restored as soon as possible to the Territory. It is hoped therefore that the troops in the field will perform their duty with alacrity, and teach the Indians that if they prefer war, we know how to carry it on—their policy shall be ours.

By Command of
    Green Clay Smith,
    Commander-In-Chief.

The reorganizing order continued Beem's single regiment of nine companies capable of flexibly adding new companies and changing officers. Adopting the regimental name, First Montana Cavalry still seems peculiar. Smith might possibly have been influenced by a combination of arriving infantry muzzle-loaders, inappropriate for cavalry use, and an Army regulation that failed to envision a Cavalry Regiment. It might have been the needed lever to deflate the number of officers. Some positions disappeared and some officers were demoted. For example, there was no longer a place for Carpenter as the Territory's Chief Ordinance Officer. Smith gave Pinney the additional duty of being Ordnance Aid-de-Camp in Helena. Pinney was already overworked from trying to make sensible orders out of the flurry of guidance from Smith. There had been Smith's order to tell people to follow orders, orders correcting each other and orders in conflict with each other. One message told Pinney to write an order sending Thoroughman 350 rifle-muskets and 1,000 rounds of ammunition with two howitzers and ammunition. Another message arriving the same day from Virginia City told Pinney to send Thoroughman 300 rifle-muskets and 4000 rounds, with two howitzers and ammunition. Both messages seemed to conflict with one earlier ordering Howie to arm the new company forming at Helena with rifle-muskets and two howitzers with ammunition and to send them east to the Musselshell. Pinney was able to write Special Order Number 2 for Howie's Musselshell expedition that never materialized. Both Pinney and Howie must have been frustrated, because all of this was happening before the expected ordnance even arrived in Helena. Rumors began circulating about deteriorating morale. Then came Smith's second General Order No. 1.

Smith seemed to need Beem's help just to organize himself enough to reorganize everybody else. When Smith's order of June 14 came from Virginia City, it had to have been a surprise. Beem's name was not signed below Smith's, but the Adjutant's handiwork shows in both form and substance. He drew largely from his previous month's inspection in the field.[351] Reactions to General Order No. 1 started tumbling onto each other. Thoroughman and

Howie, the key officers at the core of the order, both resigned as did Fisk and, eventually, Hereford and Pinney. Beidler was already refocused on his Deputy U.S. Marshal's job. On July 16, Thoroughman's Chief of Staff Blake returned in a tizzy to his *The Montana Post* publishing job in Virginia City:

> . . . having received advices that his commission was merely complimentary. Not relishing that style of business, he reported at his own office for practical duty.[352]

Major Kingsly also resigned.[353]

On the day of the reorganization, Hereford's nine-month old son died from "brain fever." This caused Smith to place Howie at the lead of Hereford's Company, expecting it to immediately depart for the Musselshell.[354] Hereford resigned but Smith refused to accept his resignation, because "it was not in proper form." The resignation stood and Civil War veteran Captain Elijah Mattock from Blackfoot City assumed command of Hereford's Company I.[355] Thoroughman resigned because he had his heart set on getting married to Mattie Boyce, which he eventually did in Virginia City on September 19.[356] Smith solved his dilemma of not having a field commander by putting Howie in charge.

On July 24, there was a parade through Helena led by "Generals Thoroughman and

Howie" followed by Curtis, at the front of a section of two howitzers and 79 fully armed men.[357] The next evening, David Allen, a 36-year old volunteer in Company I, died of bilious fever. He was buried in Helena with military honors the next day.[358] In Virginia City the same night as Allen's death, Smith wrote across Howie's new commission "Colonel First Regiment of Volunteers" and indicated the term of the commission as three months, not six. That commission with Howie's appointment arrived in Helena by dispatch courier the night of July 26.

Ignoring the Montana Militia Regiment's change of name from Cavalry, Howie recorded in his diary: "Received my commission as Colonel of the 1st Montana Cavalry."[359]

By then Sherman's commander of the Department of Dakota Terry arrived in Helena from Fort Benton on the Wells Fargo Express.[360] He had with him an entourage of regular army officers and civilians. After consulting with Smith, Terry decided it was:

> ... immediately impossible—or apparently so, for him to relieve our volunteers by Regular troops before next Spring, and it appearing necessary for the retention of an armed force for the protection of the Gallatin and Muscleshell Vallies (sic.), our troops should be reenlisted for the term of six months and be recruited to a force of 800 men.

A week later Helena's *Tri-Weekly* noted:

> The tender of this (Command) position to General Howie and his acceptance of it will be hailed with the greatest satisfaction by the volunteers and the people. His ability, energy and popularity will infuse new life into the organization, and if there is work to be done, it will receive attention. The reorganization of the militia created a great deal of dissatisfaction at first, but as it is becoming better understood there is a better feeling.[361]

Volunteers were re-enlisting or enlisting for the first time, for six months or until relieved by federal troops.[362] Captain Turner had been commissioned to open a recruiting office in Virginia City. Captain Mitchell was commissioned to recruit in Salmon City. W.J. Tagert was on the Salmon purchasing horses to mount the new recruits. Captain Deasey in Virginia City had 63 men nearly ready to ride for the Yellowstone.[363]

By the end of July 1867, Inspector General Hardie estimated the Montana Militia, present and absent, numbered 32 officers and 481 enlisted, aggregating strength of 513 men.

Kirkendall's Montana Fast Freight in Helena

26. Muster

Howie's orders from Smith were to proceed at once to the Gallatin and assume command of the forces in the field. Time was needed for re-organizing, equipping and enlisting more troops. Hugh Kirkendall hired out his mule teams, drivers and wagons, on a per diem basis starting July 28.[364] Sullivan and his men were back in the field. If any guns returned immediately to the Yellowstone with that detail, it would have been two cases of ammunition with seven cases of rifle-muskets for the 100 volunteers with no guns and the 40 volunteers needing replacements for their .577 Caliber Enfield rifle-muskets.[365] Six cases of ammunition would provide a basic load for those weapons. Kirkendall's wagons could bring additional ordnance, provisions and supplies as needed, as well as bedding, camp equipment and materials. Smith wanted the howitzers following Howie to the field.[366] That didn't happen. After the Helena parade, Curtis left with the two-gun section and crossed Foster's Bridge over the Gallatin on Monday, July 28.[367]

Howie was still in Helena on August 5 when Smith used General Order No. 3 to appoint Captain W.G. Scribner as Pinney's replacement in the Aide-de-Camp and Ordnance Officer position.[368] On August 8, Howie wrote in his diary:

> The Governor, Adjutant Beem, Colonel Sanders and Dr. Glick left this morning for Virginia City.

From this, it appears Sanders had involved himself by placing his legal services at the disposal of the returning governor.[369]

On August 10, Deasey left Virginia City for the Yellowstone bringing 26 men to add to the 34 of his company at Camp Thoroughman.[370] That same day, Mattock left from Helena for the Musselshell with 50 men. They towed a 12-pound howitzer. A number of Helena's prominent citizens, who were interested in that region's copper deposits, followed Mattock's Company.[371] As Mattock's and Foster's units left for the field, Howie arrived at Camp

Thoroughman with his column. His first priority was to raise morale:

> Much dissatisfaction existed among the men; they complaining that they had been repeatedly promised their horses, saddles, bridles, etc. at the close of their service, and that it appeared plain to them now that these promises were not to be fulfilled. I stated to them plainly that it was beyond my power and authority to make such disposition of the Government property; although I could but freely acknowledge that their pay under the regular allowance of the Government was indeed most meager compensation for their time, and services rendered.[372]

Howie congratulated his men for keeping hostiles out of the Gallatin Valley and told them to plan on taking the offensive into their winter camps farther down the Yellowstone. He argued the positive aspects of offensive action, while making clear they would be fed and sheltered through most of the approaching winter:

> Upon learning of the probability of the Command being re-enlisted for a longer term, and being directed to retain the troops in the field until further orders, it required but a few days of earnest work on my part, together with the prompt cooperation of the company & other

officers, to place the Command on a good footing for efficient service in either offensive or defensive operations.373

The question of the volunteers getting paid for their service had become an issue after the publicized statements by regular army officers. Regarding the pay question, *The Montana Post* had this to say:

> The time of many of the volunteers expiring, they are being mustered out. Nearly all are re-enlisting. On being mustered out, however, they are entitled to pay. To do this requires two things—a paymaster and –money. Neither of these we have, but if ever there is a dollar paid for this organization, or its expenses, the soldiers who are serving under the same regulations as the regulars, will be the first to receive it.

The Montana Post continued:

> . . . the authority of General Terry to Governor Smith is full authority for their enlistment. The officers, on mustering out soldiers, give them a discharge and duplicate final statements. These are vouchers for the pay due the soldiers and as they are out of money they will have to dispose of them. That there will be a discount upon them is not the less wrong

because it is true, but it is a matter unavoidable, as capital is worth interest and they cannot be redeemed until an appropriation is made by Congress. Sixteen dollars a month is very poor pay at best, and purchasers should deal liberally with the boys who have been the wall of men, staying hostilities beyond our settlements. Give them all you can for their vouchers.[374]

Some men from Companies B and E decided against re-enlisting and left for home with their government property, which included some of the newly issued arms. They rode toward Helena.

As Howie worked to stabilize his command, one militia squad still patrolled down the Yellowstone. It had stopped trader Richards from taking more of his wagons loaded with goods from the Gallatin to Fort C.F. Smith. It let Richards go by himself farther downriver to assess the situation. Later, a party of immigrants four months on the trail from Fort Leavenworth informed the patrol that Indians along the route were numerous and active. They said they had been attacked twice while camped near Fort Phil Kearny equipped with four pieces of artillery and manned by 600 Infantry, Cavalry and citizens. As the immigrants moved farther northwest under military escort, a military courier brought them word that Sioux would soon attack Fort C.F. Smith from their 2500 lodges in the vicinity.

After being menaced by Sioux, Cheyenne, Kiowa and Arapaho, their train reached the isolated fort on the Big Horn without being attacked. The immigrants left there on July 24 and said they visited with Richards on July 27. Richards told them that 40 hostiles had attacked a Wells Fargo herd and taken 280 head of stock, but that a party of Crow helped save all but 30 head.[375]

The upriver train reported to the patrol that Fort C.F. Smith had grown to a garrison of 550 that included five Infantry companies, a number of citizens and two artillery pieces. They said the garrison refused to be baited by 600 hostiles who were insulting and were demonstrating from nearby bluffs. That hostile force had expelled the Crow for refusing to help them attack the whites. The Crow, consisting of 800 lodges, were peacefully camped between the Big Horn and the Yellowstone. After hearing reports like these from downriver, Howie decided to move the Montana Militia's base camp up the Yellowstone a few miles to establish a defensive line along the river's west bank. Howie later explained how he repositioned his force and furloughed a large portion of his men:

> Up to this period the troops had been somewhat permanently stationed, in several detachments, at points commanding the most important passes leading from the enemy's country through the high mountain ranges into the threatened settlements of the Gallatin

Valley. Both officers and men could but feel conscious of having fully accomplished the grand object for which they entered the field: that of forcing back and holding in check, the savage forces, and of restoring confidence, quiet and hopefulness to the settlers of that, the most beautiful and fertile region in the Territory. The enemy frequently appeared in small or detached 'War parties,' approaching the passes held by our troops, but were in all instances, dispersed or driven back beyond the Yellowstone . . . (I furloughed) quite a number of officers and men for 15 days with instructions to proceed to Helena & Virginia Cities, recruit their Companies to the Standard number, and in due time to report back for duty at the front.[376]

While the recruiting teams were gone, Howie maintained forward patrols, one of which engaged in a fight with a grizzly bear.

    Ten of Campbell's men were camped for the night on the Boulder, about 50 miles down the Yellowstone. Three or four of the men, including their Orderly Sergeant, decided to follow some bear sign. After 150 yards they killed a large bear. While three of the men were dressing their kill, the sergeant continued by himself a couple of hundred yards and met another large bear. It weighed at least 750 pounds. He fired two rounds from his Henry, both of which struck and failed to stop the animal. As the grizzly kept approaching, the Sergeant's rifle missed fire on its third round. The bear rose on his hind legs, close enough to grab and embrace the militiaman. The bear hugged so tightly, the volunteer could not draw his revolver. With no other choice, he plunged his free hand into the grizzly's mouth and grabbed hold of its tongue. The wounded bear slashed back with his sharp claws, tearing off the man's scalp and leaving it to hang in tatters around his ears. During a fight lasting just a few minutes, the sergeant was able to throw the bear three times. Each time the enraged bruin regained its footing instantly and lunged back to fight. The other three volunteers responded to the sounds of the shots. The youngest arrived soon enough to see the sergeant draw his revolver and fire it against the bear's skull. Not yet expired, the bear took the revolver's muzzle into his mouth and chewed it like paper. The sergeant returned to camp with both of his hands seriously lacerated and his scalp hanging from his head. He mounted his horse and with one companion rode all night to the new patrolling base on the Yellowstone. Surgeon Dunlevy was able to sew on his scalp and dress his mangled hands. By the time a written report of the incident left for Virginia City, it said the sergeant was "getting along handsomely."[377]

On August 13 after hearing that some of the volunteers had walked away with government property at the end of their enlistment, Smith issued General Order No. 9.

Order 9 warned that any deserter caught selling government property anywhere in the United States would be imprisoned. That same day Howie wrote to Helena calling the former volunteers deserters and requesting help recovering the government's property.[378] In sharp contrast Nelson's Company rode into Virginia City that day and mustered out 50 men. Of these, 47 mustered back in again for six months. Completed Quartermaster and Ordnance returns went to the appropriate departments, and Nelson's Company turned immediately back for the Yellowstone.[379]

On August 17, Carpenter "and lady," returned to Virginia City from the trip they made north for him to sign the hand receipt at Camp Reynolds. They checked into Planters House. Three days following Carpenters arrival, Smith again ordered the arrest of any volunteer found selling, trading or disposing of government property. The governor ordered Lieutenant H.S. Neal in Helena to detail three privates and a corporal to the capital as an armed Provost Guard to arrest anyone found without a furlough or trying to dispose of territorial property.[380] On August 23, Hynson's 50-man Company rode into Virginia City and mustered-out. Most of that company reenlisted and were joined by 16 recruits just arriving from the Salmon.[381] That's when word surfaced in the territory's newspapers that 300 regular soldiers were moving toward Bozeman City from Fort Shaw.

The news originated the previous week

when a regular army officer, Lieutenant Josiah Chance of the 13th Infantry, stopped in Helena while the first three companies of regulars walked from Fort Shaw on the Sun to the Gallatin. Chance told a reporter that nothing was certain, but he expected the regulars would be establishing a military post between Bozeman City and the main pass from the Yellowstone. In his opinion, the new post would be used as a base of future operations for the Montana Militia.[382] From this interview with Chance, *The Montana Post* concluded the movement of regulars was part of a military buildup, including volunteers, in preparation for an offensive movement down the Yellowstone.[383] This proved to be a hasty conclusion before reality began dawning on the territory:

> We fear that unless the expedition gets off soon and cuts loose from the reach of couriers, that the recent consultation of Sherman and Company at Saint Louis, when it was determined to suspend active hostilities and send out runners convening the hostile tribes for grand Pow Wows, will result in orders from Department headquarters prohibiting any movement of the Volunteers. This consultation resulted in the adoption of a series of resolutions offered by Sherman, and orders issued to the several Department Commanders. The Indians are to be convened at two specified points. The first is to meet at Fort Laramie,

September 15, and runners are now out collecting the Indians. The Government is to feed all who assemble. The second (will be) at Fort Larned, Kansas, October 15. Department commanders are instructed to defend the great routes and settlements but not to invade Indian country. This is intended as a pacific and conciliatory measure, but the instructions to commanders to protect the great routes of travel is the most warlike order Sherman has yet issued. If he finds it so interpreted it will be at once rescinded without doubt. These Councils will be a fat thing for the traders. At the council last summer at Laramie, the sutler made a good thing, and no doubt had plenty of partners. Over two tons of lead and powder was traded to the Indians. Several thousand buffalo robes, besides innumerable furs, skins, etc. were received in exchange; the robes costing as high as twenty cents a piece. The Indians now have all the year's furs and robes on hand, and the same farce will be played to end in another tragedy as soon as the red devils are supplied with ammunition. Uncle Sam pays all expenses, the military and traders enjoy the play, and the lifeblood of the frontiersman is quaffed by the actors. These councils can all be summed up in a few words: they are damnable, outrageous, cold-blooded, avaricious conspiracies against the lives of the whites of the West, and any one who will voluntarily engage in them is an accomplice in a dastardly plot against every man, woman and child in the West. The Laramie council last summer is indictable for nearly every massacre committed this summer in the Platte Department, and now they propose another to make a sure thing on next summers massacres. Confusion to the whole assemblage.[384]

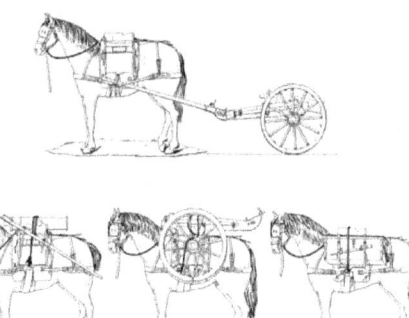

FIGURE: X-21 IDENTIFICATION: Carriage, Mountain Howitzer, 12-Pounder, Wood. SOURCE: Mordecai. REMARKS: (Top) Limbered for Draft. (Bottom) Packs. Tube and shafts (left); Carriage (center), and Ammunition Chests (right).

M1841 Mountain Howitzers Limbered & Packed

27: Ambushes

On August 27, three quarters of the militia were still on a 15-day recruiting furlough. Word came to Camp Thoroughman of an attack on a four-member gold-prospecting party. The group included Captain Weston and three others, including his brother, who were not members of the militia. Two survivors last saw Weston and another man surrounded by a large party of Indians, fighting in a situation in which they were probably going to be killed. Weston was the officer who brought in the company from the Salmon country. This news motivated Howie to take 75 men and two howitzers, configured for transport by mules, down the Bozeman Trail. At the Boulder after a day's rapid march, they blasted away with the howitzers to break up a large ambush by Indians occupying positions above and below the crossing:

> Less than half a dozen shells from our howitzers served to route them from the ambuscade—scattering them both up the stream and back onto the prairie. I divided my force, crossed them at two different places and advanced through the timber to engage them; but when we reached the open field, the Indians were all fleeing rapidly and were nearly two miles distant across the plateau.[385]

The militiamen chased the routed ambushers for eight miles but proved unable to overtake them for lack of fresh mounts. They did rescue three wounded soldiers from Fort C.F. Smith who were armed with new Springfield breech-loaders.[386]
    Those .50 caliber second Allin conversions had enabled them to kill three hostiles and save their own lives. Howie and his men found Weston's prospecting gear in an abandoned camp. Howie thought the Indians who tried the ambush on the Boulder were from Blackfoot or Bear Tooth's camps or both:

> Everything in their deserted camp goes to prove that these Indians were, and are, a 'war party' of Crows, Cheyenne and Sioux; --the head chiefs of whom are now at Laramie or vicinity, on a <u>PEACE</u> (!) Mission; --<u>after</u> a <u>reinforcement of powder & ball!!</u>

(sic.).[387]

Returning to the Boulder the raiders killed a Crow Indian, recollected by men from DeLacy's escort as being their shadow all the way to Fort C.F. Smith. The dead Indian had with him a white man's scalp.[388] Leaving at the Boulder one howitzer and their stores on the night of August 29, Howie forced a march of 50 men to the Stillwater River where they found the bodies of Weston and the other man mutilated by Indians and scattered by wolves. With rations exhausted, they turned back up the Yellowstone. At the Boulder they picked up their trains and the other howitzer and began the last 50-mile ride to their base. West of the Boulder they met Nelson riding downriver with 80 men and another howitzer. Howie noted in his diary that Captain Matthew Heart (sic.) and his men were riding with Nelson.[389] Hart's Company was down by one volunteer, Jeremiah Murphy. On July 26 at one o'clock in the early morning, he had been wounded near the left femoral artery by a ball discharged from the revolver of another volunteer, William Coe. Other men in camp had been trying to wrest drunken Coe's waving gun away from him. Coe remained in Nelson's column with Hart's Company, because the shooting had been ruled accidental by the Judge in Virginia City.[390] The combined force of 157 men, with three howitzers, rode back upriver to the new patrol base then being called Camp Thomas Francis Meagher.[391] Several hundred more men had returned to there and were waiting.

At the end of August, according to Hardie, there were 32 officers and 409 men performing service for an aggregate strength of 441.[392] In the September 2 territorial election, 259 of the men at Camp Meagher voted. Sanders received 28 fewer votes than his opponent, Cavanaugh.[393] Three days later, the number of volunteers dropped by one; a man, enlisted under the alias of C. Dunman, was killed in a gunfight with Hart.

Dunman from Salt Lake City was described as a "bad character," previously serving in the Colorado First Territorial Militia under the name of Anderson.[394] Hart enlisted him as Dunman in Salmon but discharged him once they reached the Yellowstone. After being discharged, Dunman went to Baume's Company and re-enlisted but hung around Hart's Company causing disturbances. After a few days in the new camp, Dunman confronted Hart near the stables. He said he "could lick Hart on any kind of a jump."

When Hart started toward him, the man drew his revolver catching Hart at a disadvantage. He couldn't draw his own, because he was wearing a fully buttoned overcoat. Thinking fast, Hart told the enlisted man to "Hold on a minute" while he stepped around a corner of the stable. He removed his coat and drew his own six-shooter:

The two met at the corner of the building

and fired simultaneously, both missing and both stepping back. Three times this was repeated, they (sic.) each stepping behind the building as quick as they fired. Hart had only four shots when he commenced, and was now down to the last. They stepped out again and firing almost simultaneously the ball from Hart's revolver passed through the other's wrist and into his bowels.

Fellow volunteers carried Anderson alias Dunman to his quarters where he expired the next morning. "Hart was not touched" but held for examination before a military commission and honorably acquitted.[395] In the meantime, the Montana Militia was experiencing another kind of ambush.

On August 30 without understanding that Howie and more than three companies of men were engaged on the Yellowstone, LaMotte, the regular army officer transferred to the Gallatin, made some uninformed and unfavorable conclusions.[396] This was the officer who signed the hand receipt for the territory's ordnance. He now commanded the regulars of the 13th Infantry at Bozeman City. Having just arrived in the area and without specifying his source of information, LaMotte sent this assessment through command channels at Fort Shaw:

The Montana Militia are located about eighteen miles beyond this (post) on the

Yellowstone and are as much dreaded by the people as the Indians, being a disorganized lawless set of desperados under no sort of discipline whatever. Out of about five hundred sent there, about fifty are all that remain, the rest either being on indefinite furloughs, prospecting or riding public horses back and forth between Bozeman and their camps for whisky. I understand there is an effort to turn the horses belonging to the militia over to the U.S. at the prices contracted to be paid. I would especially state that very few of them are serviceable, the best have been stolen, and the prices at which they were contracted for were from $200 to $240 while the prices paid by the contractors were $40 to $50. A considerable number of horses have been stolen lately in the vicinity and I see the Montana papers are filled with accounts of these 'Indian depredations,' I noticed, however, that in this vicinity the depredators are strongly suspected of being Montana Militia.[397]

If there had there been anything close to depredations by a volunteer or volunteers, the word would have quickly spread through the territory and the perpetrators would have been hanged. One reported instance was of a couple of officers riding back to the Yellowstone after appropriating the governor's horses.[398] Cummings had told them to take the best replacement stock they could find, and in doing so he had mistakenly sent Smith's horses to the Yellowstone. Montanans thought this humorous.

It's important to note that LaMotte's missive to his superiors diverted attention from the fact that a war party from the Blackfeet Confederacy had ridden in full paint into the Gallatin after LaMotte and his troops arrived. The war party stole a very large number of horses, removing them to the northeast, and then north, by way of Flathead Pass.[399] The war party came from near Fort Benton where 500 lodges of Bloods from Canada had quietly appeared on August 14.[400] On their dignified way to the Gallatin, the warriors scared the settlers living along the Missouri, forcing them to take shelter in Diamond City. The entire war party rode within a mile and a half of Creighton's 600 cattle grazing along the Missouri near Crow Creek. When the war-painted Indians crossed the Missouri at Indian Creek, they told the ferryman "they were going over to Twenty-Five Yard Creek" by way of the Flathead Trail.[401] LaMotte should have been spending more time doing his own job, seeing and listening and learning what was actually happening around him.

As LaMotte fired away with his uninformed opinion, a 24-hour courier from Howie, still on the Boulder, rode to Virginia City with word to round up all the furloughed volunteers.[402] That was easily accomplished. Most could see the portent. Weston and another's body had been found on the Stillwater after an attack by 200 or so hostiles. Added to the sizeable attempted ambush of Howie's force on the Boulder and the attack on the messengers from Fort C.F. Smith, a significant hostile force had moved up the Yellowstone. The volunteers knew this was the time to raid Bear Tooth's camp, kill as many Indians as possible, including Mountain Chief's renegades, and push whoever survived that attack to the other side of the Big Horn.

Virginia City's newspaper suggested that the three companies of regulars recently moved to Fort Ellis could hold the passes east of Bozeman City:

> . . . the Volunteers can cut loose from Fort Meagher and hunt Indians at their own sweet will, and may all good luck attend them.

After shortening their re-enlistment and recruiting furloughs, 125 men including most of Hynson's Company rode out of Virginia City for Camp Meagher on August 28. Another dozen followed on September 2.[403] While the last troops left Virginia City, Beem was in Helena helping to re-enlist and sign up new recruits. The Adjutant General made a very favorable impression. Then sobering news about the Hayfield and Wagon Box fights arrived.

The twin onslaughts on regulars outside of Fort C.F. Smith and Fort Phil Kearny had been impressive. Regular troops survived because they had .50 caliber breech-loading Springfields.[404] In contrast, the militia under Howie, armed with a mix of obsolete muzzle-loaders and improved weapons, were still in jeopardy of being overwhelmed like Fetterman's men. Still, Mattock's Company, well armed and equipped, had done what was necessary on the Musselshell. They established a forward patrolling base named Camp Neil Howie and:

> . . . again restored possession and prompted the further development of the valuable mines of that District.[405]

On September 12, 65 men rode out of Helena behind Curtis for Camp Thomas Francis Meagher.[406]

The officers and men returning to the Yellowstone swelled the ranks. Work started in earnest on the winter base.[407] Cummings had been able to secure ample replacements for a large number of horses destroyed by wolves. This encouraged Howie to report his command:

> ... was of such strength and efficiency as to make me confident of success, not only in the continued protection of the Gallatin Valley, but in an aggressive movement should it be ordered . . . They began working with a will . . . commenced the erection of a Fort, or such Barracks, Storehouses, etc. as would be defensible

and comfortable for winter quarters. The men were cheerful at their task, and expressed themselves satisfied with the result which, after having deprived themselves, by entering the 1st three months service, of the means of subsistence during the long winter approaching, they were thereby insured, by their reenlistment, of the necessaries of life until the working season would open next spring to offer them other and more profitable employment. Another consideration prominent among the troops was the hope of being able, when disbanded in the coming spring, to find it not only safe, but also practicable and remunerative to occupy and develop the new and rich regions of the Yellowstone & Muscleshell, as Citizens and actual settlers. The universal desire of my command to make an active campaign by marching out and striking the enemy in his own retreats, before winter should close in, was alike indulged by myself, and finally receiving orders from the Commander-in-Chief to prepare for such a movement, I began the shoeing of horses & pack animals, and all other necessary preparations for the march—while the work on our Post for winter quarters was at the same time progressing.[408]

As the men of the First Montana Cavalry, using their preferred unit designation, prepared their winter quarters and readied for a long-distance winter offensive, they failed to appreciate how they were being looked upon negatively. That was the situation when Howie, leaving Nelson in charge, rode to Virginia City. He intended to visit with Smith about procuring winter-related supplies and equipment. He returned from headquarters with the worst kind of news.

On Sunday evening September 23 at a scheduled "dress parade," Howie spoke to the volunteers standing in formation. One estimate of its size can be made from Hardie's report for the end of September. He figured that Montana's Militia stood at 32 officers and 391 men, aggregating to 423.[409] First they were informed by hearing General Terry's order read. Terry directed Smith to disband Montana's volunteer forces and to march them to their places of enlistment for mustering out. Howie then spoke with obvious disappointment when he told them, "They were no longer needed." There was only one week left before they were to be mustered out of service. The men's first reaction was confusion.

After the evening formation, the men talked and reflected for nearly two days about Terry's order and Howie's news. On Tuesday 200 men rebelled.

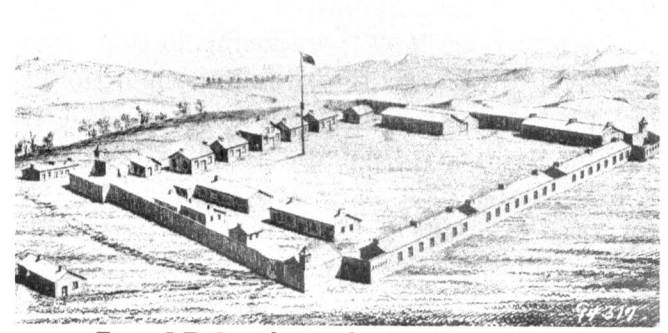
Fort C.F. Smith On the Big Horn River

28. Insurrection

The revolt at Camp Thomas Francis Meagher on the west bank of the Yellowstone near today's Livingston was substantial. The mutineers were a cohesive group of men, desperate about having to face a potentially fatal winter. They were survivors hardened by civil and Indian wars and disgusted by layers of broken promises. By accident of history, these fighters were the best armed, mounted and supplied of any similar sized group anywhere. Riding southeast out of Montana through the thickest possible concentration of Sioux, Cheyenne, Arapaho, Crow and U.S. Army forces, they were experienced, flexible and potent. Their defiant journey had begun during that Sunday night formation. Howie described the scene:

This most unwelcome and unexpected order fell harshly upon the ears of all; and produced intense disaffection among and throughout all the companies. They had been positively promised to be kept in the service a full six months from date of re-enlistment: they had had no pay, nor but little clothing, the working season was about closed, the long winter was staring them in the face, and with a large majority of the Command, the situation was indeed discouraging and almost desperate. They pled to be allowed to take their horses & accoutrements, together with sufficient rations, and go out prospecting for three weeks, when they would return, deliver up the property and be mustered out. They urged me to accompany and command them etc. etc., but as I had only the plain line of duty to follow, although I could but feel that their grievances were well-founded & painful, I could give them, as I did, but one reply: which was, that I could not grant their request, but on the contrary must insist on the carrying out of my positive instructions from the Governor. I explained to them that it was the intention of the Governor, upon their return, and so far as possible, to pay them for their services rendered.[410]

Young LaForge remembered that after the formation each volunteer was on his own to decide between packing up to go downriver or following Howie west over the pass. A few of the men who first decided to mutiny changed their minds in favor of lawfully mustering out:

> Desertion was determined merely by personal inclination. One day I met out on the road my own Company's Captain. He told me he was quitting and he advised me to do the same. His departure brought about the unofficial disintegration of our Company. Only a few of us remained to receive our formal discharge papers. After I left, Captain Hart of another Company was shot and killed by one of his men.

LaForge had been wrong about Hart getting shot by his own man, but he was right about some men in another company drowning their officer. On September 25, the Tuesday morning after the formation, 15 or 20 men from Captain Lyda's Company A abruptly departed and:

> . . . left camp and proceeded downriver, stating they were off for the states, taking their horses, guns, provisions, etc. with them. [411]

They carried less than two weeks' provisions and planned to overtake and plunder another of Richards' supply trains, bound toward Fort C.F. Smith. Some of these men threw a rope around their Captain Baume and dragged him back and forth through the water of the Yellowstone until he drowned. Baume was the Virginia City storeowner, known for being a disciplinarian, who had gone to Nevada City to identify the body of Thiebolt from the pocket knife he'd sold the young man. He had been a vigilante, later serving as a member of the Madison County Grand Jury forced to listen to Hosmer's verbal excoriation of vigilantism.[412] After the drowning, Lyda rode into Virginia City and tersely reported to *The Montana Post*:

> Captain Thomas Baume of Company A, died at Camp Meagher Tuesday morning. His body was brought to Bozeman City, and buried on Wednesday afternoon.

As this first group bolted, a much larger organization of rebels quietly started their mutiny the same morning. They spent two days longer to properly pack:

> Captain (Robert) Hughes, representing about 180 disaffected men from different companies demanded of Colonel Howie permission to go prospecting and to be supplied with the necessary outfit. Colonel Howie promised to give him an answer in one hour. Captain Hughes and his men at once took possession of all the arms, ammunition and provisions they wanted, took sixty or seventy pack animals

belonging to the Quartermaster's Department, and placed a guard over them until the afternoon, when they moved down the river one and a half miles, crossed and began packing for a long trip, intending to start on Thursday morning.[413]

This happened after Howie told the men that Governor Smith planned to divide the government property in lieu of paying the men for their services. In his report about the mutiny Howie wrote:

> . . . a majority of the men, together with several officers, called Captain Robert Hughes of Company B to lead them and then, having stealthily availed themselves of most of the revolvers and other improved arms, as well as the best and all surplus animals, moved into the camp by themselves, placed guards over the artillery, the Commissary and the Quartermaster buildings, and profusely supplied and equipped themselves for their trip. I was utterly powerless to prevent this wholesale desertion and mutiny for the reason that there was not an enlisted man upon whom I could depend to aid me in forcing them to do their duty. Those who would not engage in open mutiny strongly sympathized with and virtually countenanced it by refusing to assist me in an endeavor to quell it.[414]

With all the artillery, extra animals, ammunition, improved weapons and supplies in their possession, the men were well-armed and abundantly prepared. They had three of the territory's seven mountain howitzers. One came to the field with the first flush of Virginia City's volunteers and two came as one section of the new artillery from Helena with Curtis. The latter two were each configured for rough terrain transport on three pack animals. There were plenty of extra animals for packing or towing howitzers and ammunition and for hauling supplies. The mutineers had their pick of revolvers and breech-loading repeating carbines and rifles. They were ready to ride down the Bozeman Trail toward danger, and all but a few succeeded in riding into new lives.

Subsequent returns at U.S. military posts suggest that Hughes, the leader of the largest group, may have later entered the U.S. Army in Wyoming, Dakota or Montana Territories.[415] Some of the mutineers, according to LaForge, were killed fighting among themselves. The rest ended up scattered here and there, with some known to have gone to Nebraska. One was hanged in Wyoming. LaForge heard that they raided Fort C.F. Smith, though that seems doubtful since the regulars in defensive positions were armed with breech-loading .50 caliber Springfields and, by then, two howitzers. LaForge stuck to this story:

(The mutineers) demanded food and general entertainment that the commandant of the fort provided, owing to the greatly superior force of the visitors.[416]

Documents record the mutineers' passage through or around Fort C.F Smith. On October 10, First Lieutenant George H. Palmer stationed inside the fort recorded buying a horse from a militiaman for $55.[417] That month, mutineers joined wagons trains leaving Fort C.F. Smith for Fort Phil Kearny. On October 25, one group of mutineers fought hostiles 56 miles south of Fort C.F. Smith. That was the day Templeton, the regular army lieutenant who earlier described the Montana Militia as a 'hard set,' wrote:

. . . a train pulled out, taking all the militia with them.[418]

Montana Territorial Arsenal at Virginia City

29: Discharge

Most human beings naturally hate war, but Congress finally took notice and established the Indian Peace Commission on July 20, 1867, because war is so darned expensive. When the new commission met in Saint Louis on August 6, two of its members proved to be Sherman and Terry. Sherman was soon called back to Washington City after making strong remarks disagreeing with the new peace policy. A year later he reported:

> . . . by an executive order it was made my military duty to subordinate of all the troops subject to my command, to whatever plan of action the peace commission might adopt.[419]

By the time the Indian Peace Commission's first treaties with Southern Plains Tribes, which were never properly ratified by them, were negotiated at Medicine Lodge Creek in October, Augur had replaced Sherman. Initial meetings with Northern Plains Tribes were not productive, because Red Cloud said he wouldn't talk until Fort Phil Kearny, Fort Reno and Fort C.F. Smith were abandoned and the Bozeman Trail closed. He would not sign the Treaty of Fort Laramie for another year and only after those requirements were satisfied. In the meantime, those serving in a disciplined chain-of-command were glad to try and make peace.[420] Montana Territory in 1867 proves the point. Terry's order to discharge Montana's militia avoided one or more bloodbaths in the winter camps of the Sioux, Cheyenne, Arapaho and Crow. The volunteers were capable of such slaughter. Losing a chance to kill the feared Indians distressed the officers and men of the militia and their fellow non-Indian Montanans. For as long as it lasted, the regular army did accomplish peace.

      LaMotte's reports, combined with regular army patrols confiscating the rifle-muskets of a few former volunteers, set the stage for Terry to "disarm the militia." Governor Smith strenuously argued against it. On September 13, he sent a fruitless protest telegram to the Department of Dakota Headquarters at Saint Paul. On October 1, Colonel I.D. Reeve at Fort Shaw was able to report through his chain of command that

Montana's territorial militia had been discharged.⁴²¹ It happened quickly.

On September 26, the volunteers who decided to stay on the right side of the law rode west with Howie. At Bozeman City, they divided into those riding to Virginia City behind Nelson and those continuing down the Missouri with Howie. Mattock's Company, ordered over from the Musselshell, joined the rest at Bozeman City. Their appearance caused Howie to entertain the notion of turning around and riding back over Bozeman Pass to overtake the rebels:

> Supposing that Captain Mattock's men were not tainted with <u>'rebellion'</u> and that I could induce them to go back with me to fight Hughes' Command I made the proposition to the men, through Captain Mattock. Twenty-six (26) of them agreed to go if I would give them all the supplies that might be recaptured. I could not guarantee this, even had the force been competent—therefore had to forego this project and return to Helena.⁴²²

As the contingents rode their respective ways, the Territorial Staff's officers were busy. On September 28, Smith issued General Order 12, formally ending the Montana Militia by including Terry's directive that volunteers were "no longer required."⁴²³ On September 30, Carpenter sent to Scribner in Helena handfuls of ordnance return forms for mustering out 50 volunteers to a company.[424] This followed another letter written for the governor, as though he was completely unaware of Terry's discharge directive. From this letter, it's clear Smith felt betrayed by the federal military establishment:

> In reply to your communication of the 23rd instant, I am directed by the Governor to say that he does not feel at liberty to authorize the distribution of the Territory's Arms and Ammunition either to individuals or Corporations; and more especially as the threatening attitude of the Indian tribes on our frontiers, render it very probable that the Ordnance and Ordnance Stores at his disposal, may all be needed long before any further supply can possibly be obtained in the Spring. And further he is of opinion that while it is the especial and bounden duty of the Officer Commanding the U.S. Troops in this District to protect the U.S. Mail routes, he, as Governor has no authority to assume the responsibility of doing so in the event as is the case of the refusal of that Officer to make at least an attempt to perform same service for the people whose bread he eats. You will therefore inform Captain Gorman that the Governor respectfully declines to accede to his request to furnish twenty four (24) muskets and accoutrements and five (5000) rounds of ammunition, for the use

of the 'Northern Overland Mail Co.' I am Captain, Very Respectfully, Your Obedient Servant, A.M.S. Carpenter, Major and Chief of Ordnance.[425]

On September 28, Virginia City's volunteers arrived home. Hart rode into town with "150 to 200 men belonging to the companies of Nelson, Deasey, Hart and others." That night he checked into the International Hotel. According to the newspaper, the enlisted men "camped a mile and a half above town." The next day a board of appraisers appointed by Smith began valuing the men's horses, saddles, and equipment. On October 2, the muster-out rolls were ready. As each man was discharged, he chose to take his horse or his rations in payment of his accounts.[426] The Territorial Staff stayed busy in the middle of this furor.

Smith announced he was sending 100 rifle-muskets with requisite ammunition from the ordnance stored in Helena to Missoula. Carpenter asked for bids by October 8 to build a substantial Territorial Arsenal in Virginia City.[427] Cummings announced:

> All Claims against the Quartermaster or Commissary General must be presented on or before the 15th day of October 1867, or be forever debarred from payment.[428]

By nightfall of October 3, Virginia City finished it's mustering out and everyone seemed pleased:

The men receiving their horses at appraisement (sic.) appear to be well satisfied with the actions of the Governor, and almost without exception deported themselves in a very creditable manner. These men who withstood the temptations and inducements offered by the Hughes party to skedaddle with the government property, when it was presumed they would be set foot without a penny when they returned here deserve not only praise for their integrity and manhood, but a charitable judgment of any little sprees they may have had on their arrival here, when no harm resulted from it. Their situation is not an enviable one; the mining season is well nigh over and not a tenth of them have any money . . . they are now seeking employment we hope they may be successful in finding it. Many of them are leaving for the different camps and valleys, and by the end of the week but few of the Montana volunteers, except those who originally resided here will remain. There are bad men among them no doubt, but we would like to know any two hundred men in an organization in this or any other place where there would not be some infernal scoundrels. There are many as brave and true among them as ever straddled a broncho or swung a pick, and they have our best wishes with a hearty good will.[429]

On September 30, Helena's contingent arrived home for a longer out-processing. Mattock kept his men camped on Prickly Pear Creek 10 miles from town until they were fully discharged a week later. Helena's officers took a little longer to figure some way to compensate their men. Their solution seems unclear, but the entire town knew the matter was being addressed. Helena's *Tri-Weekly* observed:

> It is the sincere wish of all that those having the matter in charge will be successful in raising the funds for the payment of the men. Should they do so, it will be of vast benefit both to the men themselves and to society at large.[430]

Howie and his officers did what was necessary to:

> . . . sell all the government property here, and to devote the proceeds thereof to the payment of the troops. This I did, and the amount received, paid, with a few exceptions, all the enlisted men. The officers still remain unpaid.[431]

Helena's unsold weapons and accoutrements had been stored in the new shanty on the hill west of Clore Street. Seven years later Curtis wrote of this facility:

> (I was) . . . appointed by Governor Green Clay Smith as Chief Ordnance Officer for the Territory in the shape of arms, ammunition, etc. and likewise, where in the property was stored.[432]

This means Curtis, as the officer responsible for executing Smith's Missoula County order, placed five cases of Springfield rifle-muskets and ten cases of ammunition on a Worden and Company freight wagon for delivery to Missoula.[433] It means that Carpenter was either out of touch or purposefully leaving a paper trail to give a false impression.

On October 14, Carpenter sent the first military telegraph message between Virginia City and Helena. Prepaid and on a Western Union form it said:

> From Major Carpenter, Chief of Ordnance in Virginia City to Captain W.S. Scribner: Retain strong Provost Guard. Search thoroughly for secreted government property. Order Governor. A.M.S. Carpenter, Chief of Ord[434]

Either Governor Smith failed to tell Carpenter about Curtis's new ordnance responsibilities and the shanty, or Carpenter's telegram was part of an effort to maintain the image of accountability. An appearance of accountability would have been necessary for the private commercial interests in the Territory to recover from the federal government the cost of their supplies then being liquidated. Smith's decision to proceed in this fashion calls into question something else he did with regard to ordnance.

In late November Governor Smith had to justify his request for money to complete the new arsenal in Virginia City to the President of the Territorial Legislature's Council:

> Sir-the Joint resolution to make an appropriation of 5,500 dollars to pay for and complete the arsenal, now in process in this city is before your body. I made a contract with Griffith & Thompson to build the arsenal for four thousand dollars in warrants, or two thousand dollars in greenbacks. This is my personal obligation and if the Legislature does not make the appropriation, I must and will pay it. It requires 1,500 dollars more to complete the work by placing the armory over the magazine. The arms of the Territory cannot be taken care of without it. The small arms are now in an indifferent cabin, liable to rust and to be rendered useless. The artillery is out in the weather and must be ruined before spring, unless housed. The artillery could not be purchased for less than one thousand or 1,200 dollars apiece. There are four of them to be taken care of. The small arms are worth thirty-five dollars apiece and there are 1,200 or

1,500 here with some 600,000 rounds of ammunition. The Territory cannot afford to lose this valuable property, therefore I hope the Council will pass the resolution, as the debt must be paid December 1st and the armory ought to be completed at once.[435]

The legislature appropriated the required amount of money, as well as $2,500 to reimburse Smith for purchasing the lot where the arsenal was being built and for any expenses securing the property. It was a different story three weeks later when Smith returned to seek another appropriation for protecting the small arms, artillery and ammunition in Helena:

A small magazine was built in that city at the expense of the government and now holds the small arms in boxes and the ammunition. The artillery, however, as I learned last night for the first time is out doors, and being injured by exposure. Your liberality has bestowed on Virginia City a sum sufficient to secure here, and I trust in recommending an appropriation for Helena you will be equally as kind. After inquiring into the matter, I am sure the sum of 1,500, the sum appropriated to build an armory here, will be sufficient to meet the demand there. If such arrangement is not made to protect this property, then I will be compelled to remove it to the armory here. I should regret, however, to remove any of it from Helena as it may be needed in that direction anytime; and as the citizens are anxious to retain and I think should keep a portion of the arms belonging to the Territory.[436]

Smith had claimed four 12-pound mountain howitzers on hand in and around a cabin in Virginia City. People there, especially legislators, could see and count them. Now he was telling the lawmakers about recently learning the other 12-pounders were out in the weather. Either he was passing on someone else's tall tale or carefully choosing his words, "they were out in the weather." He didn't say they were in Helena. The legislature refused to appropriate the additional funds. The cost of the shanty still needed to be covered. In March 1868, *The Montana Post* announced:

> According to the instructions by Colonel Howie, from Governor Smith, the former gentleman has rented a suitable building in which to store the firearms belonging to this section. The Colonel has also engaged a man to clean them and keep them in order.

The shanty continued to hold Helena's ordnance until two weeks before the territory's first comprehensive inventory was completed in Virginia City. That's when the legislature emptied the shanty and consolidated its contents into Virginia City with this appropriation:

> Auditor is hereby authorized and directed to issue a warrant on the territorial treasurer in favor of L.M. Todd for the sum of one hundred 35 dollars for transporting nine thousand pounds of ammunition from Helena to the Arsenal at Virginia City.

On January 30, 1874, Harrison Mandell inventoried the Virginia City Arsenal's contents.[437] He must not have reviewed the War Department's *Instruction Manual for Mountain Howitzer Batteries*, because he used the wrong terminology for the equipment he identified and counted. From his report, it's possible to conclude that five of the territory's seven mountain howitzers were missing. His count revealed that of 2,580 rifle-muskets transferred in three groups from the federal government to Montana Territory, 1316 were missing. Of these 141 could be explained.[438]

    The 40 Enfields had been discarded at Camp Thoroughman in favor of the newly arriving Springfields which could use both .58 caliber Springfield and .577 caliber Enfield cartridges. The explosion at Sun River Government Farm seems to have destroyed one Springfield. Missoula County still continued to store and maintain the 100 Springfields sent there in late 1867 with 10,000 rounds of ammunition. This amounts to 141 explainable missing guns, assuming another group of rifle-muskets had been issued and returned.

In early 1868, Smith authorized distribution of 100 more rifle-muskets and 10,000 rounds of ammunition to the settlers of Trinity Gulch and the Little Prickly Pear Valley. If these were distributed as authorized, they would have included the 36 muzzle-loaders which may have been used in an unconfirmed attack on Indians at Cut Creek on the Marias. That attack was reported by only one person as happening on March 13 and would have involved settlers augmenting Healy's Sun River Rangers. If that incident did happen as alleged, then 102 Piegan probably died.[439] The estimated shortfall of weapons assumes the Prickly Pear distribution were eventually returned, as had been all the rifle-muskets distributed to the settlers in the Gallatin. The Prickly Pear Valley's ammunition would have been expended.

Allowing for 10,000 rounds still in storage at Missoula, expenditure of 10,000 rounds by the settlers north of Helena and all 19,620 rounds transferred to Montana from the Niobrara Wagon Road Company, the Territory's ammunition shortfall by the time of Mandell's inventory still exceeded 222,000 rounds and probably far more. The 65 grains of powder contained in each of the missing .58 caliber rifle-musket cartridge means an unexplained loss of at least 2,062 pounds of gunpowder, as well as the lead in the mini-balls. This amount of lost cartridges means 266,400 percussion caps also vanished. The remaining number of howitzer shells, less six rounds fired to break up the ambush on the Boulder, suggests an additional unexplained loss of 630 howitzer rounds. A portion of this missing ammunition could have gone with the three howitzers siezed by Hughes' Mutineer Command, and the rest with who ever got the other two missing howitzers. Regardless, with a half-pound charge of powder built into each round, this translates into an additional loss of 315 pounds of gunpowder. In other words, over 2,377 pounds of gunpowder seems to have been purloined from Montana Territory or transferred or traded. Then there were all the damaged rifle-muskets.

Of the muzzle-loaders counted inside the arsenal, more than 100 had been damaged. The nature of the damage was unclear. It could have resulted from hard use by cavalry of infantry weapons. Alternatively, the large number of damaged pieces might indicate an indigenous effort to experiment at converting obsolete muzzle-loaders to single-shot breech-loaders. Cutting and removing the rear top portion of each chamber was the easy part for a blacksmith or machinist. The component parts of the trapdoor extractors, if not on the commercial market, would have had to be sand cast one part at a time from Story's single copy of a first Allin conversion. The new blast furnaces at Charles Hendrie's foundry on Clore Street, 200 feet west of the shanty, would have heated the metal to a pouring temperature.[440] Rim-fire .58 caliber metal cartridges were being made commercially for the Gatling gun. An 1878 inventory of goods in T.C. Powers' Indian Trading Post at Judith

Landing included: 1 needle reloading outfit, 6 kegs of powder, 125# of trade balls (per sack), 1250 Winchester cartridges, 50 Henry cartridges, six Henry cartridge belts, 2800 needle cartridges in two different calibers and 30 needle cartridge belts. The two different calibers of needle cartridges support the possibility that both the first Allin conversion Springfield breechloaders and the second Allin conversions were in use by the Indians.[441] Even without modifications, the Civil War rifle-muskets had value for hunting.

The trade musket commonly known as the Northwest Gun had long served that purpose. First traded by the Hudson's Bay Company, smoothbore .59 caliber trade guns or fusils, fired single balls or shot with a single patch into a nine-inch group at 90 yards. Trade guns had sea-serpent plates embedded on the left side of their lightweight stocks. By the 1860's, they were available in flintlock, percussion cap or metallic cartridge variations. By comparison, obsolete Civil War rifle-muskets could be counted upon for a 400-yard effective range, and some were known to shoot well for 800 yards.

On September 23, 1867, after his men at Fort Shaw started receiving their second Allin conversion, .50 caliber breech-loaders, Reeve asked the Military Department of the Dakotas for advice on how to dispose of his obsolete rifle-muskets. He indicated that the Flathead Indian Agent wanted them.[442] The practice of handing down obsolete weapons happened at all the western military posts.

Besides the loss of 1,316 obsolete rifle-muskets and 2,081 bayonets, Mandell's inventory showed that by 1874 Montana also had 20 cases, or 400, of the .50 caliber second Allin conversion Springfield breech-loaders. To go with those were 156,000 rounds of center-fire .50 caliber metal cartridges. This ordnance remained from a federal shipment of 1,000 rifles and 200,000 rounds of ammunition sent for distribution to settlers. Because Springfield breech-loaders used a firing pin, they were being called needle-guns in the tradition of earlier European weapons that used long needles to penetrate paper cartridges. After the regulars at Fort Shaw started getting their .50 caliber Springfields, needle-guns began to permeate Montana:

> Requisitions from agency traders in Montana in the early 1870's for ammunition and spare parts for .50 caliber Springfield needle-guns, indicated the popularity of these arms as well among various tribes.[443]

In 1871, when Colonel Phillippe Trobriand at Fort Shaw explained to the Military Department of Dakota why he no longer had surplus arms, he'd already sent 42 needle-guns with wagon trains to and from Fort Peck and eight more with a surveying party. The number of breech-loaders he still retained was just enough for his own companies. This allowed for 50 carbines in hand for his mounted detachment.[444] By the time of the 1874 Virginia City Arsenal inventory, the Mountain Crow had 500 fighting men around Crow Agency. They were armed with a total of 630 breech-loaders of which 300 were needle-guns. Some of these friendly Indians were thought to be trading needle-gun ammunition to the Sioux.

Mountain Chief (center) with Owl Child (left)

30. Dreams

Dreams, even the visions of scoundrels and renegades, are more powerful than guns. Healy and Mountain Chief are proof. By 1870, the prohibition against selling guns applied only to improved repeating weapons. The territory's missing muzzle-loaders probably found their way into Indian and Métis hands. Mini-balls and paper powder cartridges for the rifle-muskets were easily sold to Indians, trappers and hunters. All of them scrounged for powder and lead to remold for their weapons.[445]

In northern Montana and western Canada, percussion caps and metal cartridges were especially scarce. The Milk River Indian Agent restricted traders from exchanging any breech-loading or metal cartridge ammunition without his approval. A trader couldn't sell more than 25 trade rifles in a year or more than 25 pounds of powder or 75 pounds of lead in a month.[446] Consequently, ammunition remained limited causing flintlock trade guns to persist. Indians concerned about being outgunned in a fight held on to their bows until they could get a breech-loader.

In 1867, the U.S. government auctioned nearly 20,000 surplus guns, including breech-loaders, from the arsenal at Fort Leavenworth. Some found their way into the hands of Indian fighters. Warriors found other ways of procurement. Stealing them became as much a matter of prowess as stealing horses. As happened to the gold miners on the Yellowstone, reported by Upson in 1866, a Sioux war party exploited the trust of woodcutters to take their Henry repeaters and kill them. All the tribes' warriors became experts at fashioning ammunition for their guns. To supply improved weapons, they resized balls and collected and reloaded empty metallic cartridges. They used cut down percussion caps for fulminators inside the reloaded metal cartridges. They packed their reloads in thrown-away ammunition boxes. In Canada, the ammunition part of the trade became singularly important. Healy has always been routinely criticized for being an infamous whiskey trader, but the essence of his success was being able to trade from a large cache of ammunition.

In the spring of 1869, one of Fort Shaw's patrols arrested Healy's friend, Floyd Keating, and two Indian boys while they were en-route to Helena from Sun River Crossing. The patrol reported finding them hauling a load of government contraband. The illegal items had been "secreted on the premises of John J. Healy of Sun River Crossing." Keating admitted to the soldiers he was acting under direction of Kennedy, Healy's confidante from the Oro Fino gold strike days. Keating said Kennedy was in Helena waiting for him and intending to distribute the government property. A short time later, both Healy brothers were arrested and charged with stealing.

Colonel George Andrews at Fort Shaw asserted that the stealing had been ongoing since autumn 1868. On March 17, Andrews wrote to the U.S. Attorney in Helena and summarized all of his allegations, but nothing came of his assertions.[447] Nor was the nature of the contraband ever revealed. Possibly by coincidence, Howie resigned as U.S. Marshal. His public explanation was that his brother, in some legal trouble in Wyoming, needed his help.

The mystery of the Fort Shaw contraband at Healy's Trading Post had already been revealed during the Battle of Sun River Crossing. That night of February 5, 1868, Pend d'Oreille horse raiders, posing as Crow, violently attacked the Healys' place. Blood Chief Many Braids, Healy's friend camping nearby, was killed with his wife and child as were four other Bloods.

That night Healy and his wife, brother Joe and interpreter Crazy Vielle, as well as Kennedy and Keating, killed two and wounded two of the attackers. As Many Braids died, Healy promised he would raise his Blood son, which he did. Several accounts of that night's fight mention a needle-gun. Healy wrote:

> We all jumped up then and I got my buffalo gun, a Prussian (sic.) needle-gun, and ran out in the direction of the corral ...

Another account tells of Healy going over to the Blood camp earlier in the evening to loan Many Braids "an expensive Swiss (sic.) needle-gun." Most telling happened years later when Healy wrote in Fort Benton's newspaper about the incident. He said nothing about a needle-gun.[448] By then the term described the .50 caliber breech-loaders in common use at Fort Shaw. Needle-guns were the first item of value, usually traded by deserters for a suit of civilian clothes.[449]

After getting no help from the regulars, Healy, Kennedy and Keating tracked the horse thieves for 14 days. After realizing the Crow identity was a ruse, they followed tracks to the right lodges in the Mission Valley. There they recovered the last of 125 stolen horses, less one left by Healy as a gift for each of the surprised thieves. It was upon the return of Healy's party from that long chase into western Montana that the soldiers knew to arrest Keating.

Needle-guns, contraband or not, could be easily traded in Helena, especially to unpaid militia officers. In exchange, they had at least 222,000 rounds of obsolete .58 caliber cartridges and lots of artillery ammunition with no howitzers stored in the shanty. This return trade explains the contents of the Healy and Hamilton wagons during a surprise inspection in November 1868.

By that time, Indian Superintendent S.F. Eastman was certain the Sun River Crossing traders, backed by Powers, were the worst sorts of whiskey traders. He wrote to Wheeler:

> (T.C.) Power has generally been at the head or foot of most of the whiskey trade while the reputations of both Healy and Hamilton does not leave a doubt as to what their intentions are in this matter.

When Blackfeet Indian Agent Pease caused a string of their wagons to be seized, he did so expecting to find liquor. Meagher's permit had ended, and Healy and Hamilton were no longer licensed to trade with Indians on the Missouri. When he was stopped, Healy protested that he had no intention of trading in Montana. He said that his wagons were the supply line for a prospecting expedition. Pease let them continue north. The Indian Agent's men could find no liquor in the wagons but did report a great amount of gunpowder and lead shot packed into them.[450]

The next spring William Wheeler, Howie's replacement as U.S. Marshal, shut down the whiskey traders coming into Montana from Canada.[451] By then, Healy was planning his big move in the opposite direction. Hudson's Bay Company was turning over to Canada its vast holding of Rupert's Land, about a million square miles extending from the Great Lakes to the Rockies. The entire region seemed up for grabs. Canada had no way to govern the vast, buffalo covered region. Fort Benton was closer than eastern Canada so the Sun River Crossing traders made their move.

Healy gained the backing of T.C. Powers, while Hamilton secured his backing from I.G. Baker. They devised a deception plan for avoiding army patrols while they crossed the Blackfeet Reservation. The regulars had been expecting Healy to make a move northwards, because he had posted a $10,000 bond for a permit to travel to the northern border. From the telegraph office at Fort Benton, Healy telegraphed to Hamilton a planned route of travel northwards knowing the regulars would monitor it. It was misleading information for the purpose of creating a diversion. After the bogus message, the army responded by sending a detachment to patrol the wrong route. Meanwhile, the Healy and Hamilton Trading party followed a different trail as authorized by their permit:

They are also privileged to take with them

a party of from 20 to 30 men and six wagons loaded with supplies, provided there are no spirituous liquors in the wagon except a small quantity, which may be taken for medicinal purposes.

According to Healy, the medicinal liquor they carried was less for the purpose of bartering than for gifting to tribal leaders to ensure their business loyalty:

We took up 50 gallons of alcohol, not so much for the value of the goods it would bring in, as thereby to secure the Indian trade.

Healy and Hamilton's venture north started Fort Hamilton or Fort Whoop-Up, thereafter also known by Canadians as "a place founded by scoundrels." The scoundrels succeeded. In the fort's first season of 1869, they profited more than $50,000. Healy's critics claim he made a rich harvest of robes from the Indians by trading them whiskey and guns. Healy contends whiskey and guns were not the secret for his success. Some whiskey was normal in the trade. According to him, his men traded no more whiskey and none worse than the Hudson's Bay Company. As for improved guns, Healy says he was not stupid enough to trade improved firearms. Breech-loaders and repeaters would have been fired at his own party. Healy pointed to the audit of Powers' books conducted by

General William Lewis, the officer who earlier had served as Sherman's eyes and ears. Lewis determined that Healy bought only two cases of improved firearms from Powers. Healy said those two cases of Winchesters were to protect himself and his men.[452] Ammunition was his secret.

Powder and ball proved essential not just to a successful robe trade but also to the very existence of Fort Whoop-Up. This became evident after August 17, 1869, when Owl Child, a member of Mountain Chief's village, murdered Malcolm Clarke in the Little Prickly Pear Valley. Clarke was a widely respected rancher living in the same place where Fisk's 1862 expedition first encountered Morgan. Owl Child killed in revenge for something that had happened earlier, some say it was the rape of his wife who was cousin to Clarke's Piegan wife. Some say it was a delayed reaction to Clarke's penchant for fist fighting that got him kicked out of West Point. This time it had been exercised against Owl Child or some of his relatives. Others say the cause came from long ago for some of his practices as a fur trader. Regardless of whether Owl Child's reasons had any merit, General Philip Sheridan didn't see things from the Indian point of view. Sherman's replacement as Commander of the Division of the Missouri, directed:

> If the lives and property of citizens of Montana can be protected by striking Mountain Chief's band, I want them struck.

Tell Baker to strike them hard.

As eventually ordered, Major Eugene Baker at Fort Ellis prepared and moved the 2nd Cavalry north for a mid-winter attack on Mountain Chief's village. This plan went forward even after the best assessment indicated that Mountain Chief had moved his village into Canada. At Fort Shaw, General Trobriand ignored the assessment and ordered Baker to follow through with the plan for an attack on Mountain Chief's village.

Baker and his men left Fort Shaw on January 19, marching into an arctic cold front with arrest warrants for Mountain Chief and 18 members of his village. Baker had been heavily drinking whiskey. As his troops approached Chief Heavy Runner's village, trying to recover from smallpox on the Marias, one of Baker's scouts said the camp was not Mountain Chief's. Baker ignored and isolated the scout. The regular troops executed an early morning slaughter of at least 173 Piegan, including 148 women and children. This number did not include survivors, who perished from exposure while struggling toward Fort Benton.

In late March as the first male relatives of the massacred began arriving in the north around Fort Whoop-Up, it was obvious there would be much trouble. An Indian woman ran ahead of a leading warrior named Cut Hand to warn everyone. Cut Hand sent word that he intended to trade only for powder and ball and use it to kill Healy, Hamilton and all other white men associated with Fort Whoop-Up.

The intended victims barricaded themselves inside the fort. After awhile, a Blood Chief named Bull's Back Fat asked to be let inside. He convinced Healy of the seriousness of the situation, but that his warriors would protect the traders who had been good to them. He said:

> Friends, you know the white soldiers cleaned out the Piegan camp over on the Marias. The hearts of all the Blackfeet, the Piegans and the Bloods, are filled with bitterness against the whites for this. Cut Hand and his Piegans have come to kill you. But you men have been kind to us and you are our traders. We Bloods were hungry when you met us and fed us. We are grateful. Now 500 of my warriors have joined our party. The Piegans will have to kill us before they kill you. They outnumber us greatly but they are our cousins, and I do not believe they will force us to fight. If they do, we will die fighting for you, white men. Open the door and look out.

When Healy and his men did look outside, they saw hundreds of Bloods stripped down and armed for battle. They were facing hundreds of angry Piegans gathered and talking in groups. As the traders checked their Winchesters, Bull's Back Fat signaled for trade to start:

The Piegans holding their weapons, with their wives hauling the furs and robes, got into a line. Warriors under Bull's Back Fat allowed only two people at a time inside the fort. Though Healy had the full array of goods to trade, including whiskey, the only items the Piegan wanted in return for their goods was gunpowder and lead shot.

Those who were early in line received 40 rounds of powder and shot for each buffalo robe. As trade continued, Healy doubled the price of powder and shot to two robes for 40 rounds. Then he doubled the price again to four robes for 40 rounds. By the time trading was completed, Healy and Hamilton had secured 1600 buffalo robes and many hides and furs from other animals. Bull's Back Fat advised those Piegans still planning to return and kill the white men, that they would have to kill his Blood warriors first. Cut Hand became a valuable friend and returned often to trade.

This passing crisis demonstrated that ammunition saved Healy and fostered long-term trading relationships.[453] For the rest of his life, Healy argued that the regular army's slaughter of Heavy Runner's village was unnecessary. He would imply that an earlier Sun River Rangers attack had already taught the Piegan a lasting lesson:

The Piegan War is reported as starting in

1870. Officially (sic.). The work was finished before the military took a hand. The Sun River Rangers were unofficial as regards the military. They were undocumented. They consisted, and in the main if not entirely, of the employees of Healy and Hamilton at the Sun River establishment.[454]

If an earlier battle did happen, it was just after Smith released muzzle-loaders to the settlers of the Little Prickly Pear Valley and before Owl Child killed Clarke. Sheridan's reaction unleashed an intent to slaughter any Indians. The reason Baker's scouts couldn't find the renegade band for which he carried 20 arrests warrants, was because the village they sought was saved by Mountain Chief's dream.

Mountain Chief is a reversed English translation of the name, Chief Mountain. Mountain Chief was born near that striking feature of the same name at the northeast corner of Glacier National Park. He came to be ranked in war honors equal to Lame Bull and just ahead of Little Dog. Though he was a south Piegan, he became a Chief of the Bloods and spent a lot of time with his band in Canada. Shortly before the slaughter of Heavy Runner's village, he dreamed that his body was lying on the ground and that people were shooting at it. When he awoke he moved his village north.

Mountain Chief's camp of 50 lodges included Brings-Down-The-Sun's family and another lodge belonging to one of his sons, a young warrior named Big Brave and his wife. Big Brave was born in 1848 on the Old Man's River in Canada. He was one of Mountain Chief's nine sons and twelve daughters. Big Brave was a great warrior riding with his brothers and cousins to steal horses and guns. They were constantly on war raids, especially against the Crow and Gros Ventre.

According to his own words, the greatest event in Big Brave's life was the battle fought by the Blackfeet against the Crees in Canada. The battle happened one year after Baker and his men massacred Heavy Runner's village. That was the same year huge amounts of ammunition were traded to save Fort Whoop-Up. This battle happened one year before Big Brave's father, Mountain Chief, died:

> My horse and myself were both covered with blood. Let me tell you about this battle. The camp was on Old Man's River. The bands were so many that they were camped on every bend of the river. My father Mountain Chief was at the upper end of the camp. I was 22 years old at the time. It was the fall of the year and the leaves had all fallen. The people were just getting up in the morning when the news came that the Crees had attacked the lower camp.
>
> I got my best horse. It was a gray horse. My

father led his band in company with Big Lake who that summer had been elected a big chief. We rode up over the ridge while in the plain below the battle was raging. As we rode down the hill slope, I began to sing my war song. I carried a shield in my hand and this song that I sung belonged to that shield. One of the medicine men dreamed that whoever held this shield would not be hit by the bullets. While singing, I put in the words, 'My body will be lying on the Plains.' When I reached the line of battle I did not stop, but rode right in among the Crees, and they were shooting at me from behind and in front. When I rode back the same way the men made a break for the coulee. As soon as the men got into the coulee, they dug a pit. I was lying about ten yards away on the side of a hill. I was singing while lying there. I could not hear on account of the roar of the guns, and could not see for the smoke. About that time they heard my whistle, and the Crees made a break for the river.

Then the Blackfeet made an onrush for the Crees and I ran over two of them before they got to the river. As they were crossing the river I jumped off my horse and took my spear and stabbed one of the Crees between the shoulders. He had a spear and I took that away from him. I jumped on my horse again, and just as I turned there was a Cree who raised his gun to fire at me. I ran over him and he jumped up and grabbed my horse by the bridle. I swung my horse's head around to protect myself and took the butt of my whip and knocked him down. When I struck him he looked at me and I found that his nose had been cut off. I heard afterward that a bear had bitten his nose off. After I knocked him down, I killed him. I jumped on my horse and just then I met another Cree. We had a fight on our horses; he shot at me and I shot at him. When we got close together I took his arrows away from him and he, grabbed me by the hair of the head. I saw him reach for his dagger, and just then we clinched. My war bonnet had worked down on my neck, and when he struck at me with his dagger it struck the war bonnet. I looked down and saw the handle sticking out, so I grabbed it and killed the other Indian.

Then we rushed the Crees into the pit again, and my father came up with one of the old muskets and handed it to me. It had seven balls in it and, when I fired it, it kicked so hard it almost killed me. I feel that I had a more narrow escape by shooting that gun than I had with the Indians. When we returned I had taken nine different scalps. The Crees who had not been scalped had taken refuge in the scant forest, and my father said to quit and go home. So we took pity on the tribe, and let them go home, so they could tell the story. I remember that we killed over three hundred and many more that I cannot remember. When we returned we began to count how many we had killed. We crossed the river and went into the pit, and they were all in a pile. Then we were all singing around the pit, and I put in the words, 'The guns, they hear me.' And everybody turned and looked at me, and I was a great man after that battle.

In the spring of 1872, Mountain Chief's camp was on the Teton when he was shot inside his own lodge, trying to break up a fight between two drunken Indians. He was buried in the Choteau Cemetery. Big Brave was given his father's name and lived a respected life at Heart Butte as the last hereditary chief of the Blackfeet Indians. As Mountain Chief, he declared his allegiance to the United States in 1913. He died in 1942 and, after a funeral at the Little Flower Mission Church, was buried in the cemetery at Browning.[455]

Endnotes

[1] Walter W. DeLacy, Map of the Territory of Montana With Portions of the Adjoining Territories. Showing the Gulch or Placer Diggings Actually Worked, and Districts Where Quartz (Gold and Silver) Have Been Discovered To January 1, 1865, updated to January 1, 1871. JPEG2000 (9.9MB) https://cdn.loc.gov/service/gmd/gmd425/g4251/g4251h/ct001859.jp2

Chapter 1: Howitzer

[2] Frederick Allen, A Decent Orderly Lynching, The Montana Vigilantes, University of Oklahoma Press, Norman, OK, page 130.
[3] Helen Winifred Melgard, "The Mullan Road: The Northern Highway of the Pacific Northwest," MA Thesis, Graduate History Department, University of California, Berkeley, CA, 1930, page 86.
[4] Jennie Cohen, "Native Americans Hailed From Siberian Highlands, DNA Reveals," History in the Headlines, www.history.com/news/native
[5] Chief Brings-Down-the-Sun Interview by Walter McClintock, The Old North Trail: Or Life, Legends and Religion of the Blackfeet Indians, 1910, Classic Reprint, Forgotten Books, 2015, page 327.
[6] Garnet Basque, "The Last Great Indian Battle," Frontier Days in Alberta, Sunfire Publications, Ltd., Langley, BC, 1992 pp. 2-9.
[7] Allen, pp. 230-31.

[8] Timothy Egan, The Immortal Irishman, The Irish Revolutionary Who Became an American Hero, Houghton Mifflin Harcourt, New York, NY, pp. 275-76.

Chapter 2: Leader

[9] Professor Thomas J. Dimsdale, The Vigilantes of Montana, Being a Correct & Impartial Narrative of the Chase, Trial, Capture & Execution of Henry Plummer's Notorious Road Agent Band, University of Oklahoma Press, Norman, OK, 1953, pp. 152-154.

[10] "64th Regiment Ohio Volunteers, Field and Staff Company (image 1838), Official Roster of the Soldiers of the State of Ohio in the War of Rebellion; "64th Regiment, Ohio Infantry," Battle Unit Details, The Civil War, National Park Service; W.F.Sanders II and Robert T. Taylor, Biscuits and Badmen, The Sanders' Story In Their Own Words, Editorial Review Press, Butte, MT, page 3; Michael Leeson's biography of Sanders in History of Montana, Chicago, Warner, Beers & Co., pp.1739-1885.

[11] Young Mary Ronan wrote of how handsome Ives looked in his Union Army overcoat, though throughout the Civil War years, Barney Hughes remembered good times prospecting and surveying with Ives.

[12] Allen, page 188.

[13] Allis B. Stuart, The Last Days of Barney Hughes, as told to Mary Narby Cottrell of Wisdom, September 17, 1941, W.P.A. Writer's Project (Montana Historical Society, Barney Hughes Vertical File), pp. 2A-3A.

[14] Keith C. Petersen, John Mullan, The Tumultuous Life of a Western Road Builder, Washington State University Press, Pullman, WA, 2014, pp.117-118.

[15] Michael P. Malone and Richard B. Roeder, Montana, A History of Two Centuries, University of Washington Press, Seattle, WA, page. 56.

Chapter 3: Judge

[16] Hezekiah L. Hosmer, Chief Justice of the Montana Territorial Supreme Court, Charge to the Madison County Grand Jury, August 7, 1866, Montana Historical Society, Helena, MT, Wilbur Fisk Sanders Papers, MC 53; Folder 3-11.
[17] L.B.Palladino, S.J., Indian and White in the Northwest, A History of Catholicity in Montana, 1831 to 1891, Wickersham Publishing Company, Lancaster, PA, 1922, page. 189.
[18] Genevieve McBride, O.S.U., The Bird Tail, Vantage Press, NY, 1984, page. 12, Fn. 12.
[19] J.W. Schultz, My Life As An Indian, Fawcett Publishing, New York, NY, 1935, pp. 100-135.

Chapter 4: Blackfeet

[20] Calf Shirt may have killed six or eight of his tribe's warriors, including some relatives. Schultz, pp. 143-144.
[21] Gordon E.Tolton, Healy's West, The Life and Times of John J. Healy, Heritage, Toronto, 2014, pp. 70-71.
[22] "Got my commission." Neil Howie Diary, September 12, 1864, Montana Historical Society, Helena, MT, Neil Howie papers,
[23] Dimsdale, pp.136-146.
[24] Hezekiah L. Hosmer to Samuel T. Hauser, letter dated June, 24, 1865, Not in Precious Metals Alone, A Manuscript History of Montana, Montana Historical Society, Helena, 1976, page 72.
[25] Tolton, page 71.

[26] Major General A.B.Dyer, Chief of Ordinance, War Department Ordinance Office, Washington D.C. to Montana Territorial Governor Green Clay Smith, Letter dated February 26, 1868, Reference Stores valued at $1,735.27 turned over to Thomas Francis Meagher.
[27] Raymond L.Welty, "Supplying the Frontier Military Posts," Kansas Historical Quarterly (May 1938): 167, in Charles G. Worman, Gunsmoke and Saddle Leather, Firearms in the Nineteenth-Century American West, University of New Mexico Press, Albuquerque, NM, 2005, page 337.
[28] Worman, page 375.

Chapter 5: Treaty

[29] Paul R.Wylie, The Irish General, Thomas Francis Meagher, University of Oklahoma Press, Norman, OK, pp. 240-243.
[30] Howie Diary
[31] Kelley Flynn, Goldpans, Guns & Grit, Diamond City from the Territorial Gold Rush to Montana Ghost Town, Hidden Hollow Hideaway Guest Ranch, Townsend, MT, 2006, pp. 32-33.
[32] Conservative estimate by James McClellan Hamilton, History of Montana, From Wilderness to Statehood, Binsford and Mort, Portland, OR, 1957, page 182
[33] Ken Robison, Confederates in Montana Territory, In the Shadow of Price's Army, The History Press, Charleston, SC., 2014, pp. 34-35.
[34] Robert Vaughn, Then and Now, Thirty Years in the Rockies, 1864 to 1900, Far Country Press, 2001, pp. 176-177.
[35] Tolton, pp. 71-72.
[36] More Indians were present than the approximate 6,500 reported in 1865 under two Indian Agents in Montana:

At Fort Benton, about 1,800 Gros Ventre, and about 6,500 of the Blackfeet Confederacy, including 1,870 Piegan, 2,150 Bloods, and 2,450 Blackfeet proper. The western agent thought he had 550 Flatheads, 990 Pend d'Oreilles, and 270 Kootenais. U.S. Bureau of Indian Affairs, Report of the Commissioner of Indian Affairs for 1865, pp. 30-31.
[37] Wylie, pp. 243-247.

Chapter 6: Irish

[38] John J. Healy, edited by Ken Robison, Life and Death on the Upper Missouri: The Frontier Sketches of Johnny Healy, Ken Robison, 2013, page 258.
[39] Tolton, pp. 65, 249 fn. 2, and 252 fn. 8: Regina Healy Mettler, Sketch of the Life of John J. Healy, by his Daughter Regina Healy Mettler, Montana Historical Society.
[40] Thomas Meagher to Commissioner of Indian Affairs, Department of Interior, Washington, D.C. Letter dated December 14, 1866.
[41] Gary R. Forney, "Thomas Francis Meagher Irish Rebel, American Yankee, Montana Pioneer," XLibris, 2003, pp. 168 & 267, fn 73: Dillon Examiner April 14, 1919. Article based upon Lyman Munson's account.

Chapter 7: Storm

[42] Howie Diary, 1866.
[43] Howie Diary, 1865.
[44] On August 2, 1859, at Fort Benton, Father Pierre DeSmet married two couples. The marriages of the two parties, Clement Cornoyer and Mary Champagne, and J. Morgan and Rose Masero, were witnessed by Colonel J. Vaughn, A. Dawson, and Francis Cabanne. Morgan and

Masero's marriage was found soon to have been null and a sacrilege, as Morgan had another wife living at the time. This was subsequently noted in the marriage record by Father Giorda. Palladino, page 302; In September 1863, 20 members from Captain James Fisk's Second Expedition stayed overnight on Little Prickly Pear Creek at the ranch of a man named Morgan. Fisk made no mention of it on his trip through the previous year. Bancroft says that at the time it was the only farm in Prickly Pear Valley. Fisk noted, "Morgan, who was the only settler there, was building a large log house so that he could take care of guests passing his place. He engaged in some farming, trapping, and trading of ponies and cattle with the emigrants. Situated as he was in the direct line of the increasing traffic over the Mullan Road, he was in a position to do a large amount of business."Melgard, pp. 85-86.; John D. "Whiskey" Brown, who badly injured his leg cutting logs for a sluice box near Helena. He found it so unbearable during the winter of 1863-64, he gave his interest in the mine to a man named Merrill "to take me as far as Malcolm Clarke's place at the head of Prickly Pear canyon. From there a man named Morgan, from Fort Benton, took me to the (Saint Peters) Mission, a distance of 55 miles, and he charged me $250 dollars, which was all the money I had. Father Ravalli was not at the Mission but Father Jurada was, he also being a good surgeon. He told me that he could break the leg all over again but it would be shorter. He operated on my leg, and by the summer of 1865 I was able to work." Vaughn, pp. 195-196,
[45] Father Kuppens said Morgan boasted of giving his guests over to Carson and his men, "Now, boys, right here is a chance for you; some of the redskins you are after are in this house." Palladino, page 206; Ibid, pp. 224-207.

[46] Edwin Tappan Adney, Healy: Incidents of Indian Fighting and Fur Trader Days in Montana, the Canadian Northwest, and Alaska, related by the late Captain John J. Healy, Manuscript draft, Woodstock, Canada, 1937.
[47] Ibid.
[48] U.S. Bureau of Indian Affairs, Report of the Commissioner of Indian Affairs for the Year 1866, pp. 196 to 204.
[49] Tolton, page 65.
[50] Schultz, page 179.
[51] Adney, page 4.
[52] Healy, page 163.
[53] Ibid, pp. 144-145.
[54] Upham to Upson, letter dated January 9, 1866.
[55] Ibid.

Chapter 8: Irregulars

[56] Certificate displayed, Montana Military Museum.
[57] Howie Diary 1866.
[58] Ibid, January 16 "traded for revolver #90750."
[59] Tolton, page 72.
[60] Palladino, page 206.
[61] Hill to Howie, Letter dated February 4, 1866.
[62] Montana Post, February 17, 1866, "Military-Officer of the 2d Montana Volunteers."
[63] Berkin planned an exploratory survey of a new road by way of Duck Creek through the Big Belts from the Musselshell mouth on the Missouri to and from Virginia City. The mouth of the Musselshell, below most big river obstructions, would seemingly cut 15 to 20 days from the river trip to Fort Benton. The new Kercheval City, would be 75 and 35 miles farther from Helena and Virginia City, respectively. Grading of the road had started so that it could be used the coming spring.

[64] The Montana Post, February 24, 1866, page 3, "Artillery."

[65] Healy, page 146, "It happened also that within the building there was a large quantity of fixed ammunition, belonging to a howitzer, the property of Diamond R Transportation Company. The howitzer had been taken to Fort Benton by the company, but the greater part of the ammunition had been left at the farm, awaiting transportation."

[66] McBride, page 15, "The Indians then set fire to the house. Shannon stayed inside until the heat fired off the loaded guns. When the flames reached some boxes of shells for a 12-pound howitzer, Shannon jumped from the window just before the shells exploded…"; Joaquin Miller, An Illustrated History of the State of Montana, Lewis Publishing Company, Chicago, IL, 1894, pp. 779-782 Says that Curtis was the individual who "raised three companies of volunteers and reported for duty, Helena being Headquarters, and that he went to the front and remained on duty until the Indians were subdued."

[67] The Montana Post, February 24, 1866, "Kerchevel City;" The Montana Post, January 13, 1866 "An Important Movement, New Roads to the Head of Navigation on the Missouri;"

[68] Howie Diary 1866, pp.5 & 6

[69] Merle Burlingame, "Montana's Righteous Hangmen Reconsidered," Montana Magazine, Autumn, 1978, page 47.

[70] The Montana Post, March 31, 1866, page 3, "Helena Letter, dated March 27, 1866."

[71] The Montana Post, April 28, 1866, "The Indians Again."

[72] Howie Diary,1866, pp. 9 &10. Two weeks later Howie received a letter from Beidler at Diamond City.

[73] Healy gives the date of the attack as the night of April 19, 1866, Healy, pp.143-147.
[74] McBride, pp. 15-16.
[75] Ibid.
[76] Tolton, page 74; Healy, pp.163-166.
[77] Trading in Canada 6 years later, Healy recovered Carson's damaged Hawken Rifle "from the Indian who gave him his death wound, I have the weapon in my possession still and value it above all price, as a memento of one of the bravest and noblest of men." Healy, pp. 165-166.
[78] Vaughn, pp. 75-77.
[79] Tolton, pp. 74-75.
[80] Healy, page 171.
[81] Big Timber Pioneer June 17, 1937 page 8: "Charles Brumfield has been invited to participate in the celebration of Montana Day at Bozeman on July 2 and to ride a horse in the parade that he broke for T.B.Story. He will use a saddle that had belonged to Nelson Story, Sr., and which was purchased in Los Angeles in 1871, and will carry an old Springfield Needle gun which Mr. Story, Sr. carried across the Plains in 1866."

Chapter 9: Disorder

[82] U.S. Constitution Fifth Amendment: "No person shall be held to answer for a capital, or otherwise infamous crime, unless on a presentment or indictment of a Grand Jury, except in cases arising in the land or naval forces, or in the militia, when in actual service in time of war or public danger;…nor be deprived of life, liberty, or property, without due process of law…;" and United States Constitution's Eighth Amendment: "…no cruel and unusual punishment."
[83] Howie Diary,1866, page 25 & Memoranda.

[84] Wylie, pp. 263-264; Howie Diary, 1866, page 29.
[85] Howie Diary, 1866, page 7.
[86] Howie Diary, 1866, page 15.
[87] Dimsdale, page 265.
[88] Langford, page 297.
[89] http://www.legendsofamerica.com/mt-fortbenton.html
[90] Helen Fitzgerald Sanders and William H. Bertsche, Jr., X. Biedler: (sic.) Vigilante, University of Oklahoma Press, Norman, 1957, pp. 134-135.
[91] Vaughn, page 80.
[92] Ibid, page 77; "Nelse Kyse, George Huber and one man, name unknown, were killed by Sioux Indians, on Squaw creek, near the mouth of Musselshell river;" The Montana Post, September 15, 1866, "Helena Items."
[93] The Montana Post, June 6, 1866, "From Fort Laramie."
[94] Wylie, page 285; Doyle, Journey's to the Land of Gold, vol. 1, pp. 7-8
[95] Union City, Christenot Mill, National Register of Historic Places, montanahistorywiki.pbworks.com
[96] Dyer to Smith, Letter dated February 26, 1868, Reference War Department Ordinance Office Hand Receipts, signed by Meagher.
[97] The least self-conscious assessment of Vigilantes in Diamond City comes to us from a little known miner in Confederate Gulch named Thomas H. Brown. In the spring of 1866, just as Daniels was hung, Brown settled at Diamond City and later recalled, "All good Masons were members of the 'Vigilance Committee.'…we were told to observe the wooden boot sign on the street in front of a cobbler's shop. If a pair of children's shoes were hanging on the heel of the boot, all was quiet; if on the instep of the boot, that was notice of a regular meeting; but if the shoes were on the toe of the boot, strap on your gun and get to the meeting place soon as

possible. The Vigilance Committee of Montana executed, perhaps one hundred criminals, but never lynched a man…. The organization grew and extended quietly and effectively until every village and mining camp, where there were Masons, had its branch committee…the only peaceful and moral places were the Masonic lodge room and the meeting place of the Vigilance Committee." Thomas H. Brown, The Romance of Everyday Life, pp. 50-52; quoted in Flynn, page 53.

[98] Flynn, pp. 86-89.
[99] www.newspapers.com/clip/3593476/william_mcglothlin_murder/
[100] Ken Robison, Confederates…,pp.147-154.
[101] immortalnobodies.blogspot.com/2015/01/william-mcglothlin-sadly-in-wrong-place.html
[102] Ken Robison, Montana Territory and the Civil War, A Frontier Forged on the Battlefield, The Historical Press, Charleston, SC., 2013, pp. 74-75.
[103] This final count conflicts with first reports of number of killed sent to Virginia City from Fort Laramie.

Chapter 10: Electricity

[104] Larry Barsness, Gold Camp, p. 195.
[105] 1866 Directions for Putting Up and Renewing the Union Local Battery, page 1: "The jar having been cleaned, set the copper in the jar, spreading it as wide as the jar will admit. Fill the pocket with pulverized vitriol, and hang on the edge of the jar where the copper is open. Having filled the porous cup with soft or rain water sufficiently full as not to overflows when the zincs are inserted, put the zinc into the porous cup, having first placed the cup inside the copper. Pour soft water slowly through the vitriol in the pocket filling up with the

pulverized vitriol, as it is reduced by the flow of water. No vitriol should be allowed to drop into either the jar or the porous cup."
[106] Barsness, page 195.
[107] Mary Cottrell, Whitefish Pilot, January 3, 1938; Hoffman Birney, Vigilantes, Kessenger Publishing Company, 1929, page 39.
[108] "Telegraph Line in Montana was Unreliable Affair; Levi Wild was the First Operator," Montana Standard, July 4, 1939.
[109] William T. Jackson, Wells Fargo Stage Coaching in Montana Territory, Montana Historical Society, Helena, MT, 1979, page 8.
[110] Between August 12 and December 25 1867, E. Creighton and Company's Western Union Telegraph Company Account shows a total expenditure of $5582.17. Besides expenditures for cash and merchandise were these payments: $42.00 for Sutterly (October 7 & 14), $28.50 for J.Tovey (October 18), $122.85 for J.Paitras (October 22), $15.72 for M. Hurlburd (November 2), $32.80 for "Maynard and B." ($32.80). Only two payments were made from the WUTC account to P.A. Largey: $66.00 (October 7) and $4228.12 (December 12), which was the last payment before closing the WUTC account. A single offset the August-December period: $5582.17 paid in by J.A. Creighton on January 6, 1868. E. Creighton and Company General Ledger, page 94.
[111] Fredericks, p. 40.
[112] The Montana Post, August 3, 1867, page 8, "From VC's Thursday Tri-Weekly, Extending the Telegraph."
[113] The Montana Post, October 5, 1867, page 8, "From VC's Saturday Tri-Weekly, The Telegraph."
[114] The Montana Post, October 19, 1867, page 8, "From VC's Saturday Tri-Weekly, The Telegraph"

[115] The Montana Post, October 19, 1867, page 8, "From VC's Tuesday Tri-Weekly, "Working."
[116] Fredericks, p. 40.
[117] The Montana Post, October 19, 1867, page 8, "From VC's Saturday Tri-Weekly, "New Office"

Chapter 11: Fetterman

[118] Barry J. Hagan, C.S.C., "Exactly in the Right Place," A History of Fort C.F. Smith, Montana Territory, 1866-1868, Arthur Clark & Company, Spokane, WA. page 73.
[119] Ibid, page 82.
[120] The Montana Post, February 9, 1867, Front Page, "Indian Massacre."
[121] The Montana Post, March 16, 1867, "From Helena's Tuesday Tri-Weekly, Fort Phil Kearney Massacre."
[122] Civil War Springfields were fired by fitting a percussion cap over a nipple, positioned where the hammer came down. The striking hammer caused ignition down a channel into the breeched powder charge, which, while standing in plain sight, had to be rammed with a rod down the barrel behind the mini-ball.

Chapter 12: Radicals

[123] www.usmarshals.gov/district/mt/profiles/howie.html
[124] News clipping, Neil Howie papers, Folder 7/7 SC 302, Montana Historical Society, Helena, MT.
[125] Ibid.
[126] The Montana Post, June 15, 1867, page 8, "From Helena's Thursday Tri-Weekly, The Military."
[127] The Montana Post, April 28, 1866, "The Indians Again."

[128] Samuel Finley Blythe (1842-1928) Find A Grave Memorial, http://www.findagrave.com/cgi-bin/fg.cgi?page=gr&GRid=24171525
[129] Twenty Second Regiment, Official Register of the United States Army for the Ohio Infantry, pp. 81-82.
[130] Report of the Proceedings of the Society of the Army of the Tennessee, page 179.
[131] Dixon Evening Telegraph, Dixon Illinois, May 4, 1888, page 4.
[132] Congressional Serial Set: "Letter from the Secretary of War Transmitting, in response to Senate Resolution of 18 January 1883, a report dated 2 instant, from the Adjutant General of the Army, and accompanying copies of papers related to the payment of the Fourth Arkansas Mounted Infantry; Baxter's Fourth Mounted Arkansas Infantry, http://www.4tharkmountedinf.com/
[133] Journal of the Executive Proceedings of the Senate of the United States, January 14, 1867, page 102.
[134] The Montana Post, May 4, 1867, page 4, "Military Orders."
[135] Wylie, page 287.
[136] The Montana Post, April 13, 1867, page 8, "Recruiting."
[137] The Montana Post, April 27, 1867, page 1, "Our Country's Defenders."
[138] Territory of Montana Certificate, signed by T.F. Meagher and Martin Beem. Montana Historical Society, Small Collection 309, Thomas Francis Meagher papers, 5/15, Misc: 1853-1867.
[139] Howie Diary 1867.
[140] The Montana Post, April 27, 1867, page 8, "From Thursday's Tri-Weekly, Something to Read."
[141] The Montana Post, April 27, 1867, page 8, "From VC's Saturday Tri-Weekly, The Indian War and Some Street Scenes."

[142] The Montana Post, April 27, 1867, page 8, "From Helena's Thursday's Tri-Weekly, Indian Massacre on the Benton Road."
[143] The Montana Post, April 27, 1867, page 8. "From Helena's Thursday Tri-Weekly, Corralled"
[144] The Montana Post, May 4, 1867, page 7, "MILITARY ORDERS."
[145] An Aide-de-Camp receives the written or verbal direction of the superior officer and converts that information into written orders.

Chapter 13: Adjutant

[146] Stearns, Harold Joseph, "History of the Upper Musselshell Valley to 1920" (1966), Theses, Dissertations, Professional Ppwers Paper 2575, page 7.
[147] genealogytrails.co/mon/gallatin/earlyhistory.html.
[148] The Montana Post, April 27, 1867, page 2, "The Gallatin Troubles."
[149] Ibid. "Preamble and Resolutions."
[150] The Montana Post, April 27, 1867, page 1, "All those planning to ride over to the Gallatin with General Meagher be on hand next Monday at 10 AM."
[151] The Montana Post, May 4, 1867, page 8, "From Helena's Thursday's Tri-Weekly, Recruiting Office."
[152] Hardie Report: A great fire in Chicago on October 8, 1871 destroyed records gathered by Inspector General of the United States Army, General James A. Hardie, from his investigation for Congress of Montana War Claims for 1867. General Hardie's report had already been completed. This, and his personal testimony to Congress, gives the most objective summary framework for analysis of available fragments of information. General Hardie's conducted his investigation in Montana over many months, conversing with nearly all key

participants. He made detailed notes, supported by documentation of the facts. He became intimately familiar with all aspects of the 1867 incident. Hardie notes: "On the 24th of April, 1867, the acting governor (Meagher), yielding to the mainly genuine but not well-founded alarm of settlers, called for six hundred volunteers for three months' service in the Gallatin Valley and on the Yellowstone River, and appointed sundry recruiting officers to enlist and command the troops, and various staff officers to organize and supply the force. From this time to the early part of July, it is not certainly known, with the want of regular muster-rolls for that period and from the unreliability of the ration-returns, how many men were actually in the service, but it is calculated that there were not more than eighty men at the end of April."

[153] The Montana Post, May 4, 1867, page 8, "Some Truth and Some Folly."
[154] The Montana Post, May 4, 1867, page 8, From Tuesday's Tri-Weekly, First In The Field."
[155] The Montana Post, May 4, 1867, page 8, "From Saturday's Tri-Weekly First in the Field."
[156] The Montana Post, May 11, 1867, page 8, "Helena from Tuesday's Tri-Weekly Adjourned War meeting."
[157] James Fisk Notes, Rocky Mountain Gazette, May 4, 1867.
[158] The Montana Post, May 4, 1867, page 8, "From Saturday's Tri-Weekly First in the Field."
[159] The Montana Post, May 4, 1867, page 8, "From Tuesday's Tri-Weekly, Rally Round the Flag Boys."
[160] The Montana Post, May 4, 1867, page 8, "From Tuesday's Tri-Weekly, Virginia City Rangers;" May 11, 1867, "Flag Presented."

Chapter 14: Gallatin

[161] The Montana Post, May 18, 1867, "From Tuesday's Helena Tri-Weekly."
[162] The Montana Post, May 11, 1867, page 1, "From the Front."
[163] The Montana Post, May 11, 1867, page 7, "Military Orders."
[164] Howie Diary, May 10, 1867, page 6.
[165] The Montana Post, May 18, 1867, page 8,"From Helena's Tuesday Tri-Weekly, Still Later."
[166] The Montana Post, May 11, 1867, page 8, "From Saturday's Tri-Weekly, The Very Latest."
[167] The Montana Post, May 11, 1867, page 1, "The Indian Movement."
[168] The Montana Post, May 11, 1867, page 8, "On It Depends Success."
[169] The Montana Post, May 11, 1867, page 1, "The Indian Movement."
[170] The Montana Post May 11, 1867, page 8, "From Virginia City's Tuesday Tri-Weekly, Indian Affairs."
[171] The Montana Post, May 11, 1867, "From Helena's Tuesday Tri-weekly," "The Great Want," and "Military."
[172] The Montana Post, May 18, 1867, page 7, "From General Thoroughman."
[173] Coordinates of Camp Elizabeth Meagher: 45°38'30"N 110°55'05"W
[174] Major General Thomas Thoroughman, Official Report to Major General Thomas Meagher, Montana Post, May 18, 1867, page 7.
[175] The Montana Post, May 25, 1867, page 8, "From VC Saturday Tri-Weekly, In Brief the Military are doing well."
[176] The Montana Post, May 18, 1867, page 8, "From Helena's Saturday Tri-weekly, Parade."

[177] The Montana Post, May 18, 1867, page 8 "From Helena's Saturday Tri-weekly, Off to the Front, Captain Lyons."
[178] Howie Diary, 1867, page 6.
[179] The Montana Post, May 25, 1867 page 8, "From Helena's Thursday Tri-weekly, Departed."
[180] Captain Reuben Foster, 1st Lieutenant Driggs, Clark D. Shockley D.C. Slocuum, J.S. Simms, A.R McLauren, Wm Rowe, T.V. Russell, Robert Hedges, J.P. White, Charles Wilson, R.C. Johnson, J.B. Dewes, J.J. Fulmer, Thoas Dunn, J. Koentz J.S. Snyder, E.B. Jones, T.G. Houghton, Henry H. Smith, Robert Buchanan, A. Welsh, Daniel Wilbur, James Williams, Abraham Dorey and Christ Yunson; Montana Post, May 18, 1867, page 8, "Gone to the Front."
[181] The Montana Post, May 18, 1867, page 8, "From Thursday's Tri-Weekly, From the Front."
[182] The Montana Post May 25, 1867, page 8, "From VC's Thursday Tri-weekly, Returned-Col. Cummings."
[183] Captain J.D. Curtis; Lieutenant Joseph Williams; Orderly Sergeant, William G. Howard, Privates: Harry R. Richards, Frederick Baker, Henry H. Wheeler, Charles Van Alstine, Thomas Cook, John Lendemann, John Bowers, Thomas Jones, Joseph J. Kane, William Smith, Robert C. Carman, Charles E. Barber, Gilead Roup, P.W. Blasdell, Charles Reynolds, James M. Kirkendall, John Hall, John Race, Charles H Metcalf, Isaac Shaw, Adam Jones, M. Higgins, John Collins, Samuel Rath, John Sullivan, Louis Valley, Joseph H. Howland and Joseph Douchequette.
[184] The Montana Post, May 25, 1867, page 8, From Saturdays' Helena Tri-weekly, The Scouts."
[185] The Montana Post, June 1, 1867, page 7, "From General Meagher;"The Montana Post, June 15, 1867, page 7, "From Gallatin."

Chapter 15: Helena

[186] The Montana Post, August 17, 1867, page 8, "From VC's Thursday Tri-Weekly, About Soldiers' Pay."

[187] The Montana Post, April 13, 1867, "From VC's Tuesday Tri-Weekly, The War Meeting."

[188] On December 2, 1867, the Territorial House and Joint Committee on the Military Operations of the Militia made this report after taking statements and examining Colonel J.J. Hull, Commissary of Subsistence, Colonel Hamilton Cummings, Quartermaster General, and Colonel A.M.S. Carpenter, Chief of Ordnance and other documents in possession of the Governor and determined. Commissary of Subsistence, for flour, bacon and other provisions, incurred a debt of $173,000; Quartermaster-General, for clothing, horses and equipments, forage, etc, incurred a debt of about $800,000; Ordnance Department, for arms, ammunition and cavalry equipments, has incurred a debt of about $50,000. "From these and other sources we estimate the whole debt incurred by the expedition to be about $1,100,000. The above purchases were made in accordance with the U.S. Army Regulations." The Montana Post, December 2, 1867.

[189] The Montana Post, May 11, 1867, page 2; The Montana Post, May 18, 1867, page 2, "Proposals."

[190] The Montana Post, May 11, 1867, page 8, "Wanted More Lightning;"The Montana Post, May11, 1867, "Appointed."

[191] Montana Historical Society, Helena, Montana, Manuscript Collection 289, Patrick Largey Family Papers.

[192] The Montana Post, May 11, 1867 page 8, "Arrivals at the Planters House."

[193] The Montana Post, May 11 1867, page 8.
[194] The Montana Post, May 11, 1867, page 8, Wanted More Lightning."
[195] The Montana Post May 11, 1867, page 8; Montana Post, May 11, 1867, "The Situation;"Montana Post, May 18, 1867, page 8 "M.M."—Bear that Character in Mind."
[196] The Montana Post, May 25, 1867, page 8, "From the Helena's Tuesday Tri-weekly, Appointment, Quartermaster General."
[197] The Montana Post, May 11, 1867, page 8, "Arms for Montana."
[198] The Montana Post, May 25, 1867, page 8, "From VC's Thursday Tri-weekly, Ordnance Department."
[199] P.A. Mullens, S.J., Biographical Sketches: Count John A. Creighton, pp. 43-44.
[200] The Montana Post, May 25, 1867, page 8,"Resignation and Appointment; The Montana Post, June 29, 1867, page 8, "Commissary General's Office, Request for Proposals."

Chapter 16: Quartermaster

[201] The Montana Post, June 1, 1867, page 8, "Assurance Doubly Sure."
[202] The Montana Post, May 25, 1867, page 8, "Arrivals and Departures; Arrivals at Planters House."
[203] The Montana Post, May 25, 1867, page 8, "From VC Saturday Tri-weekly, Moving In."
[204] Hardie Report, Item 11: Wilbur Fisk Sanders charged the Montana Territorial Militia for "rent of building for commissary office from May 1 to December 15, 1867, inclusive (7 months and 15 days), at $150 per month for a total of $1,125 General Hardie reviewed the item and

considered a "fair allowance to have been $100 per month or $750 recommended."
205 The Montana Post, May 25, 1867, page 8, "From VC Thursday's Tri-Weekly, A Deserved Compliment."
206 Melvina Lott, The History of Madison County Montana, Mrs. Melvina J. Lott, states, "John Crieghton and W.H. Sanders are said to have been the real organizers (of the Vigilantes). John S. Lott of Nevada City drafted the Vigilante oath;" Mullans pp. 39 & 40. Father Mullans, S.J. says in his formal biography of Count John A. Creighton, "In desperation, five men, among whom was Mr. John A. Creighton, met and organized as a means of self-defense, the famous Vigilance Committee. This association increased rapidly, and in the space of two years executed such summary justice upon forty-seven malefactors, that all friends of the dead outlaws either left the neighborhood, or forgot that they had ever been in sympathy with them."
207 The Montana Post, June 1, 1867, page 7."New Today, Proposals."
208 The Montana Post, June 8, 1867, page 1, "From the Front."
209 The Montana Post, May 18 1867, page 8, "From Saturdays Tri-weekly Returned."

Chapter 17: Messenger

210 James U. Sanders, Editor, Register, Society of Montana Pioneers, Constitution, Members, and Officers, with Portraits and Maps... page 132.
211 Bancroft, page 706, as noted by Flynn.
212 Captain H.H. Lyons; First Lieutenant Robert Hughes; Second Lieutenant J.J.Herrington; Sergeants George Irwin, J.E. Shaw, Joseph K. Ross, Jacob Prewitt;

Privates Robert Adams, Adam Armstrong, Robert Bringham, George Black, Thomas Behen, Frank Bush, George Bensel, George Blue, John W. Conquest, Robert Crumblin, Albert J. Carter, W. Cochran, Lewis Copeland, James Dia, John Dillon, Joseph Davism, William A. Ellis, Abraham Easterbrooks, Samuel F. Ferris, Daniel G. Frazer, Joseph Gill, D.L.Green, James Garratt, William Hallaron, Orson Hamblin, William Hale, Marlon Hall, Thomas Hafford, George W. Heller, William Hill, John Jenkins, Peter Kramer, E.G. Minard, Francis F. Marion, William Mead, James McDonald, Ed. Meagher, Oswald B. Nevin, Jere E. Obenchain, Alfred Pierce, Henry Rogers, Lewis Roberts, Charles Rathburn, Llewelly Reynolds, Charles Reid, James Smith, N. Seerles, Simon Slain, Simon Stoneberger, Charles Slaterly and John H. Thrailkill;" Montana Post May 25, 1867, page 8, "From Helena Saturday Tri-weekly, Company A;" Howie Diary, 1867, page 6.

[213] The Montana Post, May 18, 1867, page 8, "From Helena's Tuesday Tri-weekly, Lieut. Col. Biedler (sic.)."

[214] The Montana Post, May 25, 1867, page 8, "From Helena's Thursday Tri-weekly, Off for the Front."

[215] The Montana Post, June 1, 1867, page 8, "From Tuesday's Tri-weekly."

[216] The Montana Post, June 1, 1867, page 8, "In Town, X the Unknown."

[217] The Montana Post, June 1, 1867, page 8, "Arrivals at the Planters House."

[218] The Montana Post, May 11, 1867, page 8, "Letters for the Soldiers." Persons having letters for the officers and men in Gallatin Valley can have he sent direct and free of charge, by messengers from headquarters. All letters left at the Executive Office will be promptly forwarded. The first messenger leaves at 10 AM today (May 11)."

[219] The Montana Post, May 25, 1867, page 8, "Arrivals and Departures."

[220] The Montana Post, Saturday May 25 in the post, page 8: "Gone with provisions by the Richards and Boyer party, responding to letter from commander of Fort C.F. Smith, This letter being submitted to General Thoroughman, 40 men under Colonel DeLacy volunteered to escort a train through to Fort Smith. Tom Cover furnished three wagons, Richards three, the two government wagons and two others, in all ten, which were loaded and the party to start yesterday morning (May 24), the Richards and Boyer boys and Colonel DeLacy commanding. We admire the heroic generosity that actuated these men. If the militia do nothing more than accomplish the task of relieving the beleaguered garrison, they will have won imperishable laurels. May they get through safe."

[221] The Montana Post, June 1, 1867, "From Helena's Tuesday Tri-weekly, Arrived."

[222] The Montana Post, June 1, 1867, "From Helena's Tuesday Tri-weekly, Personal."

[223] The Montana Post, May 25, 1867, page 8, "From Helena's Saturday tri-weekly, Generous Offer."

[224] The Montana Post, June 1, 1867, page 8, "From Helena's Tuesday Tri-weekly, Returned."

[225] The Montana Post, February 17, 1866, "Officers of the 2nd Montana Volunteers. Neil Howie, Colonel; John Featherstun, Major; ---------Quartermaster (none since Sanders resigned); A.Z. Lawrence, Robert Hereford, C.J.D. Curtis, Joseph Cobell, Captains; Edwin Bedell A.J. Wilson, 1st Lieutenants. Recruiting office is in the Courtroom."

[226] The Montana Post, June 1, 1867, page 8, "From VC Thursday Tri-weekly, Off again, General Howie and

Lieutenant Colonel Beidler leave for Helena this morning, Bon Voyage."

[227] The Montana Post, June 15, 1867, page 8, "From Helena's Thursday Tri-weekly, Home Safe."

[228] The Montana Post, June 15, 1867, page 8, "From Helena's Thursday Tri-Weekly, The Military."

[229] Howie Diary, 1867.

[230] The Montana Post, June 22, 1867, page 8, "From Helena's Tuesday Tri-weekly, On Dit-That X Beidler and John…"

[231] The Montana Post, June 29, 1867, page 8, "From Helena's Tuesday Tri-Weekly, Painful Accident."

[232] Howie Diary, page 7.

[233] The Montana Post, June 15, 1867, page 8, "From VC's Thursday's Tri-Weekly, 'Court Proceedings.'"

[234] The Montana Post, June 22, 1867, page 8, "From Helena's Thursday Tri-Weekly, 'Vi Et Armis.'"

[235] The Montana Post, July 6, 1867, page 8, "From Helena's Tuesday Tri-weekly, Going Into Camp"

Chapter 18: Professor

[236] Mother to Carpenter, Letter dated September 30, 1852; sparedshared6.wordpress.com/2014/04/29/1852-mother-to-a-m-s-carpenter/comment-page-1/

[237] Ibid.

[238] Carpenter to Sanders letter, Montana Historical Society, Helena, MT., W.F. Sanders Papers, MC 53.

[239] The Montana Post, July 7, 1867, page 8, "Arrivals and Departures."

[240] Ronald V. Rockwell, The U.S. Army in Frontier Montana, page 115.

[241] The Montana Post, June 22, 1867, "From Helena's Thursday Tri-Weekly, General Items."

[242] immortalnobodies.blogspot.com/2015/01/william-mcglothlin-sadly-in-wrong-place.html
[243] Joaquin Miller, A Illustrated History The State of Montana, page. 321.
[244] The Montana Post Supplement, November 16, 1867, "Annual Report of the Superintendent of Public Instruction, November, 1867;" see also: Tom Stout, Montana, Its Story and Biography, American Historical Society, New York, NY, 1921, Volume I, pp. 493-494.
[245] A.M.S. Carpenter vs. Montana Territorial Auditor
[246] The Montana Post, March 23, 1867, "The Agassiz Meeting."
[247] The Montana Post, June 8, 1867, page 8, "From VC's Thursday Tri-Weekly, Appointed."
[248] Captain William R. Massie operated the Steamboat Antelope in 1867. Annalies Corbin, The Material Culture of Steamboat Passengers: Archaeological Evidence From the Missouri River, books.google.com, page 1867
[249] The Montana Post, June 22, 1867, "From Saturday's Tri-weekly."
[250] "Headquarters, District of Helena, Montana Militia, Fort Benton, MT, June 22, 1867: To Major A.M.G. Carpenter, In accordance with letters of instruction from Acting Governor Meagher, you will receive and contract for the transportation of arms and ordinance directed to Montana. (Signed) Green Clay Smith, Governor of Montana and Commander in Chief of Militia." (Attested by the signature of R.L. LaMotte, Captain 13th Infantry), Montana Historical Society, Helena, MT.
[251] The Montana Post, June 29, 1867, page 4, "From Fort Benton."
[252] The Montana Post, July 6, 1867, page 8, "From Benton."

[253] The Montana Post, July 13, 1867, page 8, "From Helena's Tuesday Tri-Weekly, Benton News."

Chapter 19: Chronicler

[254] The Montana Post, June 8, 1867, page 8, "Checked in at the Planters House June 5;" The Montana Post, June 8, 1867, "From VC's Tuesday Tri-Weekly Honorable James Tufts."

[255] The Montana Post, June 8, 1867, page 8, "From VC's Saturday Tri-weekly, Personal."

[256] The Montana Post, June 15, 1867, "From VC's Thursday Tri-weekly, Items."

[257] The Montana Post June 8, 1867, page 8, "From VC's Saturday Tri-weekly, The Winding Way."

[258] Mrs. Wilbur Fisk Sanders, Diary, Saint Joseph, Missouri to Virginia City, M.T. (April 15-July 8, 1867), Montana Historical Society, Helena, MT; W.F.Sanders Papers, MC53 Folder 3-15.

[259] Charles W. Fowler, Court Clerk, Third Judicial District, Honorable L.R.Munson, The Montana Post, July 20, 1867, page 2.

[260] The Montana Post, July 6, 1867, page 8, "From Helena's Thursday's Tri-Weekly, 'District Court, First Day.'"

[261] The Montana Post, July 6, 1867.

[262] Alexander K. McClure, Letter XXXV, Three Thousand Miles Through the Rocky Mountains, p. 329-330.

[263] The Montana Post, July 6, 1867, July 4 registrations at Planters House, page 8.

[264] Harriet Sanders Diary, page 8.

[265] The Montana Post, September 21, 1867, pp. 2 & 5, The Choteau County Council Delegate position became

a competition between Sample Orr (129 votes) and A.W. Torbett (67 votes).

Chapter 20: Handoff

[266] A.C.McClure (sic.), <u>Contributions to the Montana Historical Society, VIII</u> (1917), page 32
[267] Ibid, page 33.
[268] Ibid, pp. 26 & 27.
[269] Claire Prechtel-Kluskens, "A Reasonable Degree of Promptitude," Research Branch, NARA, www.archives.gov/publications/prologue/2010/spring/civilwarpension.html
[270] Howie Diary, 1867, page 7.
[271] <u>The Montana Post</u>, June 8, 1867, page 8, "From VC's Thursday Tri-Weekly, For the Front."
[272] <u>The Montana Post,</u> June 15, 1867, page 7, "From the Gallatin."
[273] <u>The Montana Post</u>, June 1 1867, page 8, "From Saturday's VC Tri-Weekly, The Military."
[274] <u>The Montana Post,</u> June 8, 1867, page 1, "From VC's Tuesday Tri-weekly, Camp Cummings."
[275] <u>The Montana Post</u>, June 8, 1867 page 8, "From VC's Saturday Tri-Weekly, Good."
[276] <u>The Montana Post</u>, June 15, 1867, page 8 "From VC's Tuesday's Tri-weekly, Presentation."
[277] Coordinates of Camp Green Clay Smith: 45°43'20"N 110°27'40"W (same as Camp Ida Thoroughman)
[278] On Friday, May 24, Colonel Henry Blake, appointed chief of staff to General Thoroughman, left for the field.
[279] <u>The Montana Post</u>, June 25, 1867, "From Helena's Tuesday Tri-Weekly, 'Good Appointment."
[280] <u>The Montana Post</u>, June 15, 1867, "From VC's Tuesday Tri-Weekly: (On June 11) Dr. J. Dunlevy, formerly Post Surgeon at the Flathead Agency has been

appointed surgeon of the Montana Militia and is with General Thoroughman's Command on the Yellowstone."

[281] The Montana Post, June 22, 1867, page 1, "From VC's Tuesday Tri-Weekly, Camp on the Yellowstone."

[282] The Montana Post, June 22, 1867, "From Saturday's Tri-Weekly (June 15).

[283] The Montana Post, June 15, 1867.

[284] The Montana Post, June 15, 1867, page 4, and June 29 1867, page 3, "Proclamation…"

[285] The Montana Post, June 15, 1867, page 1, "The Apportionment."

[286] Flynn, page 47.

[287] The Montana Post, June 29, 1867, page 1, "The Modifications."

[288] The Montana Post, June 22, 1867, page 8, "From Helena's Thursday Tri-Weekly, Distinguished Visitor."

[289] The Montana Post, June 22, 1867, page 8, "Another company."

[290] The Montana Post, June 22, 1867, page 8, "From Helena's Thursday's Tri-Weekly, 'Vi Et Armis;'" Coordinates of Camp Ida Thoroughman: 45°43'20"N 110°27'40"W

[291] The Montana Post, June 29, 1867, page 6, "Army News: Letter, dated June 21, 1867, Adjutant General Martin Beem to Major General Thomas Thoroughman."

[292] The Montana Post, June 22, 1867, page 8, "From Helena's Saturday Tri-Weekly, 'General Meagher.'"

[293] The Montana Post, June 29, 1867, page 4, "From Fort Benton."

[294] Date of meeting comes from Fort Benton's Overholser Historical Research Center's. Ken Robison Blog

[295] Helena Herald, June 26, 1867, "Retires From Office." "Upon arrival of Governor Green Clay Smith, General

Thomas Francis Meagher retires from office and command in Montana-his resignation having been accepted, to take full effect upon the arrival here of his Excellency (sic.) Governor Smith, or the same, had the new Secretary come first. While en-route to Benton last week to receipt and forward arms sent up from St. Louis by General Sherman, General Meagher and Governor Smith met on the road, and during a brief but friendly interview, the General formally announced the expiration of his official authority, that he therewith surrendered into the hands of the Governor, all matters pertaining to the position, and expressed the desire that Governor Smith would so relieve him. Governor Smith did not, however, relieve General Meagher at once, but retained him in service to complete his journey and carry out the object of his mission to Benton, that the battery, the small arms and ammunition necessary to the efficiency of the militia force, might be forwarded to Helena and to the field without delay. This action on the part of his Excellency, governor Smith, is an evidence of a spirit of true courtesy, and justifies us in the belief that he will cordially endorse or approve the official proceedings of the Acting Governor during his absence in the East. Such approval and endorsement, in view of the delicate responsibilities devolving upon General Meagher, will be no less gratifying to his friends than satisfactory to the people of the Territory in general."

[296] The Montana Post, June 29 1867, page 8, "From Helena's Thursday's Tri-Weekly, 'Fort Benton Arrivals.'"
[297] Ibid.
[298] Flynn, page 189.
[299] http://missoulian.com/news/state-and-regional/auction-rare-montana-ferry-token-dated-isn-t-

so-old/article_46f1c800-22e1-5563-b227-5b1120a636df.html

[300] The Montana Post, June 29, 1867, page 4, "From Fort Benton;" Flynn, page 232.

[301] Flynn, page 22,

[302] The Montana Post, June 29, 1867, page 4, "From Fort Benton."

[303] Ken Robison's Blog.

[304] The Montana Post, June 29, 1867, "From VC's Saturday Tri-Weekly Passengers from Benton;" Montana Post, July 7, 1867, page 8, "Arrivals and Departures."

[305] The Montana Post, June 29, 1867, page 8, "From Helena's Tuesday Tri-Weekly, Arrivals from Benton."

Chapter 21: Telltale

[306] Col. W. F. Sanders, "How General Meagher Met His Death," The Butte Inter Mountain, Butte, Montana, March 15, 1902, p. 16; Chronicling America: Historic American Newspapers. Library of Congress

[307] Copy of original document at Montana Military Museum, Fort Harrison, MT.

[308] The Montana Post, August 17, 1867, page 8, "From VC's Tuesday Tri-Weekly, Choteau Nominations."

Chapter 22: Shanty

[309] Answer to questions from U.S.Marshal William Wheeler, letter dated February 2, 1874, Charles J.D.Curtis, Helena, M.T. to Captain Dusold, Virginia City, M.T. Folder 1, SC 588, Charles Curtis letters, Montana Historical Society, Helena, MT.

[310] Hardie Report: According to General Hardie, who was charged with reviewing Montana's 1867 Indian War

Claims, by Mid-July 1867 the militia numbered 250 volunteers actually performing service. Of those about fifty were line or staff officers, "among the upper grades of whom there was a disproportionate degree of rank."
[311] The Montana Post, July 28, 1867, page 8, "From VC's Saturday Tri-Weekly, Hung By The Vigilantes." Charles Wilson, about 30 years old, a one time employee of Wells, Fargo and one time companion of Slade's, recently discharged from Foster's Company D, was found hung in "the little ravine back of the stone quarry" near Virginia City on Thursday morning, September 26, 1867. He is neck was broken when hung from a tripod comprised of 15 foot poles taken from a near-by fence. His feet nearly touched the short grass, his arms were tied behind him, he was fully dressed wearing even his hat the blanket he had worn for warmth from his sleeping place was on the ground beside him, and the placard on his chest read: "Vigilantes." He was cut down by the coroner at 3PM, placed in a coffin, and decently buried taken up by the side of the five road agents on the hill opposite town. Sounding authoritative, The Montana Post stated, with its dates wrong, "This was the first execution by the Vigilance committee since James Daniels was hung in Helena in the autumn of '65." It also rehashed rumors that Wilson was a member of a 'secret organization, under the close espionage of the Vigilantes, and ever active member is known.' "On the night of his execution, Charles Wilson swore into the (secret) organization one detailed for that purpose (of robbery, incendiarism and murder), and when arrested made full confession...."
[312] The Montana Post, July 13, 1867, page 2, "Fort Benton-Hurricane."
[313] The Montana Post, July 6, 1867, page 8, "From Helena's Thursday's Tri-Weekly, River News."

[314] The Montana Post, July 27, 1867, "From VC's Saturday Tri-Weekly, Ordnance Stores."
[315] The Montana Post, November 9, 1867, page 8, "Message of Governor Green Clay Smith to the Legislature of Montana Territory," This message includes a statement about the "large number of militia who deserted with stores, supplies and 250 horses, and a request for the Council and House of Representatives to pass an efficient militia law, and to hire an Ordnance Sergeant for the new Territorial Arsenal.
[316] Order of Governor Green Clay Smith to Brigadier General Neil Howie, July 4, 1867.
[317] Tolton, page 123.
[318] The Montana Post, July 13, 1867, page 7, "From The Army."
[319] Barry J. Hagan, C.S.C., "Exactly the Right Place," A History of Fort C.F. Smith, Montana Territory, 1866-1868, Arthur Clark Company, Spokane, WA, 1999, page 98.
[320] https://books.google.com/books?id=VjP_eTHLbuEC&pg=PA3&source=gbs_toc_r&cad=3#v=onepage&q&f=false

Chapter 23: Volunteers

[321] The Montana Post, July 13, 1867, "From the Army."
[322] The Montana Post, July 13, 1867, "A Hint to Horse Thieves—A Couple of Red Skins Cared For."
[323] Ibid.
[324] LaForge, pp. 17-18.
[325] Hagan, page 98 & footnote 49.
[326] The Montana Post, July 1, 1867, "From General Meagher."
[327] The Montana Post, July 6, 1867, page 8, "From VC's Tuesday Tri-weekly, A Bit of a Row."

[328] Army Navy Journal, 29 June 1867, 714:3 and 715:1; Hagan, page 90.
[329] The Montana Post, May 25, 1867, page 2, "Letter from Fort Phil Kearney (sic.)."
[330] The Montana Post, May 25, 1867, page 8, "Distinguished Visitors."
[331] The Montana Post, 1867, page 8, "From Saturday's Helena Tri-Weekly, Indian Fight on the Yellowstone."
[332] The Montana Post, June 15, 1867, "From VC's Tuesday Tri-Weekly, "To Hon. Edwin M. Stanton, from A.C. Hunt Governor. Denver, May 27, 1867;" The Montana Post, June 22, 1867, page 1, "Don't Like Him."
[333] The Montana Post, June 8, 1867, page 1, "From the Front."

Chapter 24: Settlers

[334] The Montana Post, July 20, 1867, page 3, "From Gallatin," When Colonel DeLacy's detail brought the Richards Train back from C.F.Smith, accompanying them were a few emigrants—sturdy young men who have made their way through the Indians." In 1867 10,000 passengers and 8000 tons of freight arrived at Fort Benton by water. Steamer cabin accommodation was $300; deck passage was $75. This summer a single trip of the Ida Stockdale from St. Louis to Fort Benton cleared $42,594, the largest amount ever earned by a mountain steamboat and twice the boats original cost. Robert G. Ahern, High Plains Empire, the High Plains and Rockies, page 91.
[335] The Montana Post, June 22, 1867, page 1, "Don't Like Him."
[336] The Montana Post, June 29, 1867, page 4, "Latest News From All Parts of the World."
[337] Ibid.

[338] Hardie Report.
[339] The Montana Post, July 20, 1867, page 4, "Telegraph News: The Indian War-It's Interesting to Hear Both Sides:"
[340] The Montana Post, July 20, 1867, page 6, "Military Orders"
[341] The Montana Post, July 13, 1867, Front Page, "The Indian Situation."

Chapter 25: Regiment

[342] The Montana Post, June 15, 1867, page 8, "From VC's Thursday Tri-Weekly, All Quiet on the Yellowstone."
[343] The Montana Post, July 13, 1867, page 8, "Resolutions of the Military."
[344] The Montana Post, July 20, 1867, page 8, "From Helena's Thursday Tri-Weekly, From the Front."
[345] The Montana Post, June 29, 1867, page 8, "From VC's Saturday Tri-Weekly, Items, General Thoroughman leaves…"
[346] The Montana Post, July 6, 1867, "From Helena's Tuesday Tri-Weekly, Come for Trial."
[347] "Information wanted—Of Geo. R. Ives. Was heard of last in Montana, two years ago. Any one knowing of his whereabouts will confer a favor by addressing J. Edward Ives, Bristol, Hartford County, Connecticut."
[348] The Montana Post, July 13, 1867, page 1, "From VC's Tuesday Tri-Weekly, What Was Found."
[349] The Montana Post, July 20, 1867, page 2, "Indian Affairs."
[350] The Montana Post, July 20, 1867, "Front Page, Reorganization."

[351] The Montana Post, July 13, 1867, "From VCs Saturday Tri-weekly, Arrived. Governor Smith and family."
[352] The Montana Post, July 20, 1867, page 8, "From VC's Tuesday Tri-Weekly, Personal."
[353] The Montana Post, July 27, 1867, page 8, "From VC's Tuesday Tri-Weekly, Resigning."
[354] The Montana Post, July 20, 1867, page 8, "Died."
[355] Letter, dated July 25, 1867, Colonel Beem to Captain Pinney: "His Excellency Gov. Smith directs me to state that in consequence of the informalities existing in the resignation of Capt. Robert Hereford, he is compelled to return the same and until it is sent in proper form and only accepted, he cannot recognize as vacant the position of Captain."
[356] The Montana Post, September 21, 1867, page 8, "Married."
[357] The Montana Post, July 27, 1867, page 8, "From Helena's Saturday Tri-Weekly, A Parade;" The Montana Post, August 3, 1867, page 8, "From Helena's Tuesday Tri Weekly, Presentation." page 8: "Previous to moving out of town, Captain Charles Curtis section of artillery were presented with a beautiful guidon, given them by the ladies of Gallatin Valley now resident in this city. The beautiful and accomplished miss Fanny Campbell presented it on behalf of the ladies and spoke as follows: "Captain Curtis: Permit me, in behalf of the ladies of Gallatin valley, to present through you to the gallant men of your command this small testimonial of our heartfelt gratitude for their ready response to their country's call at a time when our homes were menaced by a savage foe. Pray accept this in the spirit in which it is given with our confidence that you will defend it with honor to yourselves and us." Captain Curtis eloquently responded, promising that by no act of his or his men

should the beautiful present they had received be sullied, and that it would be defended by the best blood of the command. The guidon was then handed to General Howie, who in company with General Thoroughman headed the procession, cheers were given for the ladies of Gallatin, Captain Curtis and his company, when the procession was reformed and marched through the City.

[358] The Montana Post, August 3, 1867, page 8, "From Helena's Tuesday Tri-Weekly, Died."

[359] Howie Diary, "On July 25, I received my commission as Colonel First Montana Cavalry."

[360] The Montana Post, August 3, 1867, page 8 (from Helena's Tri-Weekly): Arrived: General Terry and suite arrived from Benton per Wells, Fargo and Co. Express on last Wednesday. The following are the names of the suite: General Terry, F. Terry, General Comstock, Major Taining, Lt. O'Toole Lt Tilford, Capt. Graves, Mr. Snow, Dr. Taylor, Col. Reeve and J.D. Taylor. General T. visits our Territory on business connected with our red neighbors and it is to be hoped that he will display as much sagacity in the consideration of this matter as he did bravery in the reduction of Fort Fisher." (Note: "In August, Major General Alfred H. Terry, then commanding the Department of the Dakota and Major General Comstock, Inspector General of the U.S. Army arrived to inspect progress of construction of Fort Shaw. (U.S. Army in Frontier Montana, pages 136-37)

[361] The Montana Post, August 3, 1867, page 8, "From Helena's Saturday Tri-Weekly, Military."

[362] Colonel Neil Howie, Commanding 1st Regiment Montana Volunteers, Helena M.T., Report of November 10, 1867, to Colonel Martin Beem, Adjutant and Inspector General, Virginia City M.T.

[363] The Montana Post, July 20, 1867, page 8, "From VC's Saturday Tri-Weekly, Recruiting."

Chapter 26: Muster

[364] Hardie Report: Kirkendall contracting to provide nine six-mule teams, wagons and drivers, July 28, 1867.
[365] While using metal detectors at the site of Camp Ida Thoroughman John Hawkins of Helena, MT (Fronteirwest@msn.com) discovered numerous pieces of discarded Enfield Rifle-Muskets, the barrels of which had been turned into fencing posts.
[366] Smith to Pinney, Undated Letter, "Howie might have to fight. Let the small arms go ahead, and if the artillery cannot go with it (illegible) 2 pieces. These matters are confidential, save to you, Howie and Fisk." (P.S.) Write me by return mail. Do not stop to buy teams and wagons, but hire them." G.C.S
[367] The Montana Post, August 3, 1867, "From VC's Thursday Tri-Weekly, Artillery."
[368] Colonel Martin Beem, Adjutant General, by Order of the Commander in Chief, General Order No. 3.
[369] The War Claims Report indicates Sanders was entitled in addition to $75 of the $150 he charged each month for rent May 1 to September 28, repayment in the amount of $358.25, to satisfy claims totaling $447.25 for services and a bake oven $149.00.
[370] The Montana Post, August 10, 1867, page 8, "From VC's Thursday Tri-Weekly, Off."
[371] The Montana Post, August 10, 1867, page 8, "From Helena's Tuesday Tri-Weekly, Military."
[372] Howie Report, November 10, 1867.
[373] Ibid.
[374] The Montana Post, August 17, 1867, page 8, "From VC's Thursday Tri-Weekly, About Soldiers' Pay."
[375] The Montana Post, August 8, 1867, page 8, "From VC's Thursday's Tri-Weekly, Latest From the Indians."

[376] Ibid, page 2.
[377] The Montana Post, August 17, 1867, page 8, "From VC's Tuesday Tri-Weekly, Fight for Life."
[378] Howie ADC Apnal to Smith ADC Scribner in Helena, Letter, dated August 13, 1867, "Col. Howie, Commanding, directs me to forward to you a descriptive list of deserters from Co's "B," and "E." As most of Co. "B" as recruited at Helena it is supposed they will probably go back there. They took with their horses, equipments blankets and arms, all Government property. These you will take and turn the over to the proper departments, taking receipts therefore and sending to Captain Robert Hughes, Co. B, and Captain Neil Campbell, Co. E."
[379] Montana Post, August 17, 1867, "From VC's Tuesday Tri-Weekly, Mustered Out, Mustered In."
[380] Smith to Neal, Commanding Recruits, Letter dated August 20, 1867, Montana Historical Society.
[381] Montana Post, August 24, 1867, "From VC's Tuesday Tri-Weekly, Items."
[382] Montana Post, August 24, 1867, page 8, "From Helena's Thursday Tri-Weekly, New Post-Lieutenant Chance."
[383] Montana Post, August 24, 1867, page 8: "Regulars for Yellowstone, We learn that Governor Smith has received information that General Terry has ordered 300 regulars from the Sun River to move to the Yellowstone. This, it is presumed, is preparatory to the expedition contemplated to be sent out, composed of the Montana Volunteers."
[384] Montana Post, September 7, 1867, "From Saturday's Tri-Weekly, Military," page 8.

Chapter 27: Ambush

[385] Howie Report, Boulder River, August 29 1867.
[386] These three wounded men were brought by the militia to Camp T.F.Meagher for care. One of them, a 30 year old John Thompson, died about two weeks later and was buried by the militia with military honors. <u>Montana Post</u>, September 21, 1867, page 8, "From VC's Tuesday Tri-Weekly, Dead-Official Communication."
[387] Howie Report, Boulder River, August 29, 1867.
[388] <u>The Montana Post</u>, August 7, 1867, page 8, "From VC's Saturday's Tri-Weekly, Military."
[389] Howie Diary, 1867, September 1. Captain Heart's (sic.) Company (K, for the short time it existed) from Virginia City arrived on the Upper Yellowstone, along with Colonel Nelson's Company.
[390] <u>The Montana Post</u>, August 3, 1867, page 8, "From VC's Tuesday Tri-Weekly, A Shooting Affray."
[391] Howie Report, Fort T.F.Meagher, September 1867.
[392] Hardie Report, pp. 33 & 34.
[393] <u>The Montana Post</u>, September 14, 1867 page 8, "From Helena's Tuesday Tri-Weekly, The Men at the Front Heard From."
[394] <u>The Montana Post</u>, September 14, 1867, page 8, "From VC's Thursday Tri-Weekly, Correction."
[395] <u>The Montana Post,</u> September 14, 1867, page 8, "From Camp Meagher;" <u>The Montana Post</u>, September 14, 1867, page 8, "From VC's Tuesday Tri-Weekly, Correction"
[396] Rockwell, page 137: "On August 15 the Companies D and F departed Fort Shaw for the Gallatin Valley to a site at present-day Bozeman to establish a new post. This post would be designated Fort Ellis in honor of Colonel A.V.H. Ellis, killed at the Battle of Gettysburg. A third company, Company G, followed them to Fort Ellis, departing Fort Shaw on August 25th."
[397] Rockwell, pp. 138 & 139.

[398] The Montana Post, August 10, 1867, page 8, "From VC's Tuesday Tri-Weekly, Too Good to Lose."
[399] The Montana Post, August 31, 1867, page 8, "From VC's Saturday, Tri-Weekly, The Front."
[400] The Montana Post, August 24, 1867, page 8, "From Helena's Tri-Weekly, Latest From Fort Benton."
[401] The Montana Post, August 10, 1867, page 8, "From VC's Saturday Tri-Weekly, A War Party."
[402] The Montana Post, September 7, 1867, page 2, "Official Report of Colonel Howie, Headquarters 1st Montana Cavalry, On the Boulder River, August 29, 1867."
[403] The Montana Post, August 31, 1867, page 8, "From VC's Thursday's Tri-Weekly, The Indian Campaign."
[404] The Montana Post, September 7, 1867, page 8, "From VC's Tuesday Tri-Weekly, War on the Border."
[405] The Montana Post, August 24, 1867, page 8, "From Helena's Tuesday Tri-weekly, From the Muscleshell (sic.)." Coordinates of Camp Neil Howie: 46°31'40"N 110°23'30"W,
[406] The Montana Post, September 14, 1867, page 8, "From VC's Saturday Tri-Weekly, For the Front and Adjutant General Beem."
[407] Coordinates of Camp Thomas Francis Meagher: 45°42'00"N 110°31'00"W
[408] Howie Report, November 10, 1867, page 3.
[409] Hardie's Report, pp. 33 & 34.

Chapter 28: Insurrection

[410] Howie Report, November 10, 1867, page 4.
[411] The Montana Post, October 5, 1867, page 8, "From VC's Tuesday Tri-Weekly, From the Yellowstone."
[412] Ken Egan, Jr., Montana 1864, Riverbend, Helena, MT, 2014, p. 209.

[413] Howie Report, November 10, 1867, page 4.
[414] Ibid, By the time of the mutiny, Howie and his men knew that .50 caliber Springfield breech-loaders saved the regulars in the August 1 Hayfield and August 2 Wagon Box fights.
[415] U.S., Returns from Military Posts, 1806-1916, see subsequent enlistments/ assignments of several Robert Hughes' in Wyoming, South Dakota and Montana.
[416] LaForge and Marquis, pp. 19-20.
[417] Hagan, page 154.
[418] Ibid.

Chapter 29: Discharge

[419] Lieutenant General W.T. Sherman, Headquarters Military Division of the Missouri, St. Louis, Misouri, November 1, 1868, Papers Accompanying Report of the General-in-Chief, freepages.history.rootsweb.ancestry.com.
[420] Rea, Tom, "Peace, War, Land and a Funeral: The Fort Laramie Treaty of 1868," WyoHistory.org
[421] Rockwell, pp.138 & 139.
[422] Howie Report, November 10, 1867.
[423] General Order Number 12, Montana Territorial Governor Green Clay Smith, September 28 1867.
[424] Carpenter to Scribner, letter dated September 30, 1867.
[425] Captain Gorman had been the manager for C.C. Huntley Stage in Fort Benton. On June 23, 1867 C.C.Huntley sold out to Wells Fargo & Company and on July 10 hauled the company's stock and equipment from the Mullan Road to the new road to the Muscleshell (sic.), with a plan to survey stations and open a stage road to carry overland mail from Minnesota to Helena the following spring. The plan would continue the mail

service in the fall months on horseback; Montana Historical Society, Small Collection 162, Folder 1/6, Volunteers (May –November 1867 General Correspondence).

[426] The Montana Post, October 5, 1867, page 8, "The Militia and International House Arrivals;" As an Example of Mustering Out: Captain John H. Evans discharged (mustered out) at Virginia City, by Lieutenant Col Nelson, witnessed by Captain Martin Beem. Final statement certified that Captain John H. Evans of Company D of the First Regiment of Montana Volunteer Forces born in Washington County in the State of Ohio aged 22 years, 5 feet 11 ½ inches, light complexion, Blue eyes light hair and by profession a Miner was commissioned by the Governor of Montana at Virginia City M.T. on the eight of May, 1867 to served during the Indian wars and is now entitled to a discharge by reason of order from Commanding Officer Department of Dakota. The said John H. Evans has pay due from enlistment to include ___ and has pay due him from that time to the present date. There I due to him --- dollars, retained pay. There is due to him ---dollars on account of clothing not drawn in kind. He is indebted to the United States Fifty-eight and no /100 for Commissary Sores, clothing, etc. He is indebted to ___laundress for Horse and Equipment appraised at fifty $50 dollars. (Total $108). Given in Triplicate at Virginia City, M.T. this tenth day of October 1867, signed John H. Evans, Captain, commanding Company.

[427] The Montana Post, October 5, 1867, page 8, "From VC's Thursday's Tri-Weekly, Armory Building."

[428] The Montana Post, October 5, 1867, page 8, "From VC's Saturday Tri-Weekly, Notice."

[429] The Montana Post, October 5, 1867, page 8, "From VC's Thursday's Tri-Weekly, Mustering Out."

[430] The Montana Post, October 5, 1867, page 8, "From Saturday's Helena Tri-Weekly, The Militia."
[431] Ibid.
[432] Curtis to Dusold, Letter Reference Your Dispatch to Marshall Wheeler Reference the Arsenal on the Hill; Montana Historical Society, Small Collection 588, Folder 1/1.
[433] November 6, 1867, minute entry: Missoula County pays Worden and Co. Freight bill for arms. $175.00
[434] Carpenter to Scribner, Telegraph dated October 14, 1867, Montana Historical Society, SC 162, Volunteers, May-November Correspondence, 1867, Folder 1/6.
[435] Governor Green Clay Smith to Honorable C.S.Bagg, President of the Council November 22, 1867, Council Journal, 4th Session Legislative Assembly, M.T.
[436] Governor Green Clay Smith message to the Montana Territorial Legislature, December 14, 1867.
[437] "Arsenal building is in good and safe order and condition. Contains there in: 90 boxes of 12 pound howitzer ammunitions (12 rounds per box of shell, spherical with primers); 7 boxes of same imperfect and damaged; 156 boxes (1000 rounds in each) of center-primed metallic cartridges (caliber 50); 508 boxes (1000 rounds in each of Springfield musket cartridges cal. 58; 20 breech loading rifled muskets cal .50; 73 boxes (20 guns in each) Springfield rifled muskets, cal. .58; 80 boxes of harnesses and infantry; 7 empty arms chests; 9 empty packing boxes; 2 twelve- pound mountain howitzers with limbers and caissons; 4 tarpaulins (damaged); 4 twelve-pound mountain howitzer caissons and chests; 4 limbers and chests; 4 boxes Springfield muskets cal. 58 (damaged); 1 lot of Springfield muskets cal. 58 damaged; 398 Springfield musket bayonets; 1 box of extra, sponges & staffs and trail hand spikes; and "A lot of damaged saddles, bridles and infantry

equipment. Respectfully submitted, Harrison Mandell

[438] U.S. War Department, Instructions for Mountain Artillery "Instructions for a mountain howitzer mounted on a prairie carriage. The mountain howitzer carriage, which is arranged for packing, being ill adapted for draught, a wider carriage, similar to that for a field piece, has been adopted for service in a prairie country, and called The Prairie Carriage. The limber has two ammunition boxes, each carrying 8 rounds. Two small boxes are placed in the axletree, one on each side of the cheeks for carrying one or more rounds of canister, and the small implements or stores for the service of the piece. The handspike is attached by a hinge to the trail and when not in use, is turned over on the stock and secured in its place by a strap. Two sponges and rammers are carried on the carriage, one attached to each cheek; the equipments and ammunitions are the same as prescribed for the howitzer on the mountain carriage. (drawing on page 36)

[439] Tolton, p. 80.

[440] "This foundry supplies a want which has been long felt, and one which has occasioned many vexatious delays, from being unable to supply the unavoidable breaks which have time to time occurred in our Quartz mills. Now, however, breakages to mill machinery, no matter of what character, can be supplied at short notice;" The Montana Post, October 19, 1867, page 8, "From VC's Tuesday Tri-Weekly, Helena Foundry."

[441] Inventory of goods, Fort Claggett, May 3, 1878.

[442] Rockwell, page 139.

[443] Charles E. Hanson, Jr. "The Post-War Indian Gun Trade," Museum of the Fur Trade Quarterly (Fall 1968): Worman, page 454, fn 61.

[444] Rockwell, page 184.

Chapter 30: Dreams

[445] Worman, page 339.
[446] Ibid, page 456.
[447] Rockwell, page 157.
[448] Tolton, pp. 84-92; Adney, pp. 19-25; Healy, pp. 182 & 183.
[449] Worman, page 117.
[450] Tolton, pp 98 & 99
[451] William R. Hunt, Whiskey Peddler, Johnny Healy, North Frontier Trader, Mountain Press Publishing, Missoula, MT, 1993, page 46.
[452] Adney, pp. 63 & 64.
[453] Tolton, pp. 103-105
[454] Adney, page 37
[455] "Mountain Chief, 'Ninna-stakka.' also known as Big Brave 'Omach-katsi,' (1848-Jan 1942), The Blackfoot Papers, A.H.W., Volume 4, The Good Medicine Foundation, Blackfeet Tribe of the Blackfeet Indian Reservation of Montana, 2006, pp. 108 – 1229.

Index

10-Mile Creek 173
10-Mile Station 93
12th U.S. Infantry 255
13th Missouri Volunteer Infantry 113, 114
13th U.S. Infantry 74, 117, 179, 305, 314
1851 Treaty of Fort Laramie 126
1855 Judith River Treaty 24, 126
1866 Fort Benton Treaty 31, 61
1867 Medicine Lodge Creek Treaties 332
1868 Treaty of Fort Laramie 332
18th U.S. Infantry 98, 255
19th U.S. Infantry 255
1st Colorado Territorial Militia 312
1st Montana Cavalry 210, 211, 286, 320
    Company A, Hynson Commanding 210
    Company B, Hughes Commanding 210
    Company C, Evans Commanding 210
    Company D, Curtis Commanding 210
    Company E, Campbell Commanding 210
    Company F, Nelson Commanding 210
1st Regiment of Montana Volunteers 320
    Company A, Captain L.M. Lyda 282
    Company B, Captain Robert Hughes 282
    Company C, Captain Charles J.D. Curtis 282
    Company D, Captain John H. Evans 282
    Company E, Captain Neil Campbell 282
    Company F, Captain John A. Nelson 282
    Company G, Captain A.F. Weston 283
    Company I, Captain Elijah Mattock (Vice
        Hereford) 283
    Company K, Captain William Deasey 283
20th U.S. Infantry 255

22nd Ohio Volunteer Infantry 112, 114
25-Yard Creek .... 126, 209. *See* Shields River
27th U.S. Infantry 255
28-Mile Springs 36, 43, 73
2nd U.S. Army Dragoons 55
2nd U.S. Cavalry 98, 255, 263, 365
3-7-77 symbol 8, 11
4th Arkansas Mounted Infantry 114, 115
54th Massachusetts Volunteer Infantry 220
64th Ohio Volunteer Infantry 15, 170, 198, 199
A.H.O.J. (Assistant Hand of Justice) .... *See* Featherstun, John
Alder Creek 83, 86, 191
Alder Gulch 87, 89, 142
Allen Corral 235
Allen, David 290
Alton, Illinois 113
Ambush 309
Anderson, Bloody Bill 86
Anderson, Private .... 313. *See* Dunman, C.
Andrews, George 357
Andrews, R.W. 69, 70, 71
Arapaho Tribe .. 24, 87, 96, 97, 127, 254, 255, 256, 257, 270, 300, 322, 332
Arizona Territory 270
Arlington Cemetery 228
Army of the Potomac 29
Army Ordinance Circular No. 13 33
Arrow Top, Blackfeet 6
Asia 4
Assiniboine Tribe .... 24. See Mountain Sioux
Augur, Christopher C. 161, 263, 332
Baker Street Ferry 213

Baker, Eugene 364, 365
Baker, I.G. 361
Baker's Massacre ..... *See* Heavy Runners' Massacre
Ball, Smith... 10, *13*
Bannack ..2, 3, 8, 9, 15, 18, 29, 119, 127, 181, 241
Bannock Tribe 23, 193, 259
Barren Lands 6
Battle of Corinth 15, 114
Battle of Ioka...114
Battle of Old Man's River................................372
Battle of Shiloh 15, 112, 114
Battle of Sun River Crossing............................357
Baume, Thomas 131, 175, 248, 250, 312, 325, 326
Bear Tooth, Crow..................... 278, 279, 310, 317
Bear's Paw Mountains 57
Beaverhead County 8, 23
Beem, Martin 112, 113, 114, 115, 116, 120, 121, 125, 137, 138, 139, 149, 161, 162, 169, 170, 171, 202, 215, 216, 276, 284, 286, 288, 289, 296, 318
Beidler, John X. . 36, 39, 49, 51, 55, 59, 65, 68, 71, 77, 81, 84, 105, 108, 122, 143, 145, 146, 150, 165, 166, 167, 168, 169, 171, 172, 173, 174, 177, 194, 196, 209, 213, 214, 216, 236, 251, 289
Belly River 28
Belt Mountains 70
Berkin, William...... 38, 59, 68, 70, 71, 77, 85, 108, 172, 177, 216
Big Brave, Blackfeet . 370, 374. *See* Mountain Chief
Big Horn County 23, 24, 96, 127, 152, 256, 272
Big Horn River 97, 238, 257, 259, 300, 301, 317
Big Horn River Ferry 239
Big Lake, Piegan............................. 22, 26, 62, 371
Bill's Saloon 183

Bird Tail Rock 35, 72
Bitterroot Mountains 7, 15
Black Hills 262
Blackfeet Confederation.. 5, 6, 22, 23, 24, 25, 26, 27, 30, 40, 46, 47, 61, 65, 69, 70, 72, 73, 118, 279, 316, 366, 371, 372, 374
Blackfeet Indian Agency..................................171
Blackfeet Indian Agent 22, 170, 360
Blackfeet Reservation 361
Blackfoot City 290
Blackfoot Tribe..256
Blackfoot, Crow 237, 258, 278, 310
Blake, Henry N. 205, 289
Blood Tribe. 25, 26, 27, 28, 30, 40, 41, 46, 47, 56, 57, 61, 65, 71, 72, 100, 316, 357, 358, 366, 367, 368, 370
Blythe, Sam 112, 113
Bollards Ferry..211
Boulder 93
Boulder River ... 237, 239, 257, 309, 310, 311, 348
Boyce, Mattie 290
Boyce, William................................ 151, 215, 221
Boyer, Mitch 99, 237
Bozeman City.....118, 122, 123, 128, 129, 138, 140, 144, 151, 201, 248, 305, 314, 317, 326, 333
Bozeman City Cemetery 250, 326
Bozeman Pass....129, 137, 151, 153, 240, 242, 247, 305, 324, 334
Bozeman Trail 5, 32, 83, 87, 92, 97, 255, 265, 309, 328, 332
Bozeman, John................................. 118, 128, 279
Brackett Creek...245
Bridge Street... 70, 71, 81

Bridger Mountains..245
Bridger Pass...................................... 129, 137, 151
Bridger, Jim..254
Brings-Down-The-Sun, Blackfeet................ 5, 370
British Possessions...... 8, 25, 28, 41, 47, 266, 270
Broadway...93, 172, 173
Brown, F.H. 98
Browning Cemetery 375
Bruce, John..189
Buffalo and Indian Independence..................... 62
Bull's Back Fat, Blood 366, 367, 368
Bull's Head Coulee 81
Bull's Head, Blackfeet 72
Burns, Thomas...209
Burrows, Thomas 239
Butte Inter Mountain 218
Byrd, John 87
Calf Shirt, Blood 28, 30
Calgary 6
Callender, F.D..229
Camp Cooke..74, 117, 160, 183, 186, 189, 220, 222
Camp Reynolds.. 179, 183, 185, 220, 229, 230, 304
Campbell, Neil... 141, 201, 205, 211, 245, 246, 282, 302
Canada ....316, 355, 356, 361, 365, 370. *See* British Possessions
Canyon Ferry 87, 157, 196
Carpenter, A.M.S. 149, 155, 156, 160, 164, 178, 179, 180, 181, 182, 183, 184, 185, 209, 212, 214, 215, 229, 230, 231, 233, 276, 287, 304, 334, 336, 337, 340, 341
Carroll and Steele 57, 66, 220
Carson, Charlie...........54, 55, 56, 65, 66, 69, 72, 73

Carson, Kit 55, 56
Catholics 16, 69, 85
Cavanaugh, James M. 197, 312
Cave Gulch Mining District 85
Chadwick, W.F. 105
Challenge Saloon 80
Chambers, James 73
Chance, Josiah 305
Charles Hendrie's Foundry 349
Cheevers, Thomas 84
Cheyenne Tribe 7, 24, 87, 97, 99, 127, 254, 255, 257, 270, 300, 310, 322, 332
Chief Mountain, Blackfeet ...... *See* Mountain Chief, Blackfeet
Choteau Cemetery 374
Chouteau County .. 23, 65, 176, 182, 183, 207, 214, 231
Chouteau County Grand Jury 65
Christenot Mill 191, 193
Christenot, Benjamin F. 83
Civil War 17, 31, 33, 44, 60, 157, 198, 199, 350
Clark's Fork of the Yellowstone River 101, 237, 239
Clarke, Malcolm 364, 369
Clarke, W.J. 85
Clinton, William M. 116, 117, 179, 220
Clore Street 236, 339, 349
Coe, William 311
Coeur d'Alene Tribe 23
Colorado Territory 255, 261, 270
Colorado Tribune 261
Columbia River 3
Comanche Tribe 257

Confederate Gulch 38, 81, 84, 165, 196, 213
Connor, Patrick 193
Content's Corner 162
Cooke, Philip 33
Copley, George 10
Couch, W.M. 185, 229, 233, 235
Cover Ranch 138
Cover, Tom 118, 279
Cree Tribe 25, 371, 372, 373, 374
Creighton and Ohle Store 90
Creighton Cattle 157, 316
Creighton, Edward 91
Creighton, John 16, 17, 87, 89, 92, 94, 157, 158, 160, 163, 164
Crow Agency 353
Crow Creek 316
Crow Tribe 7, 24, 25, 26, 47, 58, 70, 87, 96, 97, 99, 118, 127, 138, 203, 237, 257, 258, 278, 300, 310, 322, 332, 353, 357, 359, 370
Cummings, Hamilton 121, 124, 145, 149, 155, 156, 157, 159, 160, 161, 162, 163, 164, 169, 202, 209, 215, 276, 284, 315, 319, 337
Curtis, Charles J.D. 69, 73, 116, 122, 130, 149, 151, 164, 177, 210, 232, 236, 242, 258, 277, 282, 290, 295, 319, 328, 339, 340, 341
Cut Creek 347
Cut Hand, Piegan 366, 368
Cypress Hills 25
Dakota Territory 262, 270, 329, 352
Dance, Walter B. 122
Daniels, James 51, 52, 76, 77, 78, 79, 80, 108
Davis Street .... *See* Dry Gulch
Davis, Frank 205, 208

Deadman's Coulee 73, 93
Dearborn Crossing 73, 81, 120
Dearborn Crossing Cemetery 73
Dearborn Station 60, 72, 211
Deasey, William 141, 252, 283, 293, 296, 336
Deer Lodge 136
Deer Lodge County 23, 122, 139, 140
Deimling, Francis C. 120, 121
DeLacy, Walter W. 116, 137, 151, 164, 215, 278, 284
Democrat 105, 197, 274
Deserters 304, 324, 326, 327, 358
Diamond City .. 18, 38, 84, 108, 157, 175, 176, 190, 196, 213, 214, 217, 316
Diamond R Freight 38, 68, 211, 216
Dimsdale, Thomas 11, 16, 36, 78, 79, 109, 194, 277
Doran, Johnny 222
Driggs, E.U. 148, 240
Dry Fork of the Powder River 257
Dry Gulch 78, 93, 173
Duke, James K. 285
Dunlevy, James 205, 303
Dunman, C. 312, 313
Dusold, Andrew 235
Eagle Rib, Piegan 58, 64
Eastman, S.F. 359
Eastman, T.H. 221
Edgerton County .. 23, 51, 122, 139, 140, 190, 207
Edgerton, Sidney 2, 3, 8, 10, 11, 14, 15, 16, 17, 19, 28, 29, 31, 63, 166, 176
Electricity 87, 89, 90, 91
Elk Morse's Store 128, 130

Elk Tongue, Blackfeet 6
Emigrant Gulch 277
Evans, Isaac 116
Evans, John 210, 240, 282
Farmer, Charley 51
Featherstun, John ...51, 77, 78, 108, 122, 172, 173, 174, 209, 216
Fenians 48
Fetterman Massacre 97, 265
Fetterman, William J. 96, 98, 99, 100, 318
Fire-Water .... 21. *See* Whiskey
Fisk, James 3, *8*, 122, 132, 133, 159, 198, 209, 216, 236, 289, 364
Fitzgerald, James 71
Flaherty, John 84, 85
Flathead Indian Agent 351
Flathead Jack, Salish 245
Flathead Pass 129, 137, 210, 245, 316
Flatheads ....*See* Salish
Forsythe, James 199
Fort Benton.. 3, 27, 29, 35, 36, 38, 40, 41, 43, 44, 48, 52, 56, 57, 58, 59, 63, 64, 65, 66, 68, 69, 70, 71, 74, 81, 82, 92, 93, 106, 110, 116, 160, 171, 173, 177, 179, 181, 182, 183, 184, 185, 186, 188, 189, 190, 191, 205, 206, 211, 212, 213, 214, 215, 216, 218, 219, 220, 221, 223, 224, 225, 233, 235, 264, 265, 272, 291, 316, 358, 361, 366
Fort C.F. Smith .. 96, 97, 98, 99, 100, 101, 118, 138, 140, 150, 152, 164, 170, 209, 233, 237, 238, 253, 254, 255, 257, 258, 263, 270, 271, 278, 299, 300, 309, 310, 317, 318, 322, 325, 329, 330, 332
Fort Ellis 317
Fort Green Clay Smith *See* Camp Ida Thoroughman

Fort Hamilton .... *See* Fort Whoop-Up
Fort Laramie 96, 97, 98, 262, 263, 306, 310
Fort Larned 306
Fort Leavenworth 299, 355
Fort Morgan 263
Fort Peck 353
Fort Phil Kearny ... 97, 99, 117, 118, 238, 239, 254, 255, 257, 258, 263, 270, 300, 318, 330, 332
Fort Reno 97, 118, 257, 332
Fort Sedgwick 263
Fort Shaw. 220, 305, 314, 333, 351, 352, 356, 357, 358, 365
Fort Union 219
Fort Wagner 220
Fort Walla Walla 3
Fort Whoop-Up 362, 363, 366, 371
Forty-Rod .... 17. *See* Whiskey
Foster, Reuben ... 134, 135, 148, 151, 205, 241, 242, 251, 296
Foster's Bridge 295
Foster's Scout Company 240
Freemasons .... *See* Masons
Fringe, Piegan 61, 64, 74
Frodsbam, Charles 163
Gallatin City 126, 127, 128, 129
Gallatin County 23, 24, 127, 175, 240
Gallatin River 127
Gallatin Valley 75, 92, 128, 140, 144, 164, 175, 232, 247, 253, 283, 291, 297, 301, 319
Gartley, Andrew 51
Gatling Gun 349
Gibson, James 180, 194, 226
Glick, Jerome S. 296

Gorman, James 225, 335
Graham Wagon Road 38, 81, 213
Grant, Johnny 55
Grant, Ulysses S. 110, 113, 114
Grant's Army 145
Great Plains 266
Greeley, Horace 228
Green, John 263
Griffith and Thompson 341
Grizzly Bear Attack 302
Grizzly Gulch 173
Gros Ventre Tribe .. 23, 25, 26, 37, 38, 40, 41, 47, 57, 58, 70, 87, 100, 256, 257, 370
Grummond, G.H. 98
H.O.J. (Hand of Justice) .... *See* Beidler, John X.
Hamilton, Alf 39, 360, 361, 362, 366, 368, 369
Hamilton, William 183
Hanging Tree 78, 85
Hardie, James 130, 264, 293, 312, 321
Hart, Matthew . 250, 252, 311, 312, 313, 324, 336
Hastert, John 84
Hayfield Fight 318
Hazlett, William 237, 238, 239
Healy and Hamilton Trading 359, 362, 369
Healy brothers 357
Healy, Joe 56
Healy, John J. 30, 39, 40, 43, 44, 45, 46, 47, 48, 54, 55, 56, 59, 70, 74, 214, 347, 354, 356, 357, 358, 359, 360, 361, 362, 363, 366, 367, 368, 369
Healy, Mary Francis Sarsfield 45
Healy's Trading Post 357
Hearn, John 120, 121, 123, 151, 208
Heart Butte 374

Heavy Runner, Piegan 365
Heavy Runners' Massacre 365, 368, 371
Heavy Runners' Massacre 370
Helena 6, 18, 29, 36, 38, 42, 44, 51, 65, 66, 68, 69, 70, 73, 75, 76, 78, 79, 80, 81, 84, 85, 90, 92, 93, 94, 95, 105, 108, 116, 118, 130, 131, 133, 134, 136, 137, 139, 140, 143, 145, 149, 150, 157, 159, 161, 164, 166, 167, 169, 170, 172, 173, 174, 176, 184, 195, 196, 205, 207, 209, 211, 212, 214, 215, 216, 225, 233, 234, 242, 251, 264, 283, 284, 287, 290, 291, 294, 295, 296, 299, 302, 304, 305, 318, 319, 328, 334, 338, 339, 340, 343, 344, 356, 357, 359
Helena Catholic Cemetery 85
Helena Cemetery 290
Helena Herald 204
Helena Water Ditch 173
Hell Gate 127
Hell Gate River..72
Hereford, Robert .. 51, 77, 108, 145, 146, 167, 172, 173, 174, 176, 177, 190, 209, 216, 217, 283, 289, 290
Hogan, Martin..74
Horse Stealing 47
Hosmer, Hezekiah 19, 20, 21, 26, 29, 76, 105, 119, 141, 325
Hosted, Charles H. 209
Howe, Sam 219
Howie, Neil 29, 36, 37, 38, 41, 42, 43, 44, 49, 51, 59, 64, 65, 66, 69, 70, 77, 78, 79, 80, 84, 102, 104, 105, 106, 107, 108, 109, 118, 122, 130, 132, 136, 139, 140, 143, 145, 146, 157, 166, 168, 169, 170, 171, 172, 174, 175, 176, 189, 216, 235, 236,

   276, 282, 283, 284, 288, 289, 290, 291, 292, 294, 295, 296, 297, 299, 301, 302, 304, 308, 309, 310, 311, 314, 316, 318, 319, 321, 323, 324, 326, 327, 333, 334, 339, 344, 357, 360

Howie's Raid Force 317
Hudson's Bay Company 48, 350, 361, 363
Hughes, Barney 17, 90
Hughes, Robert .. 147, 205, 210, 251, 282, 326, 329
Hull, J.J. 149, 161, 209, 215, 276, 284
Hunecke and LeGree 57, 58
Hunt, Alexander C. 255, 257, 260, 261
Huntley Express Coach 212
Huntley Stage Line 173, 215, 225
Hynson, George. 131, 135, 137, 145, 148, 151, 210, 237, 276, 282, 305, 317
I.G. Baker and Company 223
Idaho Street 162
Idaho Territory 2, 15, 19, 43, 175, 208
Indian Creek Ferry 196, 316
Indian Peace Commission 310, 331
Instruction Manual for Mountain Howitzer Batteries *345*
International Hotel, Helena 252
International Hotel, Virginia City 336
Irish Brigade 31, 110
Irish Rebellion of 1848 222
Iron Eye, Lakota Sioux 99
Irwin, William L. 122
Ives, George 9, 16, 17, 90, 175, 277
Jack's Ranche 247
Jackson Street 202
Jefferson City 93
Jefferson County 139

Jefferson House 119
Jefferson River 94
Jefferson River Bridge 94
Jesuits .... 45, 54, 66. *See* Catholics
  DeSmet, Pierre 21, 44
  Giorda, Joseph 22, 23, 71
  Kuppens, Francis 35, 52, 54, 85
Johnson, Andrew 31, 91
Judith Landing 349
Judith River 24
Kansas and Pacific Railway 263
Keating, Floyd 356, 358, 359
Kennedy Ranch 36
Kennedy, Henry 59
Kennedy, John..36, 43, 71, 120, 356, 357, 358, 359
King and Gillette Freight 68, 69
Kingsly, John H 205, 282, 289
Kinney, Nathaniel J. 101
Kiowa Tribe 300
Kirby, S.R. 119
Kirkendall, Hugh 294
Kootenai Tribe 23
L.M. Todd Freight 345
LaForge, Thomas H... 240, 241, 244, 247, 248, 250, 252, 253, 324, 329
Lame Bull, Blackfeet 24, 370
LaMotte, R.S. 182, 233, 314, 315, 316, 333
Langford, Nathaniel 8, *9*, 80
Largey, Patrick 92, 93, 95, 164
Last Chance Gulch 93, 159, 173, 250
Lawrence, A.Z. 68, 69, 85, 116
Lawrence, Kansas 86
Lee's Army 145

Lewis, Jerry 134, 135
Lewis, William H. 149, 161, 162, 363
Lexington, Kentucky 109
Lincoln, Abraham 3, 19
Little Blackfoot River 55
Little Dog, Piegan 26, 40, 61, 62, 74, 279, 370
Little Flower Mission Church 375
Little Powder River 254
Little Prickly Pear Creek Canyon 36, 81
Little Prickly Pear Valley 347, 364, 369
Little Robe, Piegan 22
Little Rocky Mountains 23
Little Wolf, Cheyenne 99
Lone Bear, Lakota Sioux 99
Lyda, L.M. 282, 325
Lynch, Michael 85
Lyons, H.H. 133, 145, 146, 147, 150, 168, 251
M.M. Brand 159, 279
Mackinaw Boats 82
Madison County 8, 23, 52, 116, 139, 202
Madison County Bar Association 20, 180
Madison County Grand Jury 19, 86, 325
Madison River 127
Malcolm Clarke's Ranch 71
Mandell, Harrison 345, 348, 351
Many Braids, Blood 357, 358
Marias River 22, 28, 30, 40, 58, 62, 186, 219, 228, 347, 365, 366
Masonic Temple, Virginia City 215
Masons 8, *9*, 107
Massie, William 182
Mattock, Elijah 290, 296, 318, 333, 334, 338
McClellan, George B. 272

McClure, Alexander K. 188, 191, 193, 194, 195, 196, 197, 199
McGlothlin, William 86, 180
McGonigal, R.L. 85
McLaughlin, Michael 84
Meagher County 140, 176, 177, 207, 214
Meagher, Elizabeth 74, 148, 202, 226, 227
Meagher, Thomas F. 31, 32, 34, 35, 36, 37, 38, 40, 41, 42, 43, 44, 45, 46, 47, 48, 49, 51, 52, 54, 59, 61, 63, 64, 65, 68, 70, 71, 74, 77, 80, 84, 98, 105, 107, 109, 110, 114, 115, 116, 117, 118, 119, 120, 123, 129, 132, 133, 137, 138, 139, 140, 143, 149, 150, 152, 153, 154, 155, 158, 162, 167, 168, 169, 170, 171, 175, 177, 179, 180, 181, 185, 186, 187, 190, 193, 194, 195, 196, 202, 203, 205, 206, 207, 209, 211, 212, 214, 215, 216, 220, 221, 222, 223, 224, 225, 227, 228, 229, 232, 233, 241, 242, 251, 253, 257, 258, 259, 260, 264, 268, 276, 286, 360
Medicine Lodge Creek 332
Memoirs of a White Crow Indian 240
Messler, S. 249
Métis 56, 57, 61, 120, 237
Mexicans 6, 7, 8
Mexico 6, 266
Militia Act of 1808, Arming the Whole Body of Militia of the U.S. 230
Milk River 25, 41, 57, 58, 59, 62, 126
Milk River Indian Agent 355
Mission Valley 359
Mississippi River 266
Missoula County 23, 337, 340, 346

Missouri River 3, 4, 25, 28, 37, 40, 46, 52, 56, 85, 87, 101, 106, 107, 126, 127, 157, 189, 196, 213, 218, 219, 228, 253, 262, 270, 316, 333, 360, 364
Missouri-Kansas Border 244
Mitchell, Captain 292
Montana Territorial Code Commission 189
Morgan, John B 53, 54, 56, 66, 71, 184, 364
Mormon War 55
Mormons 269
Morse, Elkananah "Elk" 128, 175
Moses Saloon 183
Mountain Chief, Blackfeet 279, 280, 317, 354, 363, 364, 365, 369, 370, 371, 374. *See* Big Brave. *See* Chief Mountain, Blackfeet
Mountain Sioux .... *See* Assiniboine
Mr. Barnard 140
Mr. Lowe 73, 119
Mr. Reed 133
Mrs. Bartlett 135
Mrs. Hosmer 135
Mrs. McMath 135
Mullan Road ... 3, 17, 35, 41, 61, 63, 72, 74, 80, 81, 212
Munson, Lyman 37, 43, 44, 48, 49, 51, 52, 76, 77, 78, 80, 170, 175, 176, 190, 216
Murphy, Dennis 84
Murphy, Jeremiah 311
Musselshell County 176, 177
Musselshell River .. 24, 25, 69, 101, 112, 126, 175, 185, 283, 288, 290, 296, 318, 320, 333
Musselshell Valley 292
Mustering In 119, 298, 304, 305
Mustering Out .. 298, 304, 305, 324, 334, 337, 338

Mutiny 324, 325, 327
Natoya, Blackfeet Woman 6
Neal, H.S. 304
Needle-gun 75, 352, 358
Nelson, John 159, 201, 202, 205, 209, 211, 247, 248, 277, 283, 304, 311, 321, 333, 336
Nevada City 9, *12*, 16, 93, 131, 325
New Mexico Territory 270
New York City 105, 163
New York Tribune 191, 193, 195, 198, 269
Nez Pierce Tribe 23, 256, 257, 258
Niobrara and Virginia City Wagon Road Company 32, 84, 347
Northern Overland Mail Company 336
Northern Pacific Railroad 179
Northern Plains Tribes 332
Old Baldy Mountain 193
Old Man Thebeau 73
Old Man's River 370, 371
Old North Trail 5, 6, 7
Omaha 92, 164
Ordnance
   12-pound Cannister 2, 135, 160, 229, 287, 288, 328, 343, 345, 348, 359
   12-pound Shell 2, 10, 68, 135, 160, 229, 287, 288, 328, 343, 345, 348, 359
   12-pound Shot 2, 10, 68, 135, 160, 229, 287, 288, 328, 343, 345, 348, 359
   Accoutrements 229, 336, 339
   Bows and Arrows 32, 355, 373
   Breech-loading, .50 caliber Springfield Rifles, Needle-guns 75, 309, 318, 329, 350, 351, 352, 353, 358, 359

Breech-loading, .58 caliber Springfield Rifles, Needle-guns 32, 75, 349, 350
Breech-loading, Repeating Carbines 33, 118, 141, 156, 327, 328, 353
Breech-loading, Repeating Rifles 33, 141, 156, 165, 302, 327, 328, 353, 356, 363, 367
Bridles 133, 137, 156, 159, 297
Cartridges, .50 caliber Center-firing Metal, Needle-gun............ 75, 350, 352, 353, 355
Cartridges, .577 caliber paper with ball 84, 346
Cartridges, .58 caliber paper with ball . 32, 68, 69, 70, 160, 171, 229, 287, 288, 295, 336, 340, 342, 343, 345, 346, 347, 348, 354, 359
Cartridges, .58 caliber Rim-firing Copper, Needle-gun............ 32, 349, 350
Cartridges, Breech-loading Repeater Metal 350
Cartridges, Unknown Types and Caliber 120, 141, 156
Clubs............ 184
Derringers............ 183
Guns, Unknown Types and Caliber 119, 120
Howitzer, 12-pound Mountain.. 2, 3, 8, *9*, 10, *11*, *12*, 30, 34, 36, 44, 48, 49, 59, 68, 70, 71, 112, 119, 135, 238, 296, 310, 311, 343, 344
Howitzer, 4-pound Pack 39
Knives, Bayonets 230, 351
Knives, Bowie............ 183, 184, 248, 249
Knives, Daggers 79, 373
Lead.. 17, 39, 307, 310, 313, 348, 350, 355, 360, 363, 368, 371
Mountain Howitzer Battery 160, 177, 206, 229
Mountain Howitzer Battery (-) 346
Mountain Howitzer Battery (+) 2, 343

Mountain Howitzer Section....235, 283, 284, 287, 288, 290, 295, 300, 309, 328, 329, 348
Mountain Howitzer Section (+)..... 311, 327, 328, 348
Mountain Howitzer Sections (2)....235, 300, 342, 344
Muzzle-loading, .48 caliber Kentucky Rifle ...192
Muzzle-loading, .54 caliber Hawken Rifles......73
Muzzle-loading, .577 caliber Enfield Rifle-Muskets........................33, 112, 119, 295, 346
Muzzle-loading, .577 Enfield Rifle-Muskets....84
Muzzle-loading, .58 caliber Springfield (& patterned) Rifle-Muskets..... 32, 33, 68, 69, 74, 112, 119, 160, 171, 234, 287, 288, 295, 333, 335, 336, 339, 340, 342, 343, 346, 347, 349, 350, 351, 354, 369
Muzzle-loading, .59 caliber Northwest Guns.350, 355, 373
Muzzle-loading, Fusils.... *See* Ordnance, Muzzle-loading, .59 caliber Northwest Guns
Needle-guns...See
Percussion Caps.......... 32, 69, 171, 348, 355, 356
Powder... 3, 39, 68, 235, 236, 244, 307, 310, 348, 350, 355, 363, 366, 368, 371
Prairie Carriages 177, 229, 235
Quivers 32
Reloading Outfits..356
Revolvers.13, 27, 33, 34, 45, 57, 59, 74, 86, 120, 174, 223, 249, 302, 303, 311, 313, 327, 328
Rope 9, 13, 16, 53, 73, 78, 156, 246, 325, 329
Saddles 2, 133, 137, 140, 141, 156, 159, 201, 234, 297, 336
Shields 372

Spears 372
Stand of Arms . 68, 70, 84, 96, 160, 206, 229, 234
Whips 373
Orem and Marley Fight..................................... 79
Oro Cache Mine................................... 83, 191, 197
Oro Fino Gold Strike 43, 357
Orphir 28
Osborn, Patrick 84
Owl Child, Blackfeet.................. 354, 363, 364, 369
Palmer, George H. 329
Pease, William..360
Pemmican, Blackfeet 6
Pend d'Oreille Tribe 23, 37, 38, 357
Pennsylvania 197
Piegan Tribe... 5, 7, 21, 22, 25, 26, 37, 38, 40, 41,
    52, 53, 56, 57, 58, 61, 62, 64, 65, 70, 72, 87,
    100, 184, 256, 347, 364, 365, 366, 367, 368, 370
Piegan War 369
Piles, Nat 183, 184
Pinney, George 64, 65, 104, 107, 108, 173, 208,
    209, 211, 212, 215, 236, 284, 287, 288, 289, 295
Pittsburgh Landing..113
Pizanthia, Jose............................. 9, 10, *12*, 13, 16
Planters House.... 19, 157, 162, 163, 169, 178, 179,
    193, 229, 231, 304
Platte Route 263
Plummer, Henry 8
Powder River 254, 263
Powers, T.C. 360, 361, 363
Prickly Pear Creek 93, 338
Primary Battery.. 90
Pryor Mountains... 96
Quantrill, William 86, 87

Red Cloud, Lakota Sioux 82, 96, 100, 332
Red Cloud's War 82
Redferns Station 94
Reeve, I.D. 333, 351
Regulars .... See U.S. Army
Regulars and Volunteers 154
Republican 19, 29, 37, 88, 102, 107, 180, 189, 191, 196, 197, 252, 268, 269
Republican River 263
Richards, John 97, 98, 99, 237, 299, 300, 325
Rock Creek Station 212, 214
Rocky Mountain Front 4, 5, 6
Rocky Mountain News 261
Rocky Mountain Telegraph Company 94
Rocky Mountain Weekly Gazette 132, 204
Rocky Mountains 266
Rodney Street 235
Ross Pass 129
Ruby River .... See Stinking Water River
Rupert's Land .... *See* British Possessions
Russell, Charlie 4
Sacramento Union 265
Saint Ignatius Mission 72
Saint Joseph 262, 264
Saint Louis 113, 160, 233, 331
Saint Louis Arsenal 160
Saint Patrick's Day 104, 111, 112, 218
Saint Paul 333
Saint Peters Mission 22, 52, 66, 71, 74
Saint Peters Mission (New) 35, 72
Saint Peters Mission (Old) 52, 53
Salish Tribe .... 245, 246, 256. See Flathead
Salmon City 292, 312

Salmon River 175, 208, 292, 305, 308
Salt Lake City 89, 91, 92, 93, 161, 312
Salt Lake Telegraph 269
Sanders, Harriet P...199
Sanders, Wilbur F. 8, 14, 15, 16, 17, 20, 29, 64, 87, 101, 102, 104, 105, 106, 107, 108, 111, 162, 163, 169, 170, 171, 179, 180, 186, 187, 188, 189, 190, 191, 193, 194, 196, 197, 198, 199, 215, 216, 218, 233, 296, 312
Sawyer, James... 32
Scribner, Wylie 170, 190, 295, 334, 340
Shaw, Robert...220
Sheridan, Philip 364, 369
Sherman, William T. . 109, 110, 114, 138, 141, 149, 158, 161, 162, 253, 255, 260, 261, 262, 266, 268, 271, 272, 273, 274, 291, 306, 331, 363, 364
Shields River 4, 152, 209, 243, 245, 250, 251
Sioux Tribe 7, 24, 82, 87, 96, 97, 99, 100, 101, 117, 127, 128, 132, 138, 203, 237, 238, 254, 255, 256, 257, 259, 270, 272, 279, 280, 300, 310, 322, 332, 353, 356
Sixteen Mile Creek 129
Sixteen Mile Creek Pass.....................................129
Slater, John... 134, 135
Smallpox 365
Smith River 4
Smith, Charley..278, 279
Smith, Green Clay . 91, 92, 152, 182, 184, 196, 206, 211, 212, 214, 227, 235, 248, 268, 274, 276, 280, 281, 286, 288, 290, 291, 294, 295, 298, 303, 315, 321, 333, 334, 335, 339, 340, 342, 369
Smoky Hill Route 263
Snake Tribe... 23

Snider, A.J. 202
South Pass..263
Southern Plains Tribes 332
Spencer, James..249, 250
Spokane Tribe 23
Spread Eagle Bar 219
Springfield Armory................................. 32, 75
Square Butte 4
Squaw Dance 233
Stanton, Edwin 260
State of Kansas 60, 270
State of Missouri..60
State of Nebraska 270
State of Ohio 31
State of Pennsylvania 191, 194
Steamboat Abeona 162, 170, 186, 189, 219, 264
Steamboat Amaranth 233
Steamboat Antelope 233
Steamboat Ben Johnson 182
Steamboat G.A. Thompson 222, 225, 264
Steamboat Gallatin ... 183, 185, 186, 188, 189, 219, 233, 264
Steamboat Guidon 183, 226
Steamboat Ida Stockman..............................233
Steamboat J.H. Trover II 185, 233
Steamboat Octavia....................182, 183, 184, 264
Steamboat Only Chance................................264
Steamboat Yorktown............................... 189, 219
Steele, Gough 59
Sterling 196, 201
Stevens, Isaac.. 24
Stillwater River.........................239, 310, 317
Stinking Water River 30

Story, Nelson 75, 349
Stuart and Dance General Store 180
Stuart, Granville 122
Stuart, James 30
Sullivan, John 150, 177, 209, 211, 229, 249
Sun Dance 280
Sun River . 4, 5, 21, 40, 41, 44, 45, 46, 47, 53, 59, 66, 74, 179, 184, 211, 212, 215, 220, 260, 305, 346
Sun River Crossing . 53, 73, 74, 185, 211, 212, 215, 356, 360, 361
Sun River Ferry 74
Sun River Government Farm ... 30, 36, 53, 56, 59, 68, 69, 71, 346
Sun River Rangers 54, 63, 184, 347, 368, 369
T.C. Powers' Indian Trading Post 349
Tagert, W.J. 292
Telegraph ... 87, 89, 90, 91, 92, 93, 94, 98, 155, 157, 160, 161, 163, 169, 227, 262, 340, 361
Templeton, George 239, 330
Territorial 1st Volunteer Militia
   Brigader General Neil Howie Commanding 28
   Colonel Wilbur F. Sanders Quartermaster 28
   Created by Governor Edgerton 28
   Stuart's 30-Man Virginia City Company 29, 30
Territorial 2nd Volunteer Militia
   Colonel Neil Howie Commanding 67
   Created by Acting Governor Meagher 65
   Fort Benton Vigilantes 59
   Helena Officers 67
   Helena Staff 67
   Lawrence's 10-Man Helena Detail 67, 69
   Sanders Resigned Commission 67

   Sun River Rangers 45
Territorial 3rd Volunteer Militia
   1st Montana Cavalry 210, 211
   Brigadier General Thoroughman Commanding
   122
   Camp Cummings Training Facility 202, 203
   Camp Elizabeth Meagher 144, 240
   Camp Ida Thoroughman. 204, 209, 243, 245, 246,
      248, 250, 251, 276, 296
   Campbell's Sterling Company 141, 201, 209
   Completed Ordnance Shanty 264
   Created by Acting Governor Meagher 117
   Curtis' Helena Scout Company 149, 210
   Deasey's Virginia City Company 141
   DeLacy's 42-Man Relief Detail 150, 170, 209,
      238, 239, 310
   Ending Strength
      481 Enlisted and 32 Officers 293
   Flag by Mrs. Hosmer, Mrs. Bartlett, Mrs.
      McMath 135
   Flag issued by Quartermaster Cummings 202
   Fort Green Clay Smith 152
   Foster's Virginia City Scout Company ... 134, 147,
      148, 152, 232, 251
   Gallatin River Bridge 116, 151
   Gallatin Valley Local Protection Force 128
   Guidon by Mrs. Meagher 148
   Hynson's Virginia City Company A 135
   Lewis' Virginia City Company B 135
   Lyons' Helena Company A 147, 150
   Madison River Bridge 116, 152
   Montana Militia "M.M." Brand 159

   Montana's First Adjutant General .. 115, 210, 232, 289, 318
   Nelson's Virginia City Company 202
   Organized According to General Order No. 1, dated April 29, 1867 124
   Quartermaster Procurement System 155
   Staff According to General Orders, dated April 28, 1867 120
   Strong Public Support 269, 271
   Sullivan's 12-Man Ordnance Detail 177, 182, 294
   Three Missions Accomplished 259
   Three month Month Enlistments 117
   Virginia City Rangers *See* Hynson's Virginia City Company A
   Weston's Salmon River Company 208
Territorial 4th Volunteer Militia
   1st Montana Cavalry 291
   1st Regiment of Montana Volunteers 282
   6-month enlistments beginning August 1, 1867 292
   Armed Provost 4-Man Detail 304
   Baume's Drowners 325, 326
   Camp Ida Thoroughman 308, 346
   Camp Neil Howie 318
   Camp Thomas Francis Meagher 301, 303, 312, 317, 318, 319, 322, 326
   Colonel Neil Howie Commanding (Vice Thoroughman) 291
   Discharged by U.S. Army General Terry 332
   Ending Strength 391 Enlisted and 32 Officers 321
   Guidon by Ms. Fannie Campbell 290
   Hart's Salmon River Company 311, 312

Howie's Raid Force 308
Hughes' Mutineers Command 326, 327, 329, 330, 334, 337, 348
Reorganized by General Order No. 1, dated July 14, 1867 281
Territorial Acting First Lady 144
Territorial Acting Governor 31, 109, 206, 274
Territorial Acting Secretary 115
Territorial Acting U.S. Marshal 108
Territorial Arsenal . 156, 235, 337, 341, 344, 345, 353
Territorial Capital 3
Territorial Chief Justice 19, 26
Territorial Collector of U.S. Customs 105
Territorial District Judge 37
Territorial Election 312
Territorial Election Canvassing 37
Territorial Governor 3, 17, 31, 91, 212, 274
Territorial Indian Superintendent 31, 40
Territorial Legislature 88, 162, 175, 180, 181, 197, 341
Territorial Provost Guard 340
Territorial Secretary 31, 105, 188
Territorial Superintendent of Public Instruction
.... 11, 180
Territorial Supreme Court 37, 175, 176
Territorial U.S. Attorney 105, 357
Territorial U.S. Customs Inspector 166
Territorial U.S. Marshal 64, 104, 105, 107, 108, 235, 357, 360
Terry, Alfred H. 262, 266, 291, 298, 321, 331, 332, 333, 334, 335
Teton River 40, 46, 52, 53, 73, 374

The Democrat............................ 105, 106, 112, 205
The Montana Post . 91, 98, 107, 112, 113, 119, 128, 141, 142, 143, 147, 158, 168, 169, 185, 189, 193, 204, 206, 207, 208, 231, 234, 237, 260, 265, 277, 280, 289, 298, 305, 325, 344
The Shanty 232, 337, 339, 341, 343, 344, 345, 349, 359
The Vigilantes of Montana *11*, 36, 80, 277
Thoroughman, Ida 204
Thoroughman, Thomas 109, 115, 123, 134, 135, 137, 138, 143, 144, 149, 153, 158, 168, 204, 208, 209, 210, 216, 241, 283, 284, 287, 289, 290
Three Forks 126, 127
Three Suns, Blackfeet 26
Three Thousand Miles Through the Rockies......191
Tibbets, L..181
Tibeault, Nicholas 9, 325
Tiffany & Co. 163
Tongue River 254, 255
Train, George F. 269
Trinity Gulch 347
Tri-Weekly................................ 166, 173, 292, 338
Trobriand, Phillippe 352, 365
Trumbull, Walter 219
Tufts, James 105, 188, 197, 206, 212
Turner, N.L...292
Tutt and Donnell.. 70
U.S. Army 399
U.S. Army Regulations Regarding a Volunteer Regiment..286
U.S. Congress. 42, 88, 102, 103, 104, 106, 161, 162, 180, 196, 197, 199, 200, 206, 266, 267, 270, 274, 299

Union City 191, 193
Union League 103, 107
Upham, Hiram 59, 61, 63, 64, 65
Upson, Gad 22, 31, 40, 46, 59, 61, 63, 65, 170, 356
Utah Territory 161, 191, 270
Ute Tribe 257
Van Buren Street 95
Vaughn, Robert 39, 55
Vielle, Crazy 358
Vigilante Days and Ways *8*
Vigilantism 19, 20, 325
Virginia City..9, 18, 19, 29, 42, 44, 50, 52, 65, 68, 71, 77, 80, 82, 87, 89, 91, 92, 93, 94, 97, 104, 105, 111, 112, 115, 119, 123, 124, 130, 131, 133, 134, 136, 138, 139, 140, 142, 145, 149, 153, 154, 155, 156, 157, 159, 160, 162, 163, 168, 170, 171, 172, 178, 179, 185, 188, 189, 191, 193, 194, 196, 197, 201, 203, 205, 207, 214, 215, 218, 221, 226, 229, 231, 233, 234, 237, 240, 241, 242, 252, 255, 257, 262, 277, 287, 288, 290, 292, 293, 296, 302, 303, 304, 311, 316, 317, 318, 321, 325, 328, 331, 333, 336, 337, 340, 341, 343, 344, 345
Virginia City First Class Post Office 178, 180
Virmette, Paul 73
Wagon Box Fight 318
Wallace Street 86
War Meetings 115, 116, 118, 128, 131, 136, 143, 154, 155
War of Rebellion .... *See* Civil War
Washington City ... 59, 92, 102, 109, 136, 155, 189, 265, 331
Washington Territory 3
Washington, George 111

Watson, Carrie 179
Webb, Charles... 74
Wells Fargo Cattle 300
Wells Fargo Express...291
Wells Fargo Express Coach 213, 214
Western Union...................................... 89, 95, 340
Weston, A.F. 208, 209, 283, 308, 310, 317
Wheeler, William.......................................235, 360
Whiskey 17, 21, 22, 29, 57, 58, 59, 107, 109, 208, 252, 277, 311, 356, 360, 361, 362, 363, 365, 367, 374
White Tail Deer Creek 93
Wild, Levi... 91
Wiley, S.A. 94, 95
Williams, James 9
Williams, Joseph 149
Wolves 311, 319
Worden and Company Freight........................340
Wright, George..170, 224
Wyoming Territory 329, 357
Yellowstone Ferry 247
Yellowstone River ... 4, 24, 57, 101, 116, 118, 127, 128, 144, 150, 151, 152, 164, 204, 205, 208, 210, 236, 237, 238, 239, 241, 242, 245, 253, 256, 257, 258, 271, 278, 279, 294, 296, 297, 299, 301, 302, 303, 304, 305, 311, 312, 314, 315, 317, 319, 320, 322, 325, 355
Yunson, Christ........................... 148, 241, 242, 249